T0323502

and many shown as the "moral". Insightful analyses of individual cases provide an illuminating blend of scientific scrutiny with compelling storytelling."

Edwin P. Hollander, *Emeritus, CUNY, Baruch College, and University Graduate Center, USA.*

"In this book, Scott T. Allison and George R. Goethals continue their fascinating study of heroes which they began in their earlier book entitled *Heroes: What They Do and Why We Need Them.*"

Jon P. Howell, *Professor Emeritus, New Mexico State University, USA.*

Heroic Leadership

Heroic Leadership is a celebration of our greatest heroes, from well-known legends to the legions of unsung heroes who transform our world quietly behind the scenes. Now in its second edition, this book offers a compelling conceptual framework for understanding heroism and heroic leadership, drawing from theories of great leadership and heroic action.

With over 50 revised heroic leader profiles and 30 new profiles of individuals that have transformed the world, the book explores the many counterintuitive ways that heroes lead, shape, and mobilize their followers. The authors offer a definition of heroic leadership that explains how people easily misconstrue both leadership and heroism, and they provide an innovative take on why people are drawn to heroic leaders and why this can be considered a "fatal attraction." Incorporating the latest theory and research, the authors unpack the following ten categories of heroism: trending heroes, transitory heroes, transparent heroes, transitional heroes, tragic heroes, transposed heroes, transitional heroes, traditional heroes, transforming heroes, and transcendent heroes. From within these categories, the authors identify 100 exceptional individuals, describing their lives and how they exemplify the characteristics of the category they have been assigned.

Suggesting that our most cherished heroes make for our most transforming leaders, this is a vital resource for students and scholars of leadership studies, organizational behavior, and social psychology. Presenting valuable insights into the lives of both historical and modern leaders, the book is also a fascinating read for casual readers.

Scott T. Allison is Professor Emeritus of Psychology at the University of Richmond, USA. He has published extensively on heroism and leadership and has authored numerous books, including *Heroes, Heroic Humility, Conceptions of Leadership, The Romance of Heroism, The Hazards of Great Leadership,* and *The Handbook of Heroism and Heroic Leadership*. His work has appeared in USA Today, National Public Radio, the New York Times, the Los Angeles Times, Slate magazine,

MSNBC, CBS, Psychology Today, and the Christian Science Monitor. He has received Richmond's Distinguished Educator Award and the Virginia Council of Higher Education's Outstanding Faculty Award.

George R. Goethals is the E. Claiborne Robins Distinguished Professor in Leadership Studies Emeritus at the University of Richmond, USA. Previously he held academic and administrative appointments at Williams College where he served as the chair of the Department of Psychology, acting dean of the faculty, provost, and, finally, founder and chair of the Program in Leadership Studies. He taught courses on theories of leadership and presidential leadership. His recent scholarship focuses on presidential leadership, heroism, and leader–follower dynamics. He has received the Lifetime Achievement Award from the International Leadership Association and Richmond's Distinguished Scholarship Award.

Leadership: Research and Practice Series

In Memoriam
Georgia Sorenson (1947–2020), Founding Editor

Series Editor

Ronald E. Riggio
*Henry R. Kravis Professor of Leadership and Organizational Psychology
and former director of the Kravis Leadership Institute at Claremont
McKenna College*

Intentional Leadership
Becoming a Trustworthy Leader
Karen E. Mishra and Aneil K. Mishra

Leadership and Virtues
Understanding and Practicing Good Leadership
Edited by Toby P. Newstead and Ronald E. Riggio

Leadership Mindsets for Adaptive Change
The Flux 5
Sharon Ravitch and Liza Herzog

Leadership on a Blockchain
What Asia Can Teach Us About Networked Leadership
Frederique Covington Corbett

Navigating Leadership
Evidence-Based Strategies for Leadership Development
*Susanne Braun, Tiffany Keller Hansbrough, Gregory A. Ruark, Rosalie J.
Hall, Robert G. Lord, and Olga Epitropaki*

Snapshots of Great Leadership, Third Edition
Jon P. Howell, Isaac Wanasika and Maria J. Mendez

Heroic Leadership, Second Edition
An Influence Taxonomy of 100 Exceptional Individuals
Scott T. Allison and George R. Goethals

For more information about this series, please visit: www.routledge.com/Leadership-Research-and-Practice/book-series/leadership

Heroic Leadership

An Influence Taxonomy of 100
Exceptional Individuals

Second Edition

Scott T. Allison and George R. Goethals

Routledge
Taylor & Francis Group

NEW YORK AND LONDON

Cover Image: Ihor Reshetniak via Getty Images

Second edition published 2025
by Routledge
605 Third Avenue, New York, NY 10158

and by Routledge
4 Park Square, Milton Park, Abingdon, Oxon, OX14 4RN

Routledge is an imprint of the Taylor & Francis Group, an informa business

© 2025 Scott T. Allison and George R. Goethals

The right of Scott T. Allison and George R. Goethals to be
identified as authors of this work has been asserted in accordance with
sections 77 and 78 of the Copyright, Designs and Patents Act 1988.

First edition published by Routledge 2013

Library of Congress Cataloging-in-Publication Data
Names: Allison, Scott T., author. | Goethals, George R., author.
Title: Heroic leadership : an influence taxonomy of 100 exceptional
individuals / Scott T. Allison and George R. Goethals.
Description: Second edition. | New York, NY : Routledge, 2025. |
Series: Leadership: research and practice | Includes bibliographical
references and index.
Identifiers: LCCN 2024033870 (print) | LCCN 2024033871
(ebook) | ISBN 9781032358079 (hardback) | ISBN
9781032358055 (paperback) | ISBN 9781003328681 (ebook)
Subjects: LCSH: Leadership. | Heroes. | Leadership--Biography. |
Heroes--Biographpy.
Classification: LCC HM1261 .A47 2025 (print) | LCC HM1261
(ebook) | DDC 303.3/4--dc23/eng/20240917
LC record available at https://lccn.loc.gov/2024033870
LC ebook record available at https://lccn.loc.gov/2024033871

ISBN: 978-1-032-35807-9 (hbk)
ISBN: 978-1-032-35805-5 (pbk)
ISBN: 978-1-003-32868-1 (ebk)

DOI: 10.4324/9781003328681

Typeset in Sabon
by SPi Technologies India Pvt Ltd (Straive)

To the memory of two of our most cherished heroic leaders, Roberto Clemente (1934–1972) and Abraham Lincoln (1809–1865).

Contents

Series Foreword

Ronald E. Riggio One of the best ways that we are able to understand good leadership is through studying leaders who have gone above and beyond and engaged in truly heroic actions. These leaders serve as role models for those who aspire to positions of leadership, or for individuals who are thrust into situations in which they must enact leadership.

Leadership itself is a very complex social relationship. So, it makes sense to turn to the discipline of social psychology to help understand the dynamics of leading and leadership. In addition, the scientific study of heroism is quite new. That is why I am so excited for this second edition of *Heroic Leadership*, because it is authored by two eminent social psychologists who are also among the foremost experts in the study of heroism. Through profiling and dissecting the careers of heroic leaders, Scott Allison and Al Goethals, provide a state-of-the-art analysis of how and why leaders engage in heroic behavior. By emulating the actions of heroic leaders, and understanding the dynamics of heroic behaviors, the hope is that future leaders can learn to be more effective and heroic.

Ronald E. Riggio, PhD
Kravis Leadership Institute
Claremont McKenna College

Preface

This book is the latest product of a collaboration that started 40 years ago when Scott Allison was a graduate student at the University of California, Santa Barbara, and Al Goethals was on sabbatical there, visiting from Williams College. Looking back on some of our earliest collaborative work, we should have realized that at some point we would surely write about heroes. The first paper we published together, along with David Messick, was inspired by one of our heroes, the boxer Muhammad Ali. We were always fascinated by his influence and leadership outside the ring, particularly his role in changing race relations in the United States. Ali was always his own man. He insisted on being called Muhammad Ali rather than what he referred to as his slave name, Cassius Clay. At first the media refused to go along. But as we know from his long boxing career, Ali never quit. Eventually sports writers and broadcasters recognized that he was right to insist that they call him what he wanted to be called. He led the way for many, many more African Americans to use names that reflected their pride in their racial identity. There was no doubt that he was the first, and that he led the way.

As we tried to identify the qualities that made Ali an effective leader to a largely hostile white establishment, we focused on his wit and his obvious linguistic intelligence. We remembered that when Ali was once asked whether he had deliberately faked a low score on the US Army mental test, so that he could avoid the draft, he mischievously quipped, "I never said I was the smartest, just the greatest" (McNamara, 2009). That self-characterization led us to researching some of the limits on people's self-serving biases. The result was our *Social Cognition* paper, "On being better but not smarter than other people: The Muhammad Ali effect" (Allison et al., 1989).

At that point neither of us had turned to studying heroism or leadership or the connections between them. But we were inching closer in that direction. Allison's research began to focus on prosocial behavior in groups, examining the conditions under which people place their group's well-being ahead of their own individual interests. Goethals, meanwhile, was publishing work on group goals, social judgment processes, and eventually leadership. Circumstances eventually brought us both to the University of Richmond, where Allison is in the Department of Psychology and Goethals is in the Jepson School of Leadership Studies. At Richmond we began collaborating again, on both rooting for the underdog and positively evaluating people who have died. This research raised more general questions: Why do I like or admire certain people? What leads us to elevate our estimates of particular individuals? These concerns led to our first book on heroes, *Heroes: What They Do & Why We Need Them.* Although work on leadership, particularly Howard Gardner's (1995) *Leading Minds,* was always important in the way we thought about heroes, our general exploration of the psychology of heroism diverted us from focusing on the connections between leadership and heroism. Those connections are explored more fully in our review article in *Advances in Experimental Social Psychology* (Goethals & Allison, 2012).

But there was clearly much more to consider. This became increasingly clear in 2010 when we started to blog about heroes, particularly heroes who had clearly been leaders (blog.richmond.edu/heroes). Within a decade we wrote more than 150 hero profiles and attracted over a million visitors to the blog. One hundred of those hero profiles are included in this book. Profiling so many great individuals made it increasingly clear that in fact *all* of our heroes were also leaders. They might not fit traditional leader schemas or people's implicit theories of leadership, but they were clearly leaders in the sense that Gardner defined it. Either directly or indirectly, through face-to-face contact or through their accomplishments, products, and performances, they influenced and led significant numbers of other people.

Our purpose in this book is to continue exploring the various ways heroes influence us, and thereby lead. We hope to succeed in more fully developing the taxonomy of heroes that we introduced earlier, and in illustrating each of its ten types of heroes. Those types are trending heroes, transitory heroes, transitional heroes, tragic heroes, transposed heroes, transparent heroes, traditional heroes, transfigured heroes, transforming heroes and, finally, transcendent heroes. The influence and leadership of each of these types of heroes is distinct. Thinking about the different ways heroes lead helps us think more carefully about different kinds of leaders and the many different ways that each kind has an impact on followers.

We should add a word about the heroes we have selected for this volume and their assignment to one taxonomy category or another. All of them were suggested in formal surveys or in focused discussions. However, we used our own judgment in assigning them to hero types. At times the two of us did not completely agree on where to place certain individuals. It turns out they influenced different people in different ways at different times in their lives. While we acknowledge that there might be disagreement as to who really is a heroic leader, and what type of heroism they best exemplify, our overall goal is to illuminate as carefully as we can the many ways different heroes influence those who admire them.

Finally, we wish to thank the many people have helped along the way. First, we are indebted to the many colleagues at the University of Richmond, both in the Department of Psychology and the Jepson School, who have supported, or at least indulged, our interest in heroism and particular heroes. We are also deeply grateful to three friends and colleagues of ours – Rick Hutchins, Jesse Schultz, and Jeff Green – who kindly contributed five of the heroic leader profiles contained in this book.

We also are very grateful to Anne Duffy and Zoe Thomson-Kemp at Taylor & Francis for their encouragement during the entire course of this project. And we are highly indebted to series editors Ron Riggio and Georgia Sorenson for including our book in their series, *Leadership: Research and Practice*.

Scott Allison and George Goethals
September 2024

1 Introduction

Let us introduce you to Stanislav Petrov, a real-life hero whose actions exemplify the principles of heroic leadership. Most people have never heard of Stanislav Petrov, yet the heroic leadership he displayed may have been the greatest in human history. He literally saved the entire human race from total destruction.

On September 26, 1983, Petrov was working as the duty officer at Serpukhov-15, a secret command center outside Moscow responsible for monitoring Soviet military satellites over the United States. During his shift, the alarm systems suddenly went off, indicating that five Minuteman intercontinental ballistic missiles had been launched from an American base and were heading toward Moscow. The proper protocol dictated a retaliatory nuclear attack.

Petrov faced a critical decision: Should he interpret the missile attacks as real and trigger a worldwide nuclear war, or should he trust his gut feelings and evaluate the situation further? Petrov chose to honor his instincts and disregard the apparent threat.

Despite the immense pressure, here's what Petrov did:

1 **He maintained poise.** Petrov knew that the alarm systems were still in their early stages and suspected that the warning could be false. Instead of panicking, he turned the alarm off and informed his supervisor of a system malfunction.
2 **He honored a realistic mindset.** He declared his expectation that the alarm was likely a false positive, even though there was at least a 50–50 chance it wasn't.
3 **He displayed a commitment to peace.** Petrov's commitment to preventing catastrophe was unwavering. He understood the gravity of the situation and acted accordingly.
4 **He put duty to humanity before himself.** Rather than succumbing to fear or blindly following protocol, Petrov prioritized his duty to protect humanity.

DOI: 10.4324/9781003328681-1

5   **He considered the bigger picture.** His quick thinking led him to consider that if the Americans were genuinely starting a war, the attack would likely involve more than just five missiles. Petrov's broader view of the situation contributed to his heroic leadership.

Ultimately, Petrov's instincts and rational assessment proved correct: The alarm was indeed false. Had he reported it as real, the world would have plunged into nuclear devastation. His cool head, integrity, and courage saved humanity and Earth's entire ecosystem from disaster.

In Petrov's own words, "I had a funny feeling in my gut. I didn't want to make a mistake. I made a decision, and that was it." His heroic leadership reminds us that sometimes the most significant acts of heroism occur not on the world stage but within the confines of a small room that no one knows about. Stanislav Petrov's legacy offers an important lesson for leaders everywhere – a reminder that poise, maturity, commitment to principles, and critical thinking can change the course of history.

Characteristics of Heroic Leadership

Leaders who are heroic typically achieve this status by demonstrating courage, compassion, and composure during major crises. Heroic leadership can be viewed as the pinnacle of leadership, shown by leaders with extraordinary qualities who respond well to extraordinary circumstances. Heroic leaders produce transformative collective outcomes and inspire others to become their best selves. Their decisions always involve taking extraordinary risks. Franco (2017, p. 186) suggests that the term *heroic leader* should apply to "larger-than-life figures" who make tough decisions to accomplish heroic goals. These goals might include promoting social justice, transforming societies, leading military efforts in just conflicts, risking the organization's financial or safety standing to uphold moral principles, or helping a nation resolve existential threats.

Cohen (2010) identified eight universal traits of heroic leadership: integrity, knowledge acquisition, clear expectations, strong commitment, optimism, follower care, prioritizing duty over self, and leading from the front. These traits align with Allison and Goethals's (2011) "great eight" hero traits, which include wisdom, strength, caring, selflessness, resilience, reliability, charisma, and inspiration. Additionally, Cohen's characteristics are consistent with the findings of Kinsella et al. (2015), who identified 12 core hero traits: bravery, moral integrity, conviction, courage, self-sacrifice, protection, honesty, selflessness, determination, saving others, inspiration, and helpfulness.

Heroic leadership is often linked to leaders who demonstrate the exceptional qualities listed previously and who inspire others through their actions. The heroic leaders' effect on others cannot be underestimated. As legendary leadership scholar James MacGregor Burns often emphasized, to be heroic, a leader must inspire their followers to become their best selves (Burns, 1978). The specific traits of heroic leadership may differ from person to person, but there are several common elements typically associated with a particularly effective and heroic leadership style. Here are some key aspects of this heroic approach:

- **Vision and purpose:** Heroic leaders have a distinct and motivating vision for their goals. They are guided by a profound sense of purpose and a higher mission that energizes and motivates those around them.
- **Courage and resilience:** Heroic leaders show bravery and resilience when confronting difficulties. They are prepared to take risks, make tough choices, and persist through hardships. Their calm and resilient demeanor instills confidence and motivates others to overcome challenges.
- **Selflessness and sacrifice:** Heroic leaders put the needs and well-being of others before their own. They are prepared to make personal sacrifices for the greater good, showing genuine concern for their team or community. This selflessness builds trust and loyalty among their followers.
- **Integrity and ethics:** Heroic leaders demonstrate high integrity and adhere to strong ethical standards. They lead by example, ensuring their actions align with their words. This integrity garners respect and provides a moral guide for their followers.
- **Empathy and compassion:** Heroic leaders exhibit empathy and genuine concern for those they lead. They actively listen, understand different perspectives, and show compassion in their interactions. This empathy fosters a supportive and inclusive atmosphere.
- **Effective communication:** Heroic leaders are skilled communicators who can clearly convey their vision, goals, and values in an inspiring way. Through their words and actions, they motivate others to strive for excellence and achieve shared success.
- **Team building and collaboration:** Heroic leaders understand the significance of teamwork and cooperation. They cultivate a sense of belonging and create an environment where individuals feel appreciated, empowered, and motivated to share their unique skills and viewpoints. They form strong, cohesive teams that work together toward a common objective.
- **Impact and legacy:** Heroic leaders strive to make a lasting impact beyond their current leadership position. They seek to leave a positive and enduring legacy by inspiring and nurturing future leaders, driving positive change within their organization or community, and making a meaningful difference in the lives of others.

Stanislav Petrov

Image Source: Queery-54

It is important to recognize that heroic leadership isn't limited to renowned or iconic figures. Anyone can exhibit heroic leadership traits and create a positive influence within their areas of impact. This notion is consistent with Franco and Zimbardo's (2006) principle of the banality of heroism. At the time of his exceptional heroic leadership, Stanislav Petrov was an ordinary Soviet air defense worker. He had no prior history of having lived any kind of heroic life. Petrov demonstrated that an average person's calm, cool response to a major crisis can save countless lives.

Heroism and Leadership

Intuitively, being a hero isn't the same as being a leader. Or is it? Are people who are regarded as heroes also leaders? The answer depends, of course, on how one defines both heroism and leadership. When defining heroism, it is important to note that there are objective ways of defining heroes and subjective or constructivist ways. In short, there is a difference between how people perceive heroism and what heroism truly entails (Allison & Goethals 2011; Allison et al., 2017; Goethals & Allison, 2012).

Perception versus reality has long been an issue in studies of heroism. In his interviews with Bill Moyers, Joseph Campbell discussed the subjective and constructive aspects of heroism. Campbell (1988, p. 156) noted that a person could be seen as a local god to some but an enemy to those conquered by that god. He emphasized that labeling someone a hero or a monster is relative. Campbell illustrated this by stating that a German soldier who died in World War II is as much a hero as the American soldier sent to kill him. In the same vein, Franco et al. (2011, p. 99) acknowledged that heroism is a "social construction" and that "heroes of one era may prove to be villains in another time." We have argued that heroism is more than a mere social construction; it is a concept shaped by myriad constructions, including perceptual, psychological, cultural, economic, political, media, spiritual, ecological, and historical constructive forces (Allison 2023; Goethals, 2023a).

Allison and Goethals have emphasized several significant risks linked to the inherent subjectivity of heroism. First, subjectivity can create a blind spot in recognizing genuine heroism. This blind spot leads to difficulties in distinguishing heroes from villains, a phenomenon known as *hero illiteracy* (Allison & Beggan, 2023). Hero illiteracy not only distorts perceptions of heroism but also hinders individuals' ability to realize their most heroic potential. Additionally, it can result in people acting like villains while believing they are being heroic.

Second, the subjectivity of heroism leads to the prevalence of various psychological biases in how people perceive heroes. These biases cause individuals to distort reality and make incorrect social judgments about heroism. These biases fall into three categories: perceptual biases, cognitive biases, and motivational biases (Goethals & Allison, 2019). One specific bias is the heroism attribution error, which describes the tendency of people to wrongly bestow heroic status on celebrities and well-known public figures who do not deserve it (Goethals & Allison, 2025).

The third implication of the subjectivity of heroism is what Goethals and Allison (2019) termed the "romance of heroes." The word *romance* has two meanings: (1) an emotional attraction or special quality that emanates from a person, place, or thing; and (2) the tendency to exaggerate or invent details. Goethals and Allison argued that people's desire for heroes is so intense that it can be described as a romantic longing and deep emotional attraction, which can lead to mental exaggeration or the invention of heroic qualities. Essentially, people perceive what they want to see, particularly when influenced by strong emotions and motivations (Fiske & Taylor, 2017). As previously mentioned, the prominence of a hero can amplify evaluations and causal interpretations about them (Goethals & Allison, 2019).

Overall, the concept of the romance of heroism is similar to Kinsella et al. (2019) meaning-making model, which suggests that our need for heroes increases when our mental or emotional states threaten or diminish our sense of meaning. Goethals and Allison (2019) argued that situations involving danger and ambiguity exemplify such threats, leading to a heightened tendency to overattribute heroic or villainous traits to individuals. This idea aligns with social psychological research indicating that humans have a propensity to resolve ambiguity by distorting reality to fulfill their psychological needs (Fiske & Taylor, 2017).

Leadership and heroism are connected in interesting ways. We have argued that heroes are either *direct* or *indirect* leaders. Howard Gardner (1995) distinguished between direct and indirect leadership based on how leaders exert influence. Direct leaders impact their followers through face-to-face interactions and immediate, visible actions, like teachers or military commanders. Indirect leaders influence broader audiences through symbolic means, such as speeches or writings that shape cultural and social movements over time, like philosophers or political figures. This distinction highlights the different ways leaders can make an impact, either through personal engagement or broader, long-term influence.

While all heroes are leaders, not all leaders are heroes. Leadership is the superordinate category, with heroism being one of its subtypes. Leadership has always defied easy description, and the literature is full of definitions. Some scholars note that there are as many definitions of leadership as there are people attempting to define it (Schein, 1992; Stogdill, 1974; Yukl, 2013). The complexity and interdisciplinary nature of leadership make it difficult to pin down (Harvey & Riggio, 2011). Arriving at a consensus may always be a daunting challenge given that leadership encompasses processes involving the *individual* as the unit of analysis (e.g., attitudes, beliefs, biases), processes implicating the *group* as the unit of analysis (e.g., conformity, cohesiveness, interaction), and processes bridging the individual with the group (e.g., charisma). The multilayered nature of leadership makes it arguably the most talked about yet least understood phenomenon in our social world.

Exceptional Heroic Leadership

Our focus in this book is not just on leadership but on *exceptional* leadership, which we call heroic leadership. The Merriam-Webster dictionary defines *exceptional* as the quality of being superior, or of being rare. Every individual who we profile in this book possesses one of these two qualities, at least in the eyes of their admirers. Some of the leaders we discuss here will be obvious legends such as Mandela, Lincoln, King, and Gandhi. Their superior leadership is revered all around the world. But we will also focus on some obscure and unusual leaders who you've probably never heard of, and we do so to illustrate how exceptionality in the rare sense can also leave a significant mark on society.

In our previous work (Allison & Goethals, 2011; Goethals & Allison, 2012), we have argued that heroic leadership is characterized by great achievement in either the domain of *competence*, the domain of *morality*, or both. Our research has led us to conclude that people define heroic leadership as "doing the right thing at a critical moment" (Allison & Goethals, 2011, p. 9). Doing the right thing involves leaders demonstrating acts of great morality and great competence. This two-fold description of heroic leadership is consistent with research on social cognition's "big two" dimensions of person perception: (1) warmth-communion and (2) competence-agency (Fiske & Taylor 2017, p. 67). Heroes are viewed as warm, compassionate, and community-building; and they are seen as competent, agentic, and efficacious.

Heroic Leadership Narratives

Howard Gardner (1995) and Robert Sternberg (2011) have both argued that narratives are central to leadership. Leaders influence their audiences through stories marked by dynamic tension that unfold over time, and in which leaders and followers together play a central role in achieving group objectives. In Gardner's theory, the most important leader narratives are about the identities of the leader and the followers and the ways they must collaborate. Leaders are charged with the task of helping people understand who they are through stories that explain where the group has been, where it is going, and what obstacles lie in the path of getting there.

We turn to Abraham Lincoln for compelling evidence of the power of leadership narratives. Lincoln concluded his second inaugural address, often regarded as his greatest speech, by giving the nation some much-needed direction at the end of the Civil War:

> With malice toward none, with charity for all, with firmness in the right as God gave us to see the right, let us strive on to finish the work we are in, to bind up the nation's wounds, to care for him who shall have borne the battle and for his widow and his orphan, to do all which may achieve and cherish a just and a lasting peace among ourselves and with all nations.

This rhetoric was typical of Lincoln. In vivid language, he sketched a narrative of a united country working toward a common cause. In the Gettysburg Address, for example, he spoke of the nation's "unfinished work" and "the great task remaining before us." His language told stories about needing followers to perform important and noble work to achieve their future goals.

Given how much people rely on narratives to understand their worlds, it isn't surprising that there are compelling narratives about the way heroes behave. Joseph Campbell's (1949) classic book *The Hero with a Thousand Faces* argues that there is a universal *monomyth* about heroes that has emerged in heroic tales told for millennia across the globe. One central element in the monomyth is the hero venturing forth into strange and supernatural world where they encounter mysterious forces. There is almost always repeated struggle against these forces. Obstacles appear in numerous and unpredictable forms to test the prospective hero. These obstacles are not only villains and monsters, fires and floods, but also internal demons. Lust is a typical demon the hero must conquer. In the *Odyssey*, the hero Odysseus asks his shipmates to tie him to the ship's mast so that he cannot be drawn to destruction by the Sirens who arouse his sexual passions.

The hero monomyth contains the idea that other characters guide or assist the hero in a range of different ways. Often an elderly person provides direction and counsel as the hero initiates their journey into the unknown. The movie *Star Wars* capitalizes on this universal mythological feature in Alec Guinness's character Obi-Wan Kenobi, the kindly white-robed elder who counsels the young hero Luke Skywalker (Mark Hamill) to "let the force be with you." In sports, manager Leo Durocher served as a veteran guide to baseball heroes Jackie Robinson of the Brooklyn Dodgers and later Willie Mays of the New York Giants. Also, along the mythological journey, other characters, often young helpers or sidekicks, help the struggling hero. In *Star Wars*, Luke Skywalker teams up with Han Solo (Harrison Ford) and Princess Leah (Carrie Fisher). Similarly, Batman has Robin, Don Quixote relies on Sancho Panza, and Ronald Reagan leaned heavily on his wife Nancy to surmount many difficulties during his presidency. She famously commented that women are like teabags; you never know how strong they are until you put them in hot water.

Toward the end of the hero monomyth, the hero enjoys a final victory over daunting obstacles, both internal and external, which have repeatedly aligned themselves against the hero. Again, some other figure may assist. And finally, in most hero stories, the protagonist returns to their original familiar world, forever transformed and often with a boon to help transform the original world. For example, Moses is transformed from a weak to a highly empowered individual who is able to lead the exodus of the Israelites out of Egypt and across the Red Sea to Mount Sinai. He returns from the mountain with the Ten Commandments, given to him by God, thereby forever changing the world's moral code. Joseph Campbell's universal narrative of heroism – the monomyth – is familiar and easy to understand. It is this universal narrative structure that makes it so easy for people of all ages to understand the concept of hero and to identify heroes of their own.

Campbell's idea of monomyth and the idea of archetype to which we turn next both suggest cross-cultural universal understandings of heroes. Different cultures undoubtedly have different heroes. Our research participants' lists of heroes described earlier clearly reflect heroic narratives of western culture. However, while people in different societies may have different heroes, our sense is that similar dimensions of competence and morality are common across cultures. We suspect that a cross-cultural examination of hero narratives is a promising area for further research.

Archetypes and the Innate Mind

Joseph Campbell's monomyth narrative was rooted in Freudian psychoanalytic theory and Jung's theory of archetypes. For example, Campbell drew from Freud's notion of the Oedipal complex in observing that many heroes' struggles involve confrontation with father figures. In *Star Wars*, Luke Skywalker's chief antagonist, the black-clad and mysterious Darth Vader, turns out to be his father. But Jungian influences are also prominent in *Star Wars*. The Obi-Wan Kenobi figure is Jung's archetypical wise old man. Father figures permeate many hero myths. In our previous work on heroes, we have found ourselves unable to ignore the possibility that narrative structures around heroes, or hero scripts, reflect evolved, inherited Jungian archetypes (Allison & Goethals, 2011; Goethals & Allison, 2012).

One of the most important assumptions of Jungian archetypes is the idea that schemas, scripts, and narrative structures are not based entirely on experience. Jung argued that a part of our psyche called the collective unconscious was a storehouse of latent or potential images based on human evolutionary history. These latent images, or *archetypes*, prepare us for frequent encounters with meaningful situations and people. By referring to these images as latent potential, Jung meant that they were not initially conscious but could be activated when experience sufficiently matched one of them.

Jung claimed that archetypes have form but not content (Jung & von Franz, 1964). This idea is probably best understood as meaning that archetypes, much like schemas, are general outlines or shapes. Hogg (2001) describes prototypes as "context specific, multidimensional fuzzy sets of attributes" (p. 187). That description aptly captures the idea of archetype. While archetypes are very similar to schemas, or prototypes, there are two important differences. Social psychologists typically think of schemas as based on individual experience, not inherited collective experience. Jung (1969) addressed the idea of collective experience as follows: "There are as many archetypes as there are typical situations in life. Endless repetition has engraved these experiences into our psychic constitution, not in the form of images filled with content, but . . . only as forms without content, representing merely the possibility of a certain type of perception and action" (p. 48). Another difference between schemas and archetypes is that the latter, when activated, have an affective or emotional valence. We are emotionally drawn to, or repelled by, the activated archetypical images.

Jung's *mother* archetype nicely illustrates these ideas. Human infants are prepared to see mothering figures and will generally respond positively to these figures with a clear approach tendency. Jung claimed that people pay attention to, and are drawn toward or repelled from, objects, persons, and experiences that fit a latent archetypical image. It is important that Jung wrote about a number of archetypes relevant to understanding heroism, including the archetypes of *hero, demon, magic, power,* and *wise old man.* Jung also discussed the ways that archetypical images may be combined. For example, the hero and demon archetypes can both be activated by a leader such as Jim Jones or Adolph Hitler, or fictional characters such as Dracula. Their pull or appeal can stem from the activation of both those archetypes.

In summary, we make the claim that *hero* is an archetype that includes latent images of the looks, traits, and behavior of heroes, as well as the narrative structure of heroism outlined by Campbell (1949). Is there any evidence for such an idea? Research on the mysteries of inherited cognition and natural language is extremely suggestive. Infants carefully appraise features of human faces and show a remarkable ability to discriminate emotional expression in those faces (Klinnert et al., 1983). Shortly after birth, infants show a distinct preference for face-like shapes and, after as little as 42 minutes, the ability to imitate facial gestures (Carruthers et al., 2005; Johnson & Morton, 1991; Meltzoff & Moore, 1995).

Recently, Carruthers et al. (2005) have argued for a nativist understanding of the human mind, based in part on discoveries showing that a great deal of cognition is uniform, predictable, and similar across cultures, and that the human mind shares a great deal with other species. In this same vein, Marcus (2005) observes that "dozens of experiments have shown that babies come to the world able to think and reason" (p. 23). Marcus refers to research conducted by Pinker (1991) and Dehaene (1997) suggesting a "language instinct" and a "number sense." In short, there is considerable evidence supporting the idea of inherited cognitive capacities that interact with experience to produce the ways mature humans think and construct their worlds. We believe that this growing evidence of innate mindfulness is consistent with Jungian archetypal understandings of the world. Human beings may be endowed inherited, universal hero narrative structures that provide a ready basis for adopting heroes.

An innate, archetypal readiness for encountering heroic leaders suggests that human beings are wired to quickly identify leaders who seemingly fit the archetypal image of a great leader. Malcom Gladwell described this process beautifully in his best-selling 2005 book *Blink.* In a phenomenon that he calls "The Warren Harding Error," Gladwell tells the story of Ohio political operator Harry Daugherty's fascination with small-town newspaper editor Harding. Daugherty believed that Harding just "looked like a

Senator." He was tall, superbly built, with a bronzed complexion. He moved with power and grace and possessed a strong, sonorous voice. In every sense of the word he was charismatic. Harding activated people's implicit theories of leadership; he matched the template to near-perfection. Once cognitive construction filled in the blanks, Harding was assumed to have other important leadership qualities, including intelligence and integrity. Interestingly, Harding himself wasn't much fooled by the image but did not have the strength to resist Daugherty's flattery or marketing efforts.

The consequences were not good for America. Harding was elected senator in 1914, and when the Republican Party deadlocked at the 1920 convention, Harding received the presidential nomination, along with running mate Massachusetts Governor Calvin Coolidge. They were elected easily, over Democrat James Cox (and his young running mate Franklin D. Roosevelt). Harding died after two and a half years in office. He presided over a corrupt administration and is routinely at the bottom of polls of historians' ratings of presidents. He was way over his head, but for better or worse, he triggered the implicit leadership schema in the people around him.

Why Heroic Leaders Trust Their Gut Instincts

Another important point that Gladwell (2005) made in his book *Blink* is that effective leaders often make the best decisions when they follow their initial gut instincts. This would seem to contradict his cautionary tale regarding the Warren Harding error. Weren't people drawn to Harding based on their quick assessment that Harding was the spitting image of a heroic leader? How do we know whether to honor or disregard our gut feelings?

Gladwell unraveled this apparent contradiction by arguing that gut instincts lead to good decisions when they are informed by extensive expertise and experience. Professionals who have honed their skills over the years can often make accurate snap judgments because their subconscious mind recognizes patterns and cues that are not immediately obvious. You may recall that Stanislav Petrov, in the heat of the moment in his Moscow command center, reported that he had a gut feeling that the nuclear alert system was malfunctioning. His instincts told him that this attack alert contradicted his broad knowledge and good understanding of what an actual attack would look like.

Good decisions also arise from "thin-slicing," the ability to find patterns in a very narrow slice of experience. When people focus on the most relevant factors and ignore extraneous information, they can make effective quick decisions. Petrov exhibited this thin-slicing of experience. In addition, Gladwell (2005) argued that clear contexts in which the variables are limited and well understood are conducive to effective gut decisions. In such scenarios, quick judgments can often be reliable. Petrov benefited from having access to limited yet informative data that allowed him to follow his gut instinct.

Following our gut feelings can lead to bad decisions when they are influenced by biases and prejudices. Subconscious biases can skew perceptions and lead to flawed judgments. This process describes the Warren Harding error. Moreover, in complex or unfamiliar situations where leaders lack experience, arriving at a snap judgment is more likely to be disastrous. The lack of sufficient data and understanding makes quick decisions unreliable. Overconfidence in one's gut instincts, especially without sufficient expertise, can lead to poor decisions. People may ignore important information or fail to adequately analyze the situation, resulting in mistakes.

Heroes as Agents of Social Influence

Social psychology has long been defined as the study of social influence (Allport, 1985; Kassin et al., 2010; Myers, 2010; Taylor et al., 2006). As social psychologists, we thus view heroes and leadership from the perspective of how heroic leaders influence the thoughts, feelings, and behaviors of others. Only recently have scholars begun to address the issue of how heroes influence others (e.g., Bocchiaro et al., 2012) and in turn are influenced by others (e.g., Monin et al., 2008). In the following sections we briefly describe how heroes can affect the way people *feel, think*, and *act*.

Influence on Emotions

Heroes move us emotionally, and this is one aspect of heroism that sets it apart from leadership. When we earlier described the Great Eight traits associated with heroism, we noted that an important defining characteristic of many heroes is charisma and magnetism. Some of our most inspiring heroes, such as Martin Luther King, Jr., use soaring rhetoric to dare us all to join them on their heroic journeys. Other heroes, such as the New York subway hero Wesley Autrey, move us emotionally with their actions. Still others move us with their selflessness, love, and compassion, as revealed in our large survey of people's heroes (Allison & Goethals, 2011). Roughly one-third of our survey respondents listed family members as their heroes, and when asked why, respondents emphasized the love and emotional support that their parents or siblings gave them. Heroes can lifts our spirits, dreams, and aspirations (Allison & Green, 2020). We identify with them, we want to be with them, we want to be like them, and we want to bask in their successes (Cialdini et al., 1976). Leaders, of course, can do all of these things, too, but do not necessarily do so. Heroes and their heroic work produce a great emotional payoff.

Influence on Thoughts

Heroes, like leaders, also influence our worldviews. Leaders can also alter worldviews, of course, but they must be heroic leaders to do so. Heroes and heroic leaders challenge our conventional thinking and our traditional ways of viewing our lives, our surroundings, and our rules for conduct. Legendary spiritual and religious leaders made their mark by defying their society's prevailing mindsets. Confucius' moral philosophy 2,500 years ago challenged traditional views of Taoism and Legalism. According to Islamic theology, Muhammad received revelations from God, and these messages formed the basis of a new holy wisdom described in the Qur'an. According to Christian theology, Jesus of Nazareth was a revolutionary whose new moral doctrines challenged the existing moral landscape. The Dalai Lama, Desmond Tutu, Martin Luther King, Jr., Gandhi, and other spiritual leaders have all defied conventional thinking by advocating peaceful solutions to difficult, violent, intergroup conflicts.

Heroic leaders suggest new ways of looking at old situations, offering new schemas and fresh scripts for people to follow. This cognitive influence is especially apparent in the sciences, where scientific heroes suggest new paradigms that bring about revolutionary shifts in scientific thinking (Kuhn, 1962). Examples abound. Copernicus offered a new heliocentric view of the universe; Darwin forever altered the way we view the origin of species; Einstein turned our views of space and time upsidedown; and Freud stunned the world with his visionary theory of unconscious processes. Heroes also engender new ways of thinking in the business world. Henry Ford revolutionized transportation and industrial output, and Steve Jobs made computing smooth, sleek, and stylish. In each of these examples, a bold and heroic scientist or entrepreneur dared to challenge entrenched ways of thinking by completely reframing the nature of the world.

Influence on Behavior

Heroes show us how to behave well, and they urge us, either directly or indirectly, to follow their path. Oprah Winfrey is a striking example. Described as "arguably the world's most powerful woman" by CNN and Time.com, Winfrey devoted two decades during *The Oprah Winfrey Show* to promote books and literature, various forms of self-improvement, family values, and a stronger spiritual lifestyle. Winfrey's show helped propel nontraditional lifestyles (gay, lesbian, transgender) into the cultural mainstream. Her book club encouraged legions of Americans to read more; a book plugged by Winfrey sold a million more copies than it would have ordinarily. Winfrey's influence has been sweeping and legendary, and it has not gone unnoticed. She was named "one of the 100 people who most influenced the 20th Century" and "one of the most influential people" of 2004, 2005, 2006, 2007, 2008, and 2009 by *Time*. At the end of the 20th century, *Life* magazine listed Winfrey as the most influential person of her generation. Barack Obama has said she "may be the most influential woman in the country." In 1998 she made the top of *Entertainment Weekly*'s list of the 101 most powerful people in the entertainment industry. In 2003 Winfrey edged out both Superman and Elvis Presley to be named the greatest pop culture icon of all time by VH1.

Heroes do more than shape the behavior of lay people; they also inspire the actions of other heroes. Elvis Presley affected the songwriting of Chuck Berry, Fats Domino, the Everly Brothers, Little Richard, and Buddy Holly. In the 1960s the Beatles built on this foundation and took rock music to a level of creativity not seen before or since. Beatles lead guitarist John Lennon admitted that "if there hadn't been Elvis, there wouldn't have been the Beatles" (Davies, 2004, p. 256). The Beatles' groundbreaking 1967 album, *Sergeant Pepper's Lonely Hearts Club Band*, was inspired by the 1966 Beach Boys' innovative album *Pet Sounds*. "Without *Pet Sounds*," said producer George Martin, "*Sgt. Pepper* wouldn't have happened. *Pepper* was an attempt to equal *Pet Sounds*" (Davies, 2004, p. 277). Musical heroes operate much like their scientific counterparts, building on the pioneering work of their predecessors and contemporaries.

Heroes begetting heroes can also be seen in the world of sports. Tiger Woods has often attributed his success to Charlie Sifford and Lee Elder, two Black golfers who broke the color barrier on the professional golf tour. Major league baseball players routinely express their appreciation for Jackie Robinson, who in 1947 was the first Black player to be allowed to participate in major league baseball. Larry Doby, the first Black American Leaguer, viewed Robinson as a hero and always reverently referred to him as "Mr. Robinson." There is no question that in every field of human endeavor, whether in science, sports, the arts, or business, heroes exert profound effects on the behavior of others. These effects scan include emotional awe, feelings of empowerment, an innovative spirit, sheer inspiration, and a drive for self-improvement.

Influence as the Basis for Our T(r)axonomy of Heroism

Heroism assumes many different forms and thus defies simple categorization. Franco et al. (2011) proposed a taxonomy of heroism based on the types of risks that heroes take when they perform their good deeds. Of the

12 subtypes of heroes in their taxonomy, two describe heroes who take physical risks. These heroes include *military personnel* and *courageous civilians* who put themselves in harm's way to help others. The remaining ten hero subtypes feature heroes who take social risks. These heroes include *whistleblowers, scientific heroes, martyrs, good Samaritans, underdogs, political figures, religious figures, adventurers, politico-religious figures,* and *bureaucratic heroes.* As these subtypes suggest, Franco et al.'s taxonomy is driven by the context in which heroism takes place, whether military, religious, scientific, political, or moral.

We have proposed a conceptually different taxonomical framework (Goethals & Allison, 2012). We believe that the most centrally defining aspect of heroism is the nature of the influence that heroes, like leaders, have on their followers and on society. Our analysis begins with the observation that a hero's influence can differ on many significant dimensions. Influence can vary along the continua of *weak* versus *strong*; *short-term* versus *long-term*; *widespread* versus *limited*; *waxing* versus *waning*; *hidden* versus *exposed*; and *constructed* versus *authentic.* These dimensions of influence are reflected in the various categories of heroism contained in our taxonomy. Our taxonomic structure features the following subtypes of heroes: trending, transitory, transitional, tragic, transposed, transparent, traditional, transfigured, transforming, and transcendent. Because each of these subtypes share the same first two letters – "tr" – we're tempted to call our framework a *traxonomy* rather than a taxonomy. Table 1.1 displays our taxonomy and the ten hero categories within it. Next, we briefly describe each of the hero categories in our framework.

Trending Heroes

People are highly sensitive to the changing fortunes of others. This sensitivity serves as the basis for our perception of both hero formation and hero dissolution. We naturally take notice of which people in our social environment are slowly attaining heroic status and which are slowing losing it (Allison & Hensel, 2012). Rising stars and falling giants are said to be *trending heroes.* For example, the perceived impact of former US presidents is often in a state of flux as new information surfaces or as historians offer new interpretations of old information. Ulysses S. Grant is an example of one president who is trending upward. In a 2000 C-SPAN poll of US presidents, Grant was ranked as the 33rd best president. When this poll was repeated in 2009, Grant rose to 23rd, and in 2021 he rose to 20th. In the world of sports, baseball pitcher Paul Skenes is trending upward toward heroism. To become a true hero, Skenes must move beyond athletic accomplishment and begin demonstrating philanthropy and humanitarianism off the baseball field.

Table 1.1 Our Influence Taxonomy of Heroism

Type of Hero	Subtypes	Definition	Examples
1 Trending hero	• Upward • Downward	On a trajectory toward heroism	Lady Gaga Woodrow Wilson
2 Transitory hero	• True • Trivial	Enjoys 15 minutes of fame	"Sully" Sullenberger Steven Slater
3 Transitional hero		Unique to one's stage of development	Power Rangers Justin Beiber
4 Tragic hero		Falls from grace	King Lear Tiger Woods
5 Transposed hero	• Hero to villain • Villain to hero	Experiences status reversal	LeBron James Ben Wade
6 Transparent hero		Contributes behind the scenes	Firefighters, police, health workers, parents, coaches, soldiers
7 Traditional hero	• Moral • Competent • Complete	Makes exceptional contributions over time	Michael Jordan Mother Teresa Wayne Gretzky
8 Transfigured hero		Constructed hero	Chilean miners Robin Hood
9 Transforming hero	• Global • Specific	Transforms societies	Gandhi Albert Einstein
10 Transcendent hero		Transcends categories of heroism	Jesus Harry Potter John Wooden

Heroes can also trend downward. In the first ever poll of historians' rankings of US presidents, conducted by Arthur Schlesinger in 1948, Woodrow Wilson finished 4th. In the 2000 C-SPAN poll, he was ranked 6th, and later in the 2021 C-SPAN poll he had fallen to 13th. Professional athletes inevitably trend downward as their skills erode. Similarly, aging actors and actresses discover fewer opportunities for work on stage and screen. These and other fading public figures are experiencing firsthand an inescapable law of heroic gravity: What goes up must come down.

To understand the psychology of trending heroes, we note that people are sensitive to change and that the direction of change appears to matter more than one's absolute position. For example, people report that they would be happier if their 3 dollars grows to 5 dollars than if their 8 dollars shrinks to 6 dollars (Kahneman & Tversky, 1979). From an economic standpoint, this emotional response is irrational because an end state of 6 dollars is greater than an end state of 5 dollars, but psychologically we detest the trend of shrinking fortunes so much that we'd rather have less money than be trending downward. Similarly, we're more attracted to people who dislike us but are starting to warm up to us than we are to people who like us but are becoming critical of us (Aronson & Linder, 1965). Human beings show a strong sensitivity to the direction of change in many judgment contexts, and included among these contexts is our perceptions of rising or falling heroes.

Transitory Heroes

Some heroes come and go in what seems like a blink of an eye. American artist Andy Warhol once quipped that "in the future, everyone will be world-famous for 15 minutes" (Murphy, 2006). Warhol was describing what we call a *transitory hero*, the type of hero who enjoys a very short shelf-life. We also suggest that there are two subtypes of the transitory hero: the transitory-true hero and the transitory-false hero. In the 2013 first edition of this book, we believed that an example of a transitory-true hero was Chesley "Sully" Sullenberger, the US Airways pilot who saved the lives of 155 passengers when he successfully landed his crippled aircraft onto the Hudson River in January of 2009. Sullenberger's act was widely celebrated for a few short weeks, and we thought that it would soon be quickly forgotten. But years later, Clint Eastwood made a popular movie about Sully's accomplishment, ensuring that Sully would enjoy far more than just 15 minutes of fame.

A notable example of a transitory-false hero was Steven Slater, the JetBlue flight attendant who quit his job in frustration by screaming obscenities over the loudspeaker, grabbing a couple of beers, and sliding down the emergency chute. Slater became a folk hero to hundreds of thousands of people on Facebook and on Twitter. People resonated to the idea of quitting a thankless job in a blaze of glory. Such as act was glorified in the famous Johnny Paycheck song "Take This Job and Shove It," released in 1978. But we call Slater a transitory-*false* hero because his fame was deservedly fleeting. Slater displayed neither skill nor morality in resigning his position. He simply acted out a fantasy that attracted attention.

Transitional Heroes

Human beings experience many important phases of development throughout their lifespan. As we mature, our values, emotional states, cognitive abilities, and priorities tend to shift and evolve in significant ways. With these changes come adjustments in our preferences for heroes. People around the age of 40 tells us that their *transitional heroes* from the turn of the millennium were the Power Rangers, the Spice Girls, Michael Jordan, and the Backstreet Boys. These middle-aged people now openly admit that they have largely outgrown these heroes. As authors of this book and products of the mid-20th century, we gravitated in our youth to personal heroes who were professional athletes and artists such as Willie Mays, Jerry West, Elvis Presley, and the Beach Boys. As older adults, we now choose our heroes more carefully based on different criteria. In keeping with theories of adult development (Erikson, 1959), our choice of heroes is now based less on one's ability to throw a ball or hit a note. Today our heroes are Gandhi, Lincoln, King, and others who have made meaningful moral contributions to society.

Tragic Heroes

Human beings have a breathtaking ability to self-destruct and, as stated in an old aphorism, the bigger they come, the harder they fall. Tragic heroes are usually heroic leaders whose character failings bring about their downfall. Legendary playwright William Shakespeare was especially attuned to the psychological power of the tragic hero. King Lear, Hamlet, Macbeth, and Brutus are vivid examples. There is certainly no shortage of modern day Hamlets. The story of US president Bill Clinton contains some of the central elements of the tragic hero narrative. Clinton was a brilliant, charismatic president with superb political instincts. Even his detractors held a grudging admiration for him. Clinton's tragic flaw was his repeated philandering, and during his second term in office his sexual misconduct led to impeachment charges of perjury. Numerous other public figures have had their careers derailed by one or more of the seven deadly sins: pride, envy, anger, sloth, greed, gluttony, and lust. Tragic heroes attract our sympathy, and sometimes even our anger, and they remind us of just how fragile one's heroic status can be.

Transposed Heroes

Sometimes heroes unexpectedly, and overnight, become villains. In the Batman comic book and movie franchise, the character of Two-Face illustrates the concept of a *transposed hero*. Two-Face was once Harvey Dent, the virtuous district attorney of Gotham City and an ally of Batman. After a criminal throws acid on his face, hideously scarring him, Dent loses his sanity and becomes a crime boss. LeBron James may serve as a real-world example of this kind of transposition. A basketball great, James was the toast of Cleveland until he left the team in what was perceived to be an arrogant, disrespectful manner. Literally overnight, James was transposed from the role of hero to the status of villain (Bradley, 2010). In sporting contexts, a hero who fails to perform at a crucial moment during competition becomes what is called a *goat*. When Boston Red Sox first-baseman Bill Buckner mishandled a simple ground ball during the 1986 baseball world series, he allowed the opposing team to win the championship. To this day, almost 30 years later, Buckner is considered a goat or villain despite enjoying a long and distinguished career as a ballplayer.

Sometimes villains can quickly become heroes, although this status reversal is more rare than the hero-to-villain conversion. An example of an individual who changes from sinner to saint is the great Christian philosopher St. Augustine (Augustine of Hippo, 1998). We also see it in Russell Crowe's character of Ben Wade in the 2007 film *3:10 to Yuma*. Interestingly, Wade later converts back to villain status, thus again underscoring the temporal vicissitudes of hero and villain status. It is important to note that there is an important difference between tragic heroes and transposed heroes. While both these hero subtypes can involve a fall from grace, the tragic hero is a sympathetic figure whose life or career ends in shambles. In contrast, transposed heroes often make calculated choices to achieve a complete status reversal, and they may actually thrive in this new role.

Transparent Heroes

Transparent heroes are arguably our most important, most abundant, and most under-appreciated heroes. They quietly perform heroic deeds behind the scenes, outside of the public spotlight. We call them transparent because they invisibly go about performing society's most virtuous and loving actions. Transparent heroes are our parents who make great sacrifices for us. They are the teachers who mold our minds, the coaches who teach us discipline and hard work, the healthcare workers who heal us, emergency first responders who save us, and military personnel who protect us.

Transparent heroes are paradoxically our most abundant heroes and yet also our must unsung heroes. To determine the relative abundance of transparent heroes, we asked 50 participants to estimate the prevalence of the hero subtypes in our taxonomy. The results showed that participants estimated that 65% of all heroes are transparent – the invisible individuals among us whose heroic work often goes unnoticed. No other category of heroes came close to matching this percentage; the next highest percentage was 13% for traditional heroes, whom we describe next. Transparent heroes may be invisible and unsung, but they are judged to be widespread throughout our society.

Traditional Heroes

The *traditional hero* is an individual who closely matches our schema or prototype of a hero and who also follows the life path of the hero in classic literature. They are the person whose life story parallels the monomythic hero journey as described by Campbell (1949). This journey features a hero who is expelled from their ordinary world, encounters formidable obstacles, battles a dark adversary, receives assistance from unlikely sources, returns forever transformed, and offers a boon to society. Because Campbell's model of the hero's journey is derived from mythological legends from all corners of the globe, we are more likely to find the purest instances of this traditional hero in fictional stories. The heroic tales of Luke Skywalker, Batman, and Harry Potter are all narratives of the traditional hero. But many real-world heroes, such as Abraham Lincoln and Oprah Winfrey, also have important elements of the traditional hero. It is not unusual for public figures to emphasize elements of the traditional heroic script in their own lives to engender support from the public and to further their own political causes. Individuals who have done so with some success are J. K. Rowling, Barack Obama, David Geffen, and Celine Dion.

Transfigured Heroes

People are hungry for heroes, and at times this hunger motivates people to construct heroes, to see heroic elements where none exist, or to turn a mildly heroic tale into an extremely heroic one. Heroes who benefit from these constructions or exaggerations are called *transfigured heroes*. One prominent example is the story of Jessica Lynch, a former private in the US Army who fought in the Iraq War. Lynch was injured and captured by Iraqi troops, and she was later rescued by American special forces personnel. Her story was a simple one. During a battle she was wounded by a grenade and was unable to fight back because her weapon jammed. But shortly after her rescue and return to America, the *Washington Post* published an article about Lynch entitled, "She Was Fighting to the Death" (Loeb, 2003). The article reported that Lynch's unit was ambushed and that she "shot several enemy soldiers" and "continued firing at the Iraqis even after she sustained multiple gunshot wounds and watched several other soldiers in her unit die around her." The article provided a stirring account of a courageous hero performing magnificently under dire conditions.

The only problem with the *Washington Post* story is that it never happened. Lynch herself has repeatedly denied that any of these heroic events occurred. "That wasn't me. I'm not about to take credit for something I didn't do . . . I'm just a survivor." Lynch blames the *Washington Post* and the military for using her to promote a false heroic narrative. "They used me to symbolize all this stuff. It's wrong. I did not shoot, not a round, nothing. I went down praying to my knees. And that's the last I remember" (Campbell, 2012).

Transfigured heroes are credited with performing more heroic behaviors than they truly performed because of our deep-seated need for heroes and to see heroism where none exists. We are especially likely to crave heroism in difficult situations, and we will mentally create heroes or exaggerate heroism even when objective facts fly in the face of our constructions. Psychologists have long known that human beings love to embellish heroic stories and imbue them with drama, excitement, and inspiration. Moreover, people have little use for dissonant elements that might diminish the heroic narrative. Transfiguration describes the mental tricks we play on ourselves in the service of quenching our thirst for heroes.

Transforming Heroes

Our conceptualization of the transforming hero borrows heavily from the seminal work of James MacGregor Burns, who first used the term *transforming* to describe exceptional leadership (Burns, 1978, 2003). According to Burns, transforming leadership occurs when both leaders and followers engage in a mutual effort to raise levels of motivation and morality. The transforming leader is able to articulate a clear vision, offers a plan to attain the vision, exudes confidence, leads by example, and empowers followers to make the vision a reality. We believe that virtually all transforming leaders are also transforming heroes. Martin Luther King, Jr., is an ideal example of a transforming hero as seen in his charisma, expression of lofty ideals, and ability to stir followers to action. Heroes who are transforming can be more influential than any other subtype of hero.

We distinguish between heroes who transform entire societies (transforming-global heroes) and heroes who transform smaller subcultures within societies (transforming-specific heroes). As chief architect of the civil rights movement in North America and elsewhere around the world, King is clearly a transforming-global hero. Other globally transforming heroes include Nelson Mandela and Mahatma Gandhi. Examples of transforming-specific heroes are Albert Einstein, who transformed the field of physics; Elvis Presley, who transformed popular music; and Steve Jobs, who transformed personal computing.

Transcendent Heroes

We acknowledge that some heroes belong in more than one of the subtypes of our taxonomy. Consider Oprah Winfrey. Her life story possesses many of the elements of the monomythic hero journey described by

Campbell (1949), making her a traditional hero. She has also transformed television, making her a transforming hero. Another hero who defies simple categorization is legendary basketball coach John Wooden. He, too, is both a traditional and a transforming hero, and one could also argue that he is also a transparent hero for his behind-the-scenes mentoring of so many young men for so many decades. What are we to do with heroes who cannot cleanly fall into one category? We call them *transcendent heroes*. Their contributions feature a complexity or depth that transcends our taxonomic structure.

Jesus of Nazareth is most certainly a transcendent figure. The transcendent heroism of Jesus is derived from his transforming influence on western culture and also from his life story mirroring the path of the traditional hero. Elements of Campbell's traditional hero's journey in the life of Jesus include a born calling, a humble birth in a manger, help from disciples, a tumultuous clashing with the status quo, the crucifixion, and the rising from the dead to save the world. Jesus may also be considered a transfigured hero, depending on one's beliefs about the veracity of biblical accounts of his divine nature.

Because they are able to satisfy the criteria for multiple categories of heroism, transcendent heroes would appear to be the most influential of all the heroes in our taxonomy. But this is not necessary the case. A hero could conceivably be both trending and transitory, as when a rock singer enjoys one hit song (trending upward) but then disappears from the music radar screen (transitory). One-hit wonders of this type could be called transcendent because they meet the criteria for more than hero type, but they are hardly more influential than a transforming hero such as Martin Luther King, Jr. We thus argue that truly transcendent heroes must combine transforming heroism with at least one other type of heroism in our taxonomy. Thus transforming heroism is a necessary but not sufficient condition for transcendency. In this way transcendent heroes occupy supreme status of influence among all the heroes in our taxonomy.

Organization of This Book

In this book we profile over 100 heroes, many of whom you probably know and some of whom you likely don't know. These heroes come from all walks of life and represent many different domains of heroic activity. Some are heroes from fiction, and others are real-life legends. Some are heroes without question, while others will leave you wondering why we included them among the 100 profiles. We assure you that all 100 individuals, even the ones that engender puzzlement, have been listed as heroes by at least some of the many people we've surveyed about heroism.

We've arranged these hero profiles by the taxonomical category in which they fall, beginning with the hero category that we believe is the least influential on society – trending heroes – and ending with the hero category that we believe carries the greatest influence – transcendent heroes. In our conclusion, we attempt the daunting task of making sense of heroism as it relates to the complex field of leadership studies. We will examine important areas of overlap between heroism and leadership, and we will also identify key areas of difference between these two important phenomena.

The 100 profiles that follow comprise the vast majority of this book. Readers of these profiles will not agree that all 100 people profiled here are heroes. Heroism, after all, is often in the eye of the beholder (Allison & Goethals, 2011). As authors of this book, we don't believe that all 100 of these individuals are heroic leaders, but we've included them because they've all been mentioned by our survey respondents as heroes. In addition, they provide us with a way of illustrating how our "traxonomy" of heroism works. We hope you agree that the individual lives we describe are fascinating illustrations of leadership, heroic or otherwise, in all its many forms.

2 Trending Heroes
Gaining or Losing Heroic Status

People are highly sensitive to changing fortunes. We monitor our own changing fortunes, of course, but we also show great sensitivity to the shifting fortunes of others. We want to know who's doing better and who's doing worse than they were before. Is my favorite athlete or sports team having a good year? Is China's economy still growing rapidly? Are public schools in decline? Did my neighbor buy a new car? This sensitivity to changing fortunes is the foundation of our perceptions of trending heroes.

Trending heroism reflects the reality that most heroes are not created in an instant. It takes time to accumulate a resume of heroic success and accomplishment. We propose that as natural observers of human behavior, people are sensitive to cues indicating that hero formation is occurring. People take notice of the individuals around them who are experiencing rising fortunes and growing accolades. Conversely, people also show sensitivity to the reverse process, namely, heroism in decline. When heroes stumble – an all-too frequent occurrence – people are highly responsive to the stumble and watch carefully for signs indicating whether the stumble is merely an aberration or the beginning of the end of heroism.

Why are we so sensitive to trends in heroism? We're naturally drawn to changes in our social environment because they may have implications for our own well-being. Long ago, famous social psychologist Leon Festinger theorized that our sensitivity to others' outcomes fulfills our drive to know where we stand in relation to others (Festinger, 1954). We also find changes in others' fortunes to be a source of drama or entertainment (Kim et al., 2008). Unexpected changes in fortunes can be especially dramatic, as when underdogs triumph and established powerhouses fail (Goldschmied & Vandello, 2009; Goldschmied & Vandello, in press; Vandello et al., 2007). Historically unsuccessful sports teams that finally enjoy some success are said to be plucky underdogs, up-and-coming programs, rising upstarts, and Cinderella stories (Allison & Goethals, 2011). We seem to have fewer labels for fallen giants. We briefly revel in their misfortune, as befitting our

DOI: 10.4324/9781003328681-2

schadenfreudian tendencies, but our focus is usually more on celebrating the unexpected successes of the downtrodden.

Heroism can trend quickly, or it can trend slowly. Our sensitivity to changes in others' fortunes may be so great that we may rarely view anyone, especially heroes, as homeostatic over time in terms of their status or outcomes. Fortunes, it seems, are always fluctuating. People in general, but especially heroes, seem prone toward experiencing small victories and minor setbacks on a daily basis. The only exception to this rule may occur in our perceptions of dead heroes. Research has shown that our judgments and impressions of the dead tend to resist change (Eylon & Allison, 2005). Dead heroes tend to be frozen in time. Living heroes, however, are inevitably in the process of being formed, knocked down, resurrected, or dying.

In this section of the book, we discuss four trending heroes. Two of them are trending upward: Ulysses S. Grant and Sigmund Freud. One is trending downward: Woodrow Wilson. And one, Arnold Schwarzenegger, has experienced a roller coaster of trendiness, having gone up and down and then upward again.

Ulysses S. Grant: The Reappraised Hero

A proposal years ago by a number of Republicans wanting to honor Ronald Reagan by putting his image on the $50 bill might have had the unintended effect of further raising the stature of the man who is already on it. That would be another Republican, Ulysses S. Grant. People can

Ulysses S. Grant, the 18th president of the United States.

Source: Brady-Handy Photograph Collection, Library of Congress

argue about which president, Reagan or Grant, best exemplifies the principles of the GOP. But if the party is truly the party of Lincoln, it is important to remember that there is no Republican who fought harder and more effectively for Lincoln's principles than did Grant. It isn't even close.

Lincoln's principles were saving the Union and freeing slaves. He eventually came to believe that the best way to accomplish the first was to undertake the second. He argued that freeing slaves, and arming them in the Union cause, was an indispensable necessity to winning the war and saving the country. Grant became president less than four years after Lincoln's assassination and worked hard to continue a Reconstruction policy, like Lincoln's, that protected the rights of African Americans. He struggled successfully to secure ratification of the Fifteenth Amendment to the Constitution, guaranteeing Black people the right to vote, and in 1875 he supported a civil rights bill that anticipates in many ways the civil rights bill that was finally passed and signed into law by Lyndon Johnson nearly 90 years later.

Besides continuing Lincoln's policies as vigorously as he could, Grant deserves credit for overseeing international negotiations that preserved the peace when the United States could ill afford another war and for paving the way for economic expansion in the last quarter of the 19th century.

At the time of the move to put Ronald Reagan on the $50 bill, Sean Wilentz wrote in *The New York Times*, "Though much of the public and even some historians haven't yet heard the news, the vindication of Ulysses S. Grant is well under way." In 2000 a C-Span survey of historians ranked Grant 33rd among all US presidents. That in itself was an improvement over mid-20th-century polls that put Grant near the bottom, with Warren G. Harding and James Buchanan. In 2021 another C-Span survey ranked Grant 20th and placed him in 6th place on the dimension called "Pursued equal justice for all." Some argue that he should be ranked behind only Lincoln, Harry Truman, and Lyndon Johnson on that aspect of leadership.

Most interesting in the debate about Reagan and the corresponding reassessment of Grant is that our appraisals of presidents, among many other leaders, often change. A 2009 book by Joan Waugh entitled *U.S. Grant: American Hero, American Myth* shows that Grant was regarded by most Americans, in the South as well as the North, as a mythical, heroic figure for many years after his death in 1885. Then so-called "lost cause" historians elevated Robert E. Lee, denigrated Reconstruction, and turned Grant into a drunk and a "butcher." This period in history overlaps the tightening of Jim Crow laws in the South and the often overlooked segregationist policies of President Woodrow Wilson. Now people are looking at Grant through new lenses as a result of a number of recent biographies, which themselves pick up on themes of early or mid-20th century writers who were ignored during the heyday of the "lost cause" perspective.

To some extent, most all heroes and villains are the subject of myth. We construct charismatic, heroic, or villainous images of prominent people. In cases like Grant's, their reputation rises, falls, and rises again. Many of them thus qualify as trending heroes. It will be fascinating to see as the sesquicentennial of the Civil War unfolds how Grant's reputation as a military hero is appraised and reappraised, and whether those reappraisals affect his standing among the nation's 43 presidents.

Sigmund Freud: The Vindication of a Battered Theory

We often look to Albert Einstein as a shining example of a hero who transformed the way we think about the world. There are, of course, other scientists as well. Copernicus forever changed the way we view our solar system, proposing that celestial objects rotate around the sun rather than the earth. Darwin transformed our thinking about the origin of plant and animal species, proposing that processes of natural selection govern the evolution of life. To this list of transforming thinkers we add the name of Sigmund Freud, one of the most controversial and divisive figures in the history of science.

Freud was the first modern scientist to offer a theory of the human personality, a theory that was viewed as provocative, perverse, and counterintuitive. Human beings and their behavior, he said, are driven by dynamic, unconscious psychological conflicts. Our unconscious desires for sex and aggression (the id) often collide with our drive for moral perfection (the superego) and our flawed attempts to fulfill these motives within the constraints of reality (the ego). To ward off the inevitable anxiety that results from these conflicting demands, we use *defense mechanisms* – unconscious distortions of reality that keep us functioning.

Freud's theory was especially controversial in its emphasis on unconscious sexual urges, especially desires in early childhood for our opposite-sex parent. Many alternative schools of thought about human nature, such as behaviorism and humanism, were developed as a base of opposition to Freud. Over the past century, Freudian theory lost much of its luster and became a frequent source of disrespect, and even ridicule, within the academic community. A *Newsweek* article called him "history's most debunked doctor" (Adler, 2006), and W.H. Auden wrote in his 1973 poem, *In Memory of Sigmund Freud*, "if often he was wrong and, at times, absurd, to us he is no more a person now but a whole climate of opinion."

But over the past two decades, Freud has seen some measure of vindication. A number of recent psychological studies have supported his idea that people's judgments occur automatically and without awareness. Drew Westen, a psychologist at Emory University, said that before Freud, "nobody realized that our conscious mind is the tip of the mental iceberg." Freud was also correct about denial and other defense mechanisms. "The research is crystal-clear that we look the other way not to see what makes us uncomfortable," Westen said.

Freud is also getting more credit for anticipating work on the role of depletion of psychic energy in everyday tasks. Psychologist Roy Baumeister and his colleagues found that when people spend time resisting the temptation to eat chocolate, they are less persistent in solving problems as compared to people who are allowed to eat chocolate (Baumeister & Tierney, 2011). Freud is also given credit for establishing the field of psychotherapy and for being the first psychologist to recognize the importance of early childhood experiences in shaping adult behavior.

Because they dare to change the world, transforming heroes can ruffle feathers, rattle sensitivities, and become subject to the vicissitudes of public and professional opinion. Sigmund Freud's audacious theory of human nature attracted its share of critics, but it also triggered a voluminous amount of research, much of which has supported Freud's claims about the role of unconscious processes in shaping human judgments. As with many transforming figures, Freud and his reputation are likely to remain in flux for years to come. But at the present moment, his theories of the unconscious are considered prescient.

Woodrow Wilson: A Hero Trending Downward

Our evaluations of heroes are often in flux, with some heroes gaining popularity and others slipping downward in their reputations. As we've noted, heroes whose images are rising or falling are said to be *trending heroes*. We've argued that Sigmund Freud is trending up. His explorations of the unconscious and its effects on both conscious thought and overt behavior seem increasingly relevant to modern psychologists. Another individual, a hero to many in America, seems to be trending down. He is the 28th president of the United States, Woodrow Wilson.

For many years Wilson was near the top of presidential rankings. For example, in the first such poll of historians, conducted by Arthur Schlesinger in 1948, Wilson was fourth. In a 2000 C-SPAN poll he was ranked sixth, but in the 2021 C-SPAN poll he had fallen to 13th.

Why is Woodrow Wilson trending down? Will his ratings rebound back upward, or are they likely to stay depressed? Some insight comes from the leadership characteristics that historians judged in the two C-SPAN polls. Wilson improved on only one, Vision, moving from fifth to fourth. But on Crisis Leadership, Economic Management, International Relations,

Relations with Congress, and Performance Within Context of Times his ratings fell. However, the biggest drop was on Pursued Equal Justice for All. He went from a not very good 20th to the bottom half, 37th.

Despite a highly acclaimed and mostly favorable biography of Wilson published in 2009 by John Milton Cooper, there seems to be more focus on Wilson's racial and segregation policies. Wilson was a southerner, the first elected after the Civil War, and only the second Democrat, and his cabinet was mostly southern, some highly racist. One argument, for example, for segregating the post office during Wilson's administration was reported to have been that railroad cars carrying mail were not big enough for two bathrooms. It was unthinkable that Black and white employees might use the same facilities. Wilson was certainly preoccupied by other issues and may not have been as racist as his segregation policies suggest. Furthermore, he needs to be understood in the context of his times. He served as president during the height of Jim Crow. For whatever reasons – justified or not – his standing is slipping.

If the explanation is "Equal Justice for All," as suggested by C-SPAN, what are we to make of that? It may be that in an increasingly diverse society that has elected an African American president, historians and others are both more sensitized to issues touching on race and more critical of those perceived to retard progress on that front.

Another explanation may lie in increasing debate about the wisdom of Wilson's policies in shaping the Treaty of Versailles following World War I. Did the treaty's harsh treatment of Germany make Nazism more likely? Undoubtedly these issues will be debated for years to come, and presidential ratings will rise and fall. At the moment, a president once widely regarded as heroic is being assessed more negatively. He is still in the top 15, but his drop in the ratings is of note. At present, he is a trending hero heading down.

Arnold Schwarzenegger: Trending Up, Down, and Up Again

In the aftermath of the devastating 2007 wildfires that ravaged Southern California, Arnold Schwarzenegger, then serving as the governor of California, took decisive action that underscored his commitment to public service and leadership in times of crisis. Amid the chaos and destruction, Schwarzenegger visited the affected areas, meeting with firefighters, emergency personnel, and displaced residents. His presence and words of encouragement were not just symbolic; they were backed by swift executive actions to mobilize state resources, streamline the response efforts, and ensure that all necessary aid reached those in need. Schwarzenegger's proactive and hands-on approach during the wildfires highlighted his dedication to the safety and well-being of Californians, demonstrating the heroism of a leader who steps up in times of dire need to provide support and hope. This incident exemplifies his broader commitment to public service and his ability to inspire through action.

Arnold Schwarzenegger can be considered a hero due to his remarkable journey from an immigrant with limited English skills to a globally recognized figure in bodybuilding, acting, and politics. His story embodies the American Dream, demonstrating how hard work and determination can lead to extraordinary success. As a seven-time Mr. Olympia, he revolutionized bodybuilding and inspired countless individuals to pursue fitness. His transition to Hollywood brought him fame as a beloved action star in iconic films such as *The Terminator*. Beyond entertainment, Schwarzenegger's political career as the governor of California showcased his dedication to public service and advocacy for environmental issues, including pioneering initiatives to combat climate change. His resilience, versatility, and commitment to making a positive impact highlight his heroic qualities and enduring legacy.

Schwarzenegger's pathway to heroism has been neither smooth nor perfect. His critics have accused him of demonstrating the *Peter principle* – the tendency of people to rise to their level of incompetence. He rose to great professional heights, but his career appeared to unravel when he made some questionable decisions as governor of California. To make matters worse, while governor, Schwarzenegger showed poor judgment in his personal life as well. He stepped down as governor, his heroic status damaged, and then spent the next 15 years doing good public service to recapture much of that status. Today, Schwarzenegger is trending back upward as a hero.

During the 1970s, Arnold Schwarzenegger became a bodybuilding legend, winning an unprecedented seven Mr. Olympia contests. When his bodybuilding career ended, he made it his goal to become a star of motion pictures, an ambition that was met with derision by most observers. After all, Schwarzenegger sported a thick Austrian accent, was a stiff public speaker, and lacked any experience on stage or in film. With hard work and savvy, Schwarzenegger proved his critics wrong and went on to become one of the most highly sought-after leading men in Hollywood during the 1980s and 1990s. While achieving remarkable success as a bodybuilder and an actor, Schwarzenegger also enjoyed great triumphs as a businessman. He made millions of dollars from many different business ventures and in real estate investment.

In conclusion, Schwarzenegger's journey from a small village in Austria to global stardom and influential political leadership epitomizes the essence of heroism. His relentless pursuit of excellence in bodybuilding, film, and public service highlights his versatility and determination. Schwarzenegger's commitment to fitness revolutionized an industry, his iconic roles in cinema have inspired generations, and his tenure as governor of California show-cased his dedication to environmental causes and crisis management. Beyond his professional achievements, his resilience, ability to overcome adversity, and unwavering commitment to making a positive impact on society solidify his status as a hero. Arnold Schwarzenegger's legacy is a testament to the power of ambition, hard work, and the enduring impact one individual can have on the world.

3 Transitory Heroes
Hero Today, Gone Tomorrow

There's no better illustration of Andy Warhol's quip about everyone's 15 minutes of fame than examples of transitory heroes. These heroes are people who we admire for some significant action or achievement but for only a short period of time. They don't last because their heroism has no lasting effect other than to be a reminder of something we once applauded. Also, in many cases their heroism was created by a single act that becomes overlooked in our busy ongoing lives. Or they may not have demonstrated sustained effort or commitment.

Take, for example, the heroic actions of Charles Ramsey. In May 2013, Ramsey became a national hero when he helped rescue three women—Amanda Berry, Gina DeJesus, and Michelle Knight—who had been held captive for years in a house in Cleveland, Ohio. Ramsey's candid interviews and memorable quotes, such as mentioning his surprise to find out the women were being held captive, made him an instant media sensation. He was praised for his quick thinking and bravery. Despite the initial media frenzy and public admiration, Ramsey gradually disappeared from the public eye as the news cycle moved on. He achieved something great, but that accomplishment had no impact on most people after a few months.

Former Congresswoman Gabrielle Giffords of Arizona is another example of a transitory hero. Giffords was shot by a lone gunman at a rally in her congressional district in Tucson, Arizona, in January 2011. Six people were killed. Her courageous recovery from the assassin's bullet and her struggle to regain full brain function inspired many. But her bravery and tenacity are being quickly forgotten. There is too much happening too fast in today's world for a story even as moving as hers to retain much impact. This is particularly interesting because her struggle was not simply one of a single heroic moment. Her fight to recover continues.

Both Ramsey and Giffords clearly acted in ways that fit people's mental lists of the defining characteristics of heroes. We have shown that those lists include dimensions of both competence and morality and most often images of struggle and sacrifice against nearly insurmountable odds.

DOI: 10.4324/9781003328681-3

Ramsey displayed tremendous courage, and Giffords' struggle to stay alive and to regain nearly normal functioning was equally impressive. She inspired her congressional colleagues and the whole nation when she went to the capitol to cast a crucial vote and also when she appeared at President Barack Obama's State of the Union address just a year after being shot.

Even though Ramsey's and Giffords' heroism is fleeting, we regard them as true heroes. They exemplify heroism's essential qualities. In contrast, we think some transitory heroes are better regarded as false heroes. Even though they are publicly acclaimed, their "heroic" actions do not meet standards of competence or morality. They do satisfy needs we need to understand, but they do not provide genuine inspiration or authentic models of high achievement. A good example is Steven Slater, the JetBlue flight attendant who shouted obscenities at his passengers, stole some beer, and exited down the aircraft's evacuation slide. He immediately gained notoriety and celebrity and was a "folk hero" to many. Millions know the frustrations of air travel, for flight attendants as well as passengers, and could empathize with the impulse to tell off the airlines. They'd like to do it themselves. Also, people have more general fantasies of telling off their bosses, expressed so succinctly in Johnny Paycheck's noted song, "Take This Job and Shove It." Thus Steven Slater expressed feelings many of us experience ourselves. We know that they are not particularly admirable. We know that they don't express our best selves. But they are real nonetheless. Freud would argue that naming people who vicariously express those feelings "heroes" is similar to expressing socially unacceptable feelings through jokes. Freud emphasized the ways that humor (as well as dreams and slips of the tongue) bypass normal inhibitions and allow people to express impure thoughts. Admiring and making heroes of people who express our private frustrations or unacceptable impulses seems similarly Freudian. To the extent such people are heroes, we regard them as false heroes.

The profiles that follow include a wide range of heroes who for a short time attracted attention for their heroic acts. They come from a truly wide range of backgrounds and occupations, and they underline how widespread heroism is, even when it is fleeting. We first consider Abu Ghraib whistleblower Joe Darby, who revealed sadistic torture of war prisoners by US military police in Iraq. Next, we describe the career accomplishments of Mae Jemison, NASA's first Black woman astronaut; this profile was written by our good friend and colleague Rick Hutchins. We then cover the life of Civil War general Benjamin Butler, who gave emancipation an important early nudge forward by declaring escaped slaves "contraband of war" and refused to return them to their Southern owners; Christa McAuliffe, the school teacher who perished in the space shuttle *Challenger* explosion in 1986; the men and women who lent a hand to stem the disaster stemming from the Fukushima earthquake and tsunami in 2011; Liu Xiaobo, winner of the 2010 Nobel Peace Prize; Fred Korematsu, the civil rights worker who protested the prison camp internment of Japanese Americans living on the West Coast during World War II; and Eugene Goodman, who saved the lives of government officials during the January 6, 2021, insurrection. All are exceptional individuals who won our acclaim, at least for the time we paid attention.

Joe Darby: The Heroic Whistleblower of Abu Ghraib

Heroes are not always admired for their actions. Sometimes a heroic act is controversial, receiving high acclaim from some but contempt from others. One type of hero that often attracts both extreme approval and extreme condemnation is the *whistleblower* (Bocchiaro et al., 2012). Joe Darby is a courageous man whose story follows the classic pattern of the whistleblower. In January 2004, while serving in the US Army at the Abu Ghraib prisoner of war camp in Iraq, Darby discovered photographs of prisoners being abused by American soldiers. The abuse was physical, sexual, and emotional in nature, and it was obviously illegal and outrageous. "It violated everything I personally believed in and all I'd been taught about the rules of war," he said. When asked what was going through his mind when he first saw the photos, Darby simply said, "Disbelief. I tried to think of a reason why they would do this."

Darby turned the images over to authorities and wanted to remain anonymous, but his name became known after Secretary of Defense Donald Rumsfeld publicly identified him during a Senate hearing. It was at this point that things got ugly for Darby. The army decided to send him home, but a security assessment of his hometown revealed that it wasn't safe for him to return there. "There were a lot of threats, a lot of phone calls to his wife," said a local army veteran. "The overall threat of harassment or criminal activity to the Darbys was imminent." His wife Bernadette recalls that "we did not receive the response I thought we would. People were mean, saying he was a walking dead man; he was walking around with a bull's-eye on his head. It was scary." Darby and his wife now reside in protective military custody at an undisclosed location.

One of Phil Zimbardo's central tenets of heroism is that heroes have to be active when others are passive (Zimbardo, 2012). From this perspective, the opposite of heroism isn't villainy; it is apathy. Joe Darby clearly had the courage to take action while others remained silent. Human rights worker Carroll Bogert has said that "torture flourishes in the dark, and what Darby has done is to shine a light on what was happening in a place that was dark. Darby told the truth. Telling the truth doesn't always make you popular. And I think a lot of public opposition has come down on his head for the fact that he told the truth. But I think that history will put him in a good light."

Fortunately, Darby has received some much-deserved recognition for his courageous actions. In May 2004, he was profiled as the Person of the Week by anchor Peter Jennings on ABC's *World News Tonight*, and in December 2004 he was selected by ABC News as one of their People of the Year. Darby was also featured on *60 Minutes* in 2007, and he received a John F. Kennedy Profile in Courage Award in 2005. There is no doubt that as with many whistleblowers, Darby paid a steep price for his heroic actions. There will always be people who question Darby's motives or who believe that his whistleblowing betrayed his country. But many more will agree with what Edmund Burke is reported to have said: "All that is necessary for the triumph of evil is that good men do nothing."

Mae Jemison: Living Heroic Dreams

Not all heroes are created in a moment of crisis or deadly peril. Sometimes a life will simply grow to heroic proportions. Mae Jemison is just such a hero, a polymath who has dreamed great dreams and made them come true, and in so doing has shown us the greatness inherent in us all.

Mae Jemison, MD, is best known as the first female African American astronaut. In 1987, inspired by watching Nichelle Nichols' portrayal of Uhura on *Star Trek*, she joined the NASA astronaut program. For five years she trained for spaceflight, supported launch activities at the Kennedy

Mae Jemison

Source: NASA, July 1, 1992

Space Center, and worked at the Shuttle Avionics Integration Laboratory before flying her first and only space mission on the space shuttle *Endeavor* in 1992 as a life sciences mission specialist.

If this were Jemison's only notable contribution, she would still be a hero worthy of the record books. However, this Renaissance woman's life was remarkable long before her historic shuttle flight and continues to be remarkable to this day.

As a little girl, she was enamored of the arts and sciences. As early as kindergarten, she assumed that she would one day travel in space and that she would grow up to be a medical doctor (her interest in medicine, she says, began as a childhood fascination with pus). Her love for science was equaled by her love of the arts, which manifested itself most strongly as a passion for dance. She began training in a wide range of dance styles at the age of nine, and for a time she wanted to be a professional dancer (and she has indeed choreographed and produced several shows of modern jazz and African dance).

Somewhat precocious, she graduated high school and entered Stanford University at the age of 16. Four years later, she graduated with a BS in chemical engineering and a BA in African studies. Four years after that, she received her doctor of medicine degree from Cornell Medical College. When she completed her medical internship, she spent two years in Liberia and Sierra Leone as a medical officer with the Peace Corps.

Following her historic career at NASA, Jemison started her own company, the Jemison Group, which develops science and technology for use in daily life. She also founded the Dorothy Jemison Foundation for Excellence, named for her mother, which promotes various projects such as international science camps for children and adults. Several years later, she founded BioSentient Corp, a company which is working to commercialize a patented NASA biofeedback technology. She has also served on the board of directors of Gen-Probe Inc; as an honorary member of Alpha Kappa Alpha, a sorority founded in 1908 at Howard University to promote scholarship among Black women; as a professor-at-large at Cornell University; and as a professor of environmental studies at Dartmouth University.

To put it briefly, she has lived a life devoted to the betterment of humanity through the arts and sciences. In 1993, her interest in *Star Trek* came full circle when she appeared as a guest on an episode of *Star Trek: The Next Generation*. She also appeared on television in 2006 as the subject of a profile on the show *African American Lives* for PBS. Since her historic mission on the space shuttle *Endeavor* in 1992, Mae Jemison has touched the lives of millions of Americans and given inspiration to countless women, minorities, and young people. However, just as there have been no limits in her own life, there are no boundaries to the dream she represents, and she has become a role model for all people, all around the world. She is the embodiment of the spirit that will take us to the stars.

Heart-Wrenching Heroism at the Fukushima Nuclear Power Plant

When terrorists struck New York's twin towers on September 11, 2001, the world witnessed extraordinary acts of heroism from emergency personnel who sacrificed their lives to save innocent civilians. A decade later, the world witnessed a similar act of heroic sacrifice, although at a much slower and more agonizing pace than seen on 9/11. Every day, many workers at the Fukushima nuclear plant willingly exposed themselves to life-endangering radiation levels and terrible living conditions in a heroic effort to avert a nuclear meltdown.

The decommissioning of the Fukushima plant is a massive, multidecade effort involving the safe removal of radioactive materials, dismantling the reactors, and decontaminating the site. This process is expected to take 30 to 40 years or more, led by heroes who put themselves in harm's way for the greater good.

The nuclear plant was damaged by the massive earthquake that struck northern Japan in early March 2011. Weeks after the disaster, nightmarish details about what was going on at the Fukushima plant began to surface. According to news reports, the workers were "furiously connecting electrical cables, repairing instrument panels and pumping radioactive water out." Some workers were accidentally exposed to dangerously high levels of radiation. All worked long shifts under extreme stress. And many of them fully expected to die as a result of their repair efforts.

The Fukushima workers ate only two meals each day – "a carefully rationed breakfast of 30 crackers and vegetable juice and for dinner, a ready-to-eat meal or something out of a can" (Lee & Hancocks, 2011). In addition, because fresh uncontaminated water was in short supply, the workers had only wet wipes to clean themselves. If this weren't enough, many of the workers lived with the burden of their own personal tragedies weighing heavily on them. "My parents were washed away by the tsunami, and I still don't know where they are," one worker wrote in an email. "Crying is useless," said another worker. "If we're in hell now, all we can do is crawl up towards heaven."

Japanese authorities did everything in their power to assist and support the Fukushima workers. The task of repairing the facility and cleaning up radioactive spills took many months and by necessity involved putting the workers in harm's way. The heroism of these men is being recognized around the world, especially among Japanese civilians living nearby whose lives (and livelihoods) benefited the most from the noble sacrifice being made.

Time is an important concept in understanding heroism. A heroic act sometimes requires a split-second decision, such as Wesley Autrey's decision to save a man who fell onto a set of New York train tracks. But there are times, such as in Japan since 2011, when heroism involves a long-term commitment to place the welfare of others ahead of one's own welfare. One could argue that our greatest heroes are these latter heroes – those who understand full well, after ample deliberation, that their daily actions may be costly to themselves but who plow forward because they know their actions are absolutely essential for the collective well-being.

As with many heroes, the Fukushima workers downplayed their contributions. "In reality we are not heroes," said one worker, "as we are taking turns doing the work under supervision in accordance with law." Said another: "We have the option to turn down working at the plant. My family has told me to take it. It is a very difficult decision to make." But he, like the others, remained to do the job of protecting people, a job that heroes know they must do.

Randy Pausch: The Hero Who Dared Us to Live Our Dreams

Some heroes tug at our heartstrings by the way they live, and some by the way they die. Randy Pausch was a hero who did both. Pausch lived his life to the fullest, contributing significantly to the betterment of society and creating ways to fulfill even his most outlandish childhood dreams. Told by doctors at the age of 46 that he had terminal cancer, Pausch used the same unbridled enthusiasm that served him so well in life to make his final months immeasurably rich and inspiring to us all.

Randy Pausch was a professor of computer science at Carnegie Mellon University in Pittsburgh. Although a highly acclaimed faculty member, he was largely unknown to most people outside his profession and university community. In 2006, his doctors gave him the devastating diagnosis of pancreatic cancer. With only months to live, Pausch was invited by Carnegie Mellon to give the "Last Lecture" – a speech in which eminent professors impart their final words of wisdom as if it were their last chance to do so. In Pausch's case, it truly was his last chance.

The lecture was entitled "Really Achieving Your Childhood Dreams," and it vaulted Pausch into the public spotlight. He opened his speech by informing the audience of his death sentence, but he relaxed the crowd with his trademark smile, the familiar bounce in his step, and his genuine enthusiasm. His last lecture focused on his many childhood ambitions, such as experiencing zero gravity, becoming Captain Kirk, playing professional football, and designing computer-based theme park rides for Disneyworld. Pausch spoke passionately about the importance of having dreams and of having fun in the pursuit of those dreams. "I don't know how to not have fun," he said. "I'm *dying* and I'm having fun. And I'm going to keep having fun every day I have left. Never lose the child-like wonder."

Pausch also implored his audience to persevere in life. "Never give up," he said "Brick walls are there for a reason: they let us prove how badly we want things. Don't bail. The best of the gold is at the bottom of the barrels of crap." Pausch emphasized the importance of helping others, nurturing relationships, and remaining loyal to friends. "Do the right thing," he said. "When you do the right thing, good things have a way of happening." He added: "If you lead your life the right way, the karma will take care of itself. The dreams will come to you." At the conclusion of his lecture, Pausch received a lengthy standing ovation from a tearful, grateful audience.

Pausch's last lecture found its way onto YouTube, where it quickly went viral. Millions of people were moved by his inspiring life and by the courage with which he approached his terminal illness. His remaining months were very full and rich. Oprah Winfrey invited him to give an abridged version of his lecture on her show. He co-authored a *New York Times* bestselling book entitled *The Last Lecture*. The Pittsburgh Steelers heard of his dream to play in pro football and invited him to practice with them. J.J. Abrams, the director of 2009's *Star Trek* movie, heard that Pausch wanted to be Captain Kirk and permitted him to play a small part in the movie. During these last few months, Pausch underwent numerous painful procedures and treatments in an attempt to thwart his cancer. But he succumbed to his illness in July 2008 at the age of 47.

After first being diagnosed with terminal cancer, no one would have blamed Randy Pausch if he had simply disappeared from sight and spent private time with his family. Heroes, however, eschew the easy path. They selflessly share their time, their wisdom, and their love for others in an effort to make the world a better place. In fact, Pausch himself admitted that his intended audience for his Last Lecture was his three young children, ages 3, 6, and 7, to whom he wanted to leave a lasting legacy about how to live a good life. He surely did that and more.

Gabrielle Giffords: Heroic Recovery from Trauma

As college professors, we sometimes required our students to read *Into Thin Air*, Jon Krakauer's gripping account of the May 11, 1996, Mount Everest disaster in which eight climbers were killed in a blizzard during their descent. Several heroic rescues occurred on the mountain that day, but one climber who didn't save any of the others is often viewed by our students to be the greatest hero of the tragedy. The climber's name is Beck Weathers, a Texas physician who sustained severe injuries on the mountain. Weathers was left for dead by his fellow climbers, yet somehow he managed to save *himself*.

Heroes, it seems, are not always the people who save others or who perform actions that make the world a better place. Heroes can also be individuals who survive horrific ordeals and triumph over great pain and injury. Presumed to be too close to death to be rescued, Beck Weathers roused himself from his hypothermic slumber and in near blindness stumbled on frostbitten feet back to his expedition's camp. For years he endured numerous painful surgeries to treat severe injuries that left his face and limbs disfigured. Today he is back practicing medicine. There are countless other examples of heroes who prevail over personal setbacks and tragedy – people who suffer crippling injuries as victims of accidents, crimes, or illness.

The story of Gabrielle Giffords follows this heroic narrative of recovery from trauma. On January 8, 2011, Giffords, a US representative from Arizona, held an open meeting with her constituents outside a suburban supermarket in Tucson. A crazed gunman appeared from the crowd and shot her in the head. The bullet passed through the left side of her brain, but somehow it did not kill her. Giffords' intern, a young man named Daniel Hernandez, tended to her injuries and was hailed for his heroic actions after the incident.

While we applaud the heroism of Hernandez and others who come to the aid of the sick and injured, we also believe that the long difficult journey of the sick and injured makes them heroes as well. Giffords' road to recovery has been supremely challenging and will remain so for many years. At first, simply surviving her injury was the main goal. The next huge breakthrough was responding to simple commands by moving a finger. Giffords then overcame a significant hurdle by learning to breathe again on her own and later being able to sit up in bed.

The long-term rehabilitation process for someone with Giffords' injuries is "grueling," according to Dr. Christina Kwasnica, director of the Neuro Rehabilitation Program at St. Joseph's Hospital in Phoenix. "It's hard work. One of the hardest parts is realizing how long the road is." Years after the shooting, Giffords is still bravely immersed in various therapies to improve her ability to speak, read, write, and walk. Indications suggest that she is doing remarkably well, thanks to hard work, perseverance, and a supportive family. Giffords' recovery from her gunshot wounds is a testament to her resilience and determination. While she continues to face challenges, her progress and advocacy work highlight her strength and dedication to making a positive impact on society. Her story is one of hope and inspiration, showing that even in the face of severe adversity, one can make significant strides and contribute meaningfully to important causes.

The heroic journey can take many different forms. The conventional view of heroes is that they save others from suffering, but inevitably we all find ourselves on the receiving end of a serious setback. In these instances, the most heroic act we can perform is to save ourselves.

Benjamin "Beast" Butler: Hero for a Moment

General Benjamin Butler is described in James McPherson's masterful history of the Civil War era, *Battle Cry of Freedom*, as the "ubiquitous" Benjamin Butler. Butler was a so-called political general from Massachusetts who was given a military position in the Union army because of his connections in Congress and his ability to raise troops in his home state. He served in Virginia early in the war, then oversaw martial law in New Orleans after it was captured by Union forces in 1862. It was there that he acquired the unflattering nickname "Beast Butler" for his harsh treatment of civilians. He also was called "Spoons Butler" after being accused of stealing silver from the owners of New Orleans homes he commandeered during his tenure in the Crescent City.

In 1864, Butler was back in Virginia but badly bungled several critical military assignments, infuriating Union commander Ulysses S. Grant. Once Lincoln was re-elected in November 1864, Butler's political clout no longer mattered, and Lincoln allowed Grant to sack him.

Nothing thus far sounds very heroic about Butler, in terms of either the dimensions of competence or morality that we have stressed are essential to the perception of heroism. However, Butler did take a far-reaching step early in the war that paved the way for Lincoln's Emancipation Proclamation of January 1, 1863. While emancipation was long in coming, and resulted from many forces and events, Butler's contribution was timely and crucial.

It happened in May 1861, the month immediately following the Confederate attack on Fort Sumter. That attack opened the actual fighting, which would last for over four years. Butler was stationed at Fort Monroe in Hampton, Virginia. The fort was essentially an island in the waters of Hampton Roads, connected to the mainland by a narrow strip of sand. Three slaves escaped from where they were working on rebel fortifications and ran down the ribbon of beach to the fort. The slaves' owner was a Confederate Colonel who came to Fort Monroe under a white flag of truce, demanding that Butler return the three slaves. He argued that the Fugitive Slave Act of 1850 required that Butler do so.

You might imagine how Butler, a savvy politician, reacted. He said, effectively, now let me see. You are an officer in the army of a self-declared nation that is trying to cast off the authority of the United States, but you'd like me to apply the laws of those United States for your benefit. Butler reminded the officer that the South regarded slaves as a "species of property" and it was a long-standing principle of warfare that enemies seize each other's property. Butler then declared the escaped slaves as "contraband of war" (i.e., captured property) and kept them at Fort Monroe.

Word spread in the African American community, and soon hundreds of escaped slaves arrived behind Union lines at Fort Monroe, now known among slaves as the "freedom fort." Similar escapes happened in other parts of the Confederacy. Union politicians, including Abraham Lincoln, did not know how to treat these individuals. Were they free? Were they now just slaves in Union forces? In short order the US Congress passed a number of "confiscation acts" that regulated the treatment of escaped slaves. It was quickly recognized that they could do important work for the Union, including bearing arms. Benjamin Butler's "contraband" decision thus paved the way for the emancipation policy that Lincoln announced preliminarily in September 1862 and formalized in the Emancipation Proclamation of 1863. Butler's crucial contribution has generally been overlooked and overshadowed by his incompetence and self-aggrandizement. But he does earn the appellation "transitory hero."

Liu Xiaobo: A Hero of Peace, Democracy, and Human Rights

Heroic journeys can assume many different forms. People can enjoy instant heroism through a single act, as in the case of New York subway hero Wesley Autrey. Or people can, through a steady commitment of doing good works, construct a resume of heroism that reaches a crescendo of accomplishment and acclaim. Such is the case of Liu Xiaobo, a Chinese intellectual, writer, and human rights activist whose passion for peace and justice earned him the 2010 Nobel Peace Prize for his long-term dedication to promoting positive social change.

Because of his strident advocacy of human rights in China, Liu spent much of his life either in a Chinese jail or in exile abroad. The Chinese government imprisoned him several times for participating in the 1989 Tiananmen Square protests, for expressing his opposition to China's one-party Communist system, and for seeking the release of prisoners jailed for participating in various demonstrations. Liu's final jail sentence stemmed from his role in organizing and disseminating a document called *Charter 08*, which calls for 19 changes to improve human rights in China. These reforms include establishing an independent legal system, granting citizens the freedom to assemble peacefully, and eliminating the Communist Party's grip on the nation.

Over the years, Liu's endorsement of political change in China has attracted increasing attention and admiration both inside and outside his country. The Norwegian Nobel Peace Prize committee in Oslo, Norway, was particularly interested in Liu's career. On October 8, 2010, the committee awarded him the Nobel prize – and $1.5 million – for "his long and non-violent struggle for fundamental human rights in China."

Not surprisingly, the Chinese government took quick action to suppress any news of the award. Broadcasts of the announcement in China by CNN were blacked out, and coverage of Liu Xiaobo's accomplishment on popular Internet sites was removed. Moreover, electronic posts about Liu on China's Twitter-like service were quickly deleted, and any cell-phone text messages with the Chinese characters for Liu Xiaobo were removed.

These repressive actions, of course, had the effect of earning Liu even greater heroic status. We know from our studies on heroism that among our most revered heroes are underdogs who make significant self-sacrifices in the service of others. Liu's life story fits this heroic script to perfection. China's attempts to diminish Liu and his Nobel Prize–winning work gave him greater fame and highlighted the urgency of his cause.

Was Liu any more of a hero after having won the Nobel Prize than he was prior to winning it? In our research, we have found that most people believe that it is the heroic work that makes a hero, not societal recognition. But some people believe that a central criterion for heroism is, indeed, recognition. Certainly, after having won the Nobel Prize, Liu and his dedication to social change in China are now known to millions more people. Today we celebrate his sacrifice and heroism and the Nobel Committee's acknowledgment of his work.

In summary, Liu Xiaobo is considered a hero for his advocacy for democracy and human rights, for his authorship of *Charter 08*, for receiving the Nobel Peace Prize, and for his unwavering commitment to his cause that came at great personal cost. His death in 2017 was mourned by freedom-lovers worldwide.

Christa McAuliffe: Lost Hero of the Space Shuttle *Challenger*

People often report that they can remember exactly where they were and what they were doing at the time they receive the news of a shocking event. Psychologists call this *flashbulb* memory. If you are an American born before 1995, you probably have a flashbulb memory of the terrorist attacks on September 11, 2001. If you were born before 1980, you have a flashbulb memory of the crash of the space shuttle *Challenger*, which occurred on January 28, 1986.

Any deadly accident qualifies as a great tragedy, but what made the *Challenger* crash so especially poignant was the loss of one highly acclaimed crew member, Christa McAuliffe. Even prior to the shuttle's launch, the American public had embraced McAuliffe as a bold and generous hero about to embark on the kind of adventure that is usually the stuff of dreams.

McAuliffe was a New Hampshire high school teacher selected by NASA with great fanfare to become the first civilian in space. NASA screened 11,500 applicants and chose McAuliffe because of her teaching excellence, bubbling optimism, and boundless energy. She wrote on her application, "I watched the Space Age being born and I would like to participate" (Burgess, 2000, p. 20). NASA asked McAuliffe to assume the role of teacher in space and transmit lessons back to earth about experiencing zero gravity and other space-related phenomena.

Millions of McAuliffe's fans, many of them school children, were glued to their television sets to witness the launch of her shuttle. A mere 73 seconds after the *Challenger* took off into space, it exploded. The nation was in grief-stricken shock. Six other heroic crew members lost on that day were Francis R. Scobee, Michael J. Smith, Judith A. Resnik, Ronald E. McNair, Ellison S. Onizuka, and Gregory B. Jarvis.

In the aftermath of the tragedy, the best of human nature quickly surfaced. Letters, poetry, postcards, and words of sympathy flooded the mailboxes of the surviving members of the McAuliffe family. These loving words came from people from all walks of life, especially teachers and school children. The letters came from all corners of the globe: the town of Hamilton, Scotland; the Belgian town of Zele; the city of Sydney, Australia; the ancient Egyptian city of Heliopolis; along with Paris, London, Athens, and Hong Kong. Many more came from around the United States. Each letter conveyed the hurt, the sorrow, and the powerful influence that Christa McAuliffe had on people's lives.

McAuliffe's husband Steven said that remembrances of Christa were "comforting and inspirational for our family." Within hours of the tragedy, President Reagan gave a moving speech in honor of the *Challenger*'s crew. "We mourn seven heroes," Reagan told the grieving public. He spoke especially to children: "I know it's hard to understand, but sometimes painful things like this happen. It's all part of the process of exploration and discovery."

Perhaps the most powerful legacy of Christa McAuliffe was her passion for teaching. "I touch the future," she said. "I teach." With these words, McAuliffe recognized that teachers leave their marks on the world long after they are gone. Quite remarkably and by accident, NASA engineer Jerry Woodfill stumbled across McAuliffe's unfinished lesson plans 21 years after *Challenger* crashed. These lessons are now available online for any school or teacher to use and for anyone to see.

Nearly 40 years after McAuliffe's untimely end, she is still viewed as a hero to many people who admired her for pursuing her dream to participate in space flight and to share her knowledge with others. "She was the ultimate teacher," said Dennis Van Roekel, president of the National Education Association. "She not only engaged in this extraordinary venture to captivate the imagination of students, Christa wanted to elevate the teaching profession so students would aspire to teach" (Burgess, 2000, p. 177).

The Heroism and Leadership of Fred Korematsu

Heroes show leadership by taking steps to save or improve our lives. A hero's leadership can be *direct*, as when the leader interacts directly with followers, or it can be *indirect*, as when the leader's works and deeds provide an example or model for others. Two of the 20th century's greatest indirect leaders were Rosa Parks and Fred Korematsu. Parks became a civil rights hero when she refused to vacate her seat on a Montgomery, Alabama, bus in 1955. Korematsu's indirect leadership is not as well known but is no less important.

Korematsu was an ordinary 22-year-old American living in Oakland, California, when Japan attacked Pearl Harbor on December 7, 1941. In the weeks that followed, Americans feared another Japanese attack on the West Coast of the United States. Racial discrimination against Japanese Americans, already a problem before Pearl Harbor, became intensified. Korematsu was fired from his job as a welder in a shipyard simply because of his ancestry.

Ten weeks after the attack, President Roosevelt issued Executive Order No. 9066, which required all people of Japanese ancestry along the entire Pacific coast, including all of California and most of Oregon and Washington, to leave their homes and report to internment camps. At the time, most Americans supported Roosevelt's decision. Even the *Los Angeles Times* defended it: "While it might cause injustice to a few to treat them all as potential enemies," wrote the editor, "I cannot escape the conclusion . . . that such treatment . . . should be accorded to each and all of them while we are at war with their race."

Most Japanese Americans complied with Executive Order 9066 to demonstrate their loyalty to America and its laws. But Korematsu recognized the inherent injustice of the decree. "I was just living my life, and that's what I wanted to do," he said in a 1987 interview.

Korematsu did not turn himself in to authorities. Consequently, he was arrested, jailed, convicted of a felony, and sent to the Topaz internment camp in Utah. While imprisoned at the camp, Korematsu appealed his conviction, arguing that his constitutional rights had been violated. The court ruled against him. In 1944 he appealed all the way to the Supreme Court, which upheld his conviction in a 6-3 decision, authored by Justice Hugo Black. The Court ruled that Executive Order 9066, though constitutionally suspect, is justified during times of "emergency and peril."

After the war, Korematsu waited nearly 40 years to clear his name. In 1982, he obtained suppressed government documents indicating that the forced relocation of Americans to internment camps was motivated by racism, not military necessity. With this evidence, the courts overturned Korematsu's conviction. In 1998, President Bill Clinton awarded Korematsu the Presidential Medal of Freedom, the nation's highest civilian honor. At the ceremony Clinton said, "In the long history of our country's constant search for justice, some names of ordinary citizens stand for millions of souls. To that distinguished list today we add the name of Fred Korematsu."

Heroism can take time. Leaders know when to stay the course, and heroic leaders such as Korematsu stay the course to its triumphant conclusion. "It may take time to prove you're right," he said, "but you have to stick to it." In the face of injustice, he urged people "to protest, but not with violence, and don't be afraid to speak up. One person can make a difference, even if it takes forty years."

Transitory Heroes and Villains: A Tale of Two Stevens

A recurring theme in our review of heroes is the idea that heroism is in the eye of the beholder. One person's hero is another person's villain. While we acknowledge the subjectivity of heroism, there is no denying the fact that some people are much more heroic than others. Two heroes who we profile in this book, Mahatma Gandhi and Nelson Mandela, have clearly had a far more positive and enduring impact on the world than two others we profile, Drew Barrymore and Pretty Boy Floyd.

In our taxonomy of heroism, described earlier, we suggested that some heroes are ephemeral or transitory in their influence. They are at one end of the duration-of-influence continuum, with transforming heroes who forever change society at the other end. Interestingly, this same continuum also applies to villains and the negative deeds that they do. Ephemeral villains are bad guys whose badness is minor or fleeting, whereas transforming villains (e.g., Adolph Hitler) perform acts of evil that have truly altered the world permanently.

One transitory hero who received considerable media attention years ago is the former JetBlue flight attendant Steven Slater. You may recall that Slater was the man who resigned his position in a blaze of glory. On August 9, 2010, after the aircraft on which he was working landed safely, Slater shouted obscenities at a customer who was rude to him, grabbed beer out of the plane's kitchen galley, and slid down the plane's emergency evacuation chute. Slater became a folk hero to millions of working Americans who admired him for acting out the famous Johnny Paycheck song, "Take This Job and Shove It." Slater attracted over 200,000 Facebook admirers, and people even composed songs in his honor.

Conversely, a prominent example of a transitory villain is Steve Bartman, a Chicago Cubs fan who tried to catch a foul ball during game 6 of the

2003 National League Championship series. Bartman's outstretched hands deflected the ball, possibly preventing Cubs' left fielder Moises Alou from catching it. Given new life, the batter eventually drew a walk and scored, sparking a comeback for the Florida Marlins, who won the game and the series. Bartman instantly became a target of hatred. He had to be led away from the stadium under security escort for his own safety as Cubs fans shouted profanities at him and pelted him with debris. He also received police protection after his name and address were made public on baseball message boards.

What does this tale of two Stevens tell us? It tells us that transitory heroes and villains don't enjoy the spotlight for very long. Most people today hardly remember Slater and Bartman. Unlike transforming heroes and villains, transitory individuals tend to perform actions that affect only a small, inconsequential slice of life. Transitory heroes and villains capture our attention for a brief while, but like a helium balloon with a slow leak, they soon sink to their former level of anonymity.

Eugene Goodman: A Life-Saving Hero

Some heroes are relatively ordinary people who are suddenly confronted with an emergency where they must draw on their deepest reserves of wit and will to do the right thing. During the build-up to the Cuban Missile Crisis, President Kennedy encouraged Americans to keep their heads and keep their nerve. In dire situations doing the right heroic thing depends on thinking clearly under pressure and often putting oneself in danger. During the January 6, 2021, insurrectionist attack on the US Capitol, police officer Eugene Goodman rose to the occasion. He behaved heroically and most probably saved many lives, including those of the rioters who threatened both him and US senators.

Goodman was a native of Washington, DC who served in the United States Army from 2002 until 2006. He saw combat in Iraq with the famed 101st Airborne Division and was commended for being "cool, calm, and collected." He began working with the capitol police in 2009. After 12 years of routine duty, Goodman alone faced rioters threatening members of Congress, and himself.

The January 6 attacks grew out of ex-President Donald Trump attempting to overturn the 2020 election of Joe Biden to the White House. As attempts to challenge voting in swing states were defeated, Trump grew increasingly desperate. Court rulings went against him, and he failed to stop the counting of electoral votes in the states. Perhaps the last chance was to stop the routine counting of those votes in the capitol on January 6. Trump sent out tweets imploring his supporters to protest on the morning of the count, saying "Big protest in D.C. on *January 6th*. Be there, *will be wild*!" His speech that morning urged his raucous fans to go the capitol (he said he would be there with them, but he was not) and "fight like hell" to save the country. The attack ensued, leading to several deaths.

Goodman's defining moment came when a crowd that had broken through several barriers was approaching the US Senate chamber. Goodman stood on top of a landing where there was a clear path to the chamber. Some senators had left just moments before, directed by Goodman. Then Goodman glanced toward the chamber and pushed the crowd leader back, and then backed away himself. He didn't run away from the mob but walked backward, seemingly inviting them to follow as he seemed to retreat. One account describes Goodman's action as follows:

> In short, he tricked them, willingly becoming the rabbit to their wolf pack, pulling them away from the chambers where armed officers were waiting, avoiding tragedy and saving lives. Lives which include their own.
>
> (Sturdivant, 2021, p. 1)

As he drew them further and further away from danger, he eventually led them to an open room in the capitol where other capitol police stopped at least that part of the mob.

Goodman's quick thinking and ingenious decoying saved lives. He was immediately recognized as heroic. Two weeks later Goodman accompanied Vice President Kamala Harris to the inaugural platform. Earlier that day President Trump finally left the White House. Later the Senate passed a resolution praising Goodman. The House of Representatives took no action, perhaps fearing the reaction of Trump supporters. However, two years later, on January 6, 2023, the second anniversary of the insurrection, President Joe Biden presented Goodman with the Presidential Citizens Medal.

Although Goodman rose to heroic heights that crucial day, it was not entirely a "one-off." Goodman had served bravely in the military. He level-headedness was there for his comrades to see at the time. While his heroism had a firm foundation in experience and character, it reached new levels at that crucial moment on a defining day in American history.

4 Transitional Heroes
Those Whom We Outgrow

Heroes offer inspirational models of accomplished performance and moral commitment. Throughout our lifetimes, most of us have had a long list and wide range of heroes. Some may be fleeting, and some may be lasting. Some who are no longer our heroes may have been important to us at particular points in our psychological development. But they are no longer heroes because we have moved on to other aims and aspirations. The persons who inspired us at age 10, for example, might not be psychologically relevant as adults. When we were younger, baseball All Star Willie Mays was a hero known for his amazing abilities, and his cheerful athleticism and dedicated achievement. We were inspired to work as hard and happily and effectively as Willie. Internalizing aspects of his heroism helped us develop beyond the domain in which he motivated us.

But then life changes. As a Little Leaguer we needed Willie's example. As a college sophomore, we realized his qualities no longer mattered so much. We had moved on to later stages of development with different concerns and priorities. Similarly, in high school, our favorite rock'n'roll groups mattered. As graduate students, we had moved on. Great scholars and or perhaps political leaders became our heroes. As our needs changed, so did our heroes (Allison & Goethals, 2014).

We call the heroes who helped define our identities and shape our motivations at early stages of development transitional heroes. The term transitional hero resonates with Winnicott's (1953) concept of the transitional object, defined as some prized, private object that gives a young child a sense of security and helps them take the first steps toward autonomy. An iconic example of a transitional object is Linus's dirty, well-worn blanket in the comic strip *Peanuts*. It was his source of "security and happiness" (Schultz, 1956). As we develop, we need heroes as well as objects to cling to, even if they are only revealed to us through books, magazines, records, or movies. They influence us for important parts of our unfolding lives, but not as we move past those periods.

DOI: 10.4324/9781003328681-4

As always, heroism is in the eye of the beholder. One person's transitional hero may be a long-lasting, life-span hero for another. Country and Western singer Patsy Cline was a hero to some young women only for a time but remains a hero much later in life for others. It's also true that some individuals may be transitional heroes during important youthful life passages, then fade in influence, and then perhaps reemerge later in life as a heroic figure. One of us greatly admired Elvis Presley as a preteen. Then Elvis changed, making some truly horrible movies and becoming an almost weird, overweight drug-addled caricature of himself. Elvis left the building, so to speak, and so did the author. Later, both of us realized the huge impact Elvis had on not only American but world culture. Now he has regained his heroic status in our eyes. To us, he is The King.

Our profiles of transitional heroes begins with Henry Aaron, one of the greatest baseball players of all-time. Aaron might be considered a transitional hero for his exceptional achievements on the baseball field. Athletic ability, by itself, might be deemed heroic to a young person, but most of us outgrow the need to worship heroes based on athleticism alone. What might qualify Aaron as a traditional hero – a category we turn to later in this book – resides in his resilience in the face of adversity. Aaron broke Major League Baseball's long-standing home run record while enduring significant racial discrimination and threats, demonstrating extraordinary courage and perseverance. Beyond his athletic accomplishments, Aaron used his platform to advocate for civil rights and equality, inspiring countless individuals both on and off the field. Aaron, therefore, is a transitional hero if we focus only on his athletic achievements. That's why we've included him in this section, acknowledging that he (like many heroes profiled in this book) can belong in multiple categories of our traxonomy.

Another classic example of a transitional hero is former children's television host Mr. Rogers. *Mr. Rogers' Neighborhood* on PBS provided a safe, comforting educational environment for young boys and girls for over 40 years. Fred Rogers qualifies as a transitional hero because the many of the children he meant so much to in preschool forgot him or even mocked him during their adolescent years. But Mr. Rogers wonderfully illustrates the point that some transitional figures can become heroes at more than one stage of development. Many men and women who admired Mr. Rogers as youngsters in the 1970s likely found him heroic again in the early 2000s when he served as heroes for their own children.

Reed Richards, aka Mr. Fantastic, and Iron Man perfectly exemplify the comic book superhero. Each has a complicated and inspiring, if troubled, life history and provides pleasant and even somewhat daring escapism for boys and girls (mostly boys) of a certain age. They inspire those youngsters, but for most admirers their heroism is likely to be fleeting. Again we thank Rick Hutchins for composing a very clever profile of Reed Richards.

We find Captain James T. Kirk of the *Star Trek* series among our most interesting transitional heroes. He provided a strong example of effective and mostly moral leadership. Although often distracted by attractive women, when the chips were down we could always count on Kirk to do the right thing. For one of us he was only a transitional hero, having lost favor and influence after college. For the other, he always has been and probably always will be a hero. ('Til death do us part.) The former author decided where to classify him.

As a group the heroes we describe in this chapter illustrate how our interests, motives, and aspirations change over time, and with them, our heroes.

Henry (Hank) Aaron: The Hammerin' Hero

Recently Major League Baseball recognized the 50th anniversary milestone of one of its most enduring moments, the day in 1974 that Henry "Hank" Aaron broke Babe Ruth's record of 714 career home runs. Aaron was one of baseball's giants, still holding career records for runs batted in (RBIs) and total bases. A crucial part of Aaron's legacy was the grace and class with which he performed during the chase for Ruth's record, and character with which he at least publicly ignored the flood of racist hate mail he received during those trying months. Aaron was a

Henry (Hank) Aaron, photographed with President George W. Bush as he receives the Presidential Medal of Freedom during a ceremony at the White House.

Source: Photo by Paul Morse, Courtesy George W. Bush Presidential Library & Museum

quiet, soft-spoken gentlemen who embodied the best principles of his deep Christian faith. He was a hero for his heroics as a player and his behind-the-scenes efforts for civil rights and the cause of equal justice. In the early 1970s, one mark of an African American being embraced by the dominant white culture was appearing in advertisements for mainstream commercial products. In 1973, when Aaron was on the verge of passing Ruth's record, he appeared in an ad for Brut Cologne. Dressed in a light-colored suit and tie, he spoke about the product giving 100%, just as he did playing baseball. At the end he quipped. "On the field I let my bat do the talking, off the field I let my Brut do the talking." Quiet, dignified, strong, formidable: That was the essence of Hank Aaron.

The journey to his place in American history was not easy. In fact, at the time of the commercial it was perilous. Aaron faced numerous death threats from racists who wanted to stop a Black man from eclipsing the iconic record of a white man. He had been born in Mobile, Alabama, in 1934 and learned to play baseball using makeshift equipment such as sticks and bottlecaps. His high school did not have a baseball team, so Aaron played semi-pro ball for the Mobile Black Bears and then found his way into the Negro Leagues. At age 18, he signed with the Boston Braves, who soon after moved to Milwaukee. For a time he played for the Jacksonville Braves minor league team and navigated the Jim Crow South. Often he had to eat in different restaurants and sleep in different hotels from his white teammates. He finally came up to the major league Milwaukee Braves in 1954 and the next year had the first of many outstanding seasons. In 1955 he played in his first All-Star team. Aaron led his team to the World Series title in 1957 and back to the series in 1958, though the Braves lost.

Starting in 1966 the Braves moved to Atlanta. Aaron continued his superb play and in 1972 passed second-place Willie Mays on the all-time home run list. The highly publicized pursuit of Ruth's record began. Aaron finished the 1973 season with 713 career home runs, one short of Ruth's mark. During the winter Aaron received record amounts of mail, much of it encouraging but a discouraging amount fouled by racist comments. One of the most encouraging public remarks came from Claire Ruth, the Babe's widow. She said that Ruth would have cheered Aaron on.

Aaron actually feared he might be killed before the new season began. In that case there would be no pursuit of the final record-tying and record-breaking home runs. But there were no attempts on his life during the off-season. The Braves opened the 1974 pennant race in Cincinnati. Should Aaron wait until the team got home to Atlanta? His sense of the right thing was to play. He hit the record tying 714th homer on the road and then returned to Atlanta. He then hit number 715 in his first game at home.

Aaron eventually recorded 755 home runs, a mark that is still regarded as a landmark in major league baseball history.

Henry Hank Aaron is a hero for his tremendous playing, his all-time records, and for his class and dignity. He is one of baseball's and America's all-time greats.

Fred Rogers: Love, Wisdom, and Compassion for All Ages

About 20 years ago, a friend of ours was in the throes of a major depression. As she lay listlessly on the couch one day, feeling the weight of the world on her shoulders, she flipped through the television channels and came across the classic children's television program, *Mister Rogers' Neighborhood*. Struck by the show's gentle, loving host Fred Rogers, our friend penned a letter to him, expressing her grief and hopelessness but also her appreciation for briefly lifting her spirits with his message of love and hope. A week later, to her great surprise, she received a handwritten letter back from Rogers, who thanked her for writing and gave her encouragement and support. To this day this framed letter from Rogers hangs on the wall of our friend's home, and she remains deeply grateful to him for reaching out to her during the most difficult time in her life.

Not surprisingly, Fred Rogers wrote many such letters to his fans. In an age when celebrity misbehavior and drug use capture most of the headlines, Rogers was a true gentleman whose primary mission in life was to enrich the lives of other people, especially children. As a young man, Rogers noticed during television's infancy how the new medium was being misused. "I went into television because I hated it so," said Rogers. "I thought there was some way of using this fabulous instrument to be of nurture to those who would watch and listen."

Rogers developed a show in 1968 that helped children build self-esteem, conquer their fears, and love others. *Mister Rogers' Neighborhood* encouraged children to become happy and productive citizens. It was the longest-running program on public television, lasting 33 years and finally ending its run in 2001. Rogers was an American icon of children's education and a symbol of compassion and morality. He became such a beloved figure that one day, when the media reported that his car had been stolen, the thieves immediately returned the car to the exact spot from which it was taken, with an apology on the dashboard. It read, "If we'd known it was yours, we never would have taken it."

While accepting a Lifetime Achievement Award at the 1997 Emmy Awards Show, Rogers approached the microphone and said, "All of us have special ones who have loved us into being. Would you just take, along with me, ten seconds to think of the people who have helped you become who you are. Ten seconds of silence." Tears began to flow from the eyes of many in the audience. Rogers finally looked up from his watch and softly said, "Whomever you are thinking about, how pleased they must be to know the difference you feel they've made."

Actor LeVar Burton recalls a time when Rogers was invited to a gathering at the White House, and he asked everybody, including President Clinton, to close their eyes for 60 seconds and think about someone who had helped shape them. Again people wept. "Fred felt it was critical to acknowledge those who have helped us come into being," said Burton. "And Fred's legacy is that he is that person for so many of us."

Rogers was awarded the Presidential Medal of Freedom in 2002, and one year later, after Rogers passed away at the age of 74, the US Senate approved a resolution to commemorate his life. It read, in part, "Through his spirituality and placid nature, Mr. Rogers was able to reach out to our nation's children and encourage each of them to understand the important role they play in their communities and as part of their families. More importantly, he did not shy away from dealing with difficult issues of death and divorce but rather encouraged children to express their emotions in a healthy, constructive manner, often providing a simple answer to life's hardships."

To the very end of his life, Rogers encouraged people to love one another and to appreciate the deep connections all humans have with each other. Shortly before he died, while giving a commencement speech at Dartmouth College in 2002, he said, "Our world hangs like a magnificent jewel in the vastness of space. Every one of us is a part of that jewel, a facet of that jewel. And in the perspective of infinity, our differences are infinitesimal. We are intimately related."

Reed Richards: Fantastic Family Man

Heroism is a concept that stretches from the subtle to the grandiose. Heroes come in all shapes and sizes, in both reality and fiction. From saving the Earth to toppling dictators to stopping the foreclosure on the ranch to rescuing a frightened kitten from a tree, the actions of heroes are necessary in all aspects of the human experience to cushion the wrongs that we suffer. Reed Richards is a man who is flexible enough to fill all these roles.

Demonstrating from an early age a pliable genius that was both creative and crafty, Reed used his gifts in the service of his fellow humans at every opportunity. In World War II, he served behind enemy lines in occupied France, risking his life and applying his unmatched intellect to espionage and military intelligence, doing his part to bring the conflict to a quicker end. In the Cold War with the Soviets that followed, he feared that the communists would gain prestige and prominence by winning the space race, and so he devoted all his efforts to ensuring that the United States would be the first nation to reach the moon.

It was the urgency of this effort that led to his greatest failure, as well as the most amazing development in his life and the lives of his closest friends. Refusing to wait for official clearance, Reed decided that he must go to great lengths to ensure success in this endeavor. Accompanied by his best friend, Ben Grimm, a former test pilot, his fiancee Susan Storm, and her brother Johnny, he launched his rocket into space. Unfortunately, he lacked the data to properly calculate the strength of cosmic rays, and the ship was forced down to a hard landing; all aboard survived, but, alarmingly, they had been affected by the cosmic rays. Each had been endowed with a fantastic but frightening, superpower: Ben had become a misshapen monster, Johnny could burst into flame, Sue was invisible, and Reed's body had become as stretchable and moldable as plastic.

Despite the trauma of the mission's catastrophic failure and the strange changes they had undergone, Reed was resilient enough to realize that they now possessed greater power than anyone in the world – his knee-jerk reaction, and his friends agreed, was that they must use their powers to help mankind.

In the years that followed, Reed (known now to the world as Mister Fantastic) led his team on many heroic adventures. He defended the world from conquest by his archrival and fellow genius Doctor Doom and the prince of Atlantis, the Sub-Mariner; he continued to battle communists, such as the Red Ghost; he repelled several alien invasions, notably the recurring incursions mounted by the Skrulls; ultimately, he saved the entire planet from destruction at the hands of the world-devouring Galactus. Throughout all this, no matter what menaces were demanding his attention, he never stopped seeking a cure for the disfigurement that Ben had suffered on their initial space flight.

In 1968, he had married Susan and she was pregnant with their first child; but he learned that the cosmic radiation in her body threatened the lives of her and the baby. The only cure lay in a dangerous alternate dimension called the Negative Zone and was in possession of a powerful, hostile creature called Annihilus. In the company of Ben and Johnny – who refused to let him go alone – he braved the deadly peril of the Negative Zone and returned with the cure. Of all the heroic actions performed by Reed Richards over the years, surely this is the one which defines him: He is a man who literally went beyond the ends of the Earth to save the life of his unborn child.

Though the influence of Reed Richards extends around the globe and reaches to the stars, he is ultimately a family man: Husband, father and friend. He is the person in your life who you know won't fail you when you need to be saved.

Captain James T. Kirk: The Hero Who Treks the Stars

From surveying people's beliefs about fictional heroes, we've discovered an ironic fact. "They're the only *real* heroes," summed up one of our respondents. Why are fictional heroes seemingly so real to us, and so beloved? The reason is that creators of fictional heroes ensure that their characters embody the central elements of heroism. In this way fictional heroes serve as hero *prototypes*, unmistakably capturing our view of the ideal heroic figure.

James T. Kirk, the main protagonist from the *Star Trek* franchise of movies and television, is an excellent example of the perfect male fictional hero. His character was developed by Gene Roddenberry, who created and produced the original *Star Trek* television series shown on NBC from 1966 to 1969. Roddenberry conceived of *Star Trek* as a cowboy western set in space, "a wagon train to the stars," combining elements of Buck Rogers and Flash Gordon. Set in the 23rd century, *Star Trek* portrays the future as a near-utopia in which poverty, hunger, and warfare on earth have all been overcome.

In *Star Trek*, James Kirk explores the galaxy as Captain of the *USS Enterprise*, whose mission is "to explore strange new worlds, to seek out new life and new civilizations, to boldly go where no man has gone before." The show was well ahead of its time in featuring racial and gender diversity among the crew, and using dazzling futuristic technologies such as computer discs and smartphone-like communicators.

The original Captain Kirk, played by William Shatner, was the quintessential male hero of the 1960s. As a young student, his keen intellect and brashness enabled him to win an "unwinnable" computer battle simulation called the *Kobayashi Maru*. As captain of the *Enterprise*, Kirk cleverly thinks his way out of impossibly adverse circumstances against more advanced alien life forms. The late Randy Pausch revealed that he became a better teacher, colleague, and husband because of Kirk's leadership skills. "For ambitious boys with a scientific bent," said Pausch, "there could be no greater role model than James T. Kirk."

Shatner's portrayal of Kirk was also intended to attract the attention of female fans. Kirk was handsome and a hopeless flirt around women, both human and alien. It was not unusual during fight scenes for Kirk to have his shirt ripped off, baring his upper torso. His sense of humor, playfulness, and soft romantic side also contributed to his sex appeal.

Perhaps more than any other quality, Kirk's selflessness made him a phenomenal hero. His selfless qualities were best revealed in a highly acclaimed episode, *City on the Edge of Forever*, which won a 1968 Hugo Award for best science fiction dramatic presentation. In this episode, Kirk travels back in time to the 1930s and falls in love with Edith Keeler, played by

Joan Collins. He then discovers that in the normal timeline, Edith dies in a traffic accident; otherwise, she will lead a peace movement that delays America's entry into World War II, enabling Germany to defeat the allies. Although Kirk has the ability to prevent her death, in a heart-wrenching scene he allows the fatal accident to occur, thereby saving the lives of millions.

In 2009, the Star Trek franchise received a much-needed boost with the critical and box office success of *Star Trek XI*, starring Chris Pine as James Kirk. Although Pine's portrayal of Kirk was unmistakably his own, he did retain much of Shatner's brash charisma and intelligence. In the 2020s, the television series *Strange New Worlds* features a new actor, Paul Wesley, who plays Captain Kirk in his own unique way. We look forward to following the development of James Kirk's heroic leadership in future installments of *Star Trek*.

5 Tragic Heroes
The Self-Destruction of Greatness

As we've noted earlier, heroism can be fragile and fleeting. The pedestal on which heroes stand is not a large, stable platform, but rather a tenuous, narrow ledge from which heroes can plunge if they take one small misstep. It seems that rarely a day passes when the news media fail to report a story about a hero who has self-destructed in some way. A great hero who possesses a tragic flaw that leads to their self-destruction is called a *tragic hero*.

Great playwrights throughout history have recognized that tales of tragic heroes pack considerable dramatic punch. Sophocles' story of King Oedipus contains the timeless story of a great king whose pride and impulsivity lead him to fulfill a prophecy that he would marry his mother and kill his father. Moreover, the works of Shakespeare feature many unforgettable tragic heroes, including King Lear, Hamlet, MacBeth, and Brutus.

Hubris is the most common flaw of the tragic hero. Prideful arrogance has been the undoing of many leaders who allow power to go to their heads. Lord Acton was famous for saying "power corrupts; absolute power corrupts absolutely." A surprising amount of research confirms Acton's observation. Power frees people from restraint and accountability and has the overall effect of disinhibiting goal-directed and instinctive behavior. And it sometimes leads us to disregard other people's perspectives as we focus on our own agenda. The research showing these effects is based on observations of college students in a lab setting who are made to feel momentarily more or less powerful. In one study, participants who were made to feel powerful were more likely to get up and turn off an annoying fan than others who did not feel powerful. The latter just let the fan blow on them.

Other research has shown that people who felt powerful were more likely to eat the last cookie on a plate of shared snacks. And they were less careful about getting crumbs on the table. They went about satisfying their feeding instincts in an unrestrained way. And even sexual instincts were uninhibited. Both men and women who feel powerful are more likely to flirt. This finding underscores former Secretary of State Henry Kissinger's

DOI: 10.4324/9781003328681-5

comment in 1973 that "power is the ultimate aphrodisiac." Support for this idea also comes from the real world as well as from the psychology laboratory. Presidential scholar Theodore H. White, in writing about President John F. Kennedy and First Lady Jacqueline Kennedy, noted that he "knew that Kennedy loved his wife—but that Kennedy, the politician, exuded that musk odor of power which acts as an aphrodisiac to many women" (White, 1978).

According to White, only three presidential candidates he had ever met had denied themselves the pleasures invited by that aphrodisiac—Harry Truman, George Romney, and Jimmy Carter. He was reasonably sure that all the others he had met had, at one time or another, on the campaign trail, accepted casual partners. "The noise, the shrieking, the excitement of crowds, and then the power, the silent pickup and delivery in limousines, set the glands alive in women as in men." Many politicians have ruined their political careers by cheating on their spouses, sometimes in the most embarrassing ways possible. Former US President Bill Clinton knows this all too well.

In this section of the book, we include profiles of five tragic heroes who allowed their fame, success, and power to compromise their good judgment. We begin with the aforementioned story of King Oedipus, who ascends to become the monarch of Thebes and makes the tragic assumption that his self-will can overcome an irrevocable prophecy. The more Oedipus attempts to take control of an uncontrollable situation, the more his life unravels. Next, we profile the tragic story of Bill Cosby, who was once the most popular comedian and actor in America before over 60 women accused him of rape, sexual assault, and sexual harassment.

Then we turn to a modern-day example of a tragic hero: American golfer Tiger Woods. No human being has ever been better groomed to be a sports hero – and to remain one – than Tiger Woods. Although Tiger was prepared to achieve greatness on the golf course, he was far less prepared to handle success and to live life under the media microscope. The exposure of his marital infidelities, and the media circus that followed, absolutely devastated him. Tiger's career and image on and off the golf course suffered a ravaging blow from which he may never fully recover.

Finally, we examine the life and tragedy of former US President Richard Nixon. As president, Nixon engineered some notable achievements. He was the first president to establish formal relations with China, and he ended America's long involvement in the Vietnam War. But his eternal legacy will always be his terrible mishandling of a break-in at the Watergate hotel by members of his reelection committee. Nixon's decision to cover up the incident led to a tragic downward spiral that culminated in his resignation in disgrace. The unfortunate tales of Oedipus, Woods, and Nixon underscore the hidden dangers of assuming the power and fame associated with great leadership. It appears that to be human is to be prone to intoxication by success, which is a sure recipe for tragedy.

Our final tragic hero is the unfortunate saga of Rudy Giuliani, the mayor of New York who heroically led America through the painful recovery from the September 11 terrorist attacks. For a time, he said and did all the right things, but like most tragic heroes, his ego and poor judgment led him astray. As with all tragic heroes, Giuliani has become a cautionary tale.

Rudy Giuliani: The 9/11 Hero Turned Villain

Rudy Giuliani, former mayor of New York City, candidate for the Republican nomination for president in 2008, and legal adviser to President Donald Trump, has been widely regarded as both hero and villain at different times in his career. His reputation has gone up, and then way back down. He attained heroic status during his last year as mayor in the days following the terrorist attacks on the twin towers of the World Trade Center on September 11, 2001. Giuliani rallied the city and earned the gratitude of many in New York and across the country and the world. For his leadership during those days he was named *Time* magazine's Man of the Year in 2001. He was widely known as "America's Mayor" for his perceived heroism during those tragic days. However, both before and after the 9/11 terrorist attacks he was viewed much more negatively.

During the 1980s, Giuliani was a US Attorney in New York with a reputation for being a tough crime fighter. He ran unsuccessfully for mayor in

Rudy Giuliani
Source: Gage Skidmore from Surprise, AZ, United States of America

1989 but was elected in 1993 and then reelected in 1997. His reputation was one of an uncompromising, law-and-order, no-nonsense leader. He championed "stop and frisk" policies by police and supported efforts to remove intimidating young men with squeegee bottles from stepping into the street, washing passenger windshields, and demanding money. He seemed indifferent to the racial overtones of his rhetoric and his policies. He repeatedly alienated Black leaders by reacting coldly to their concerns. When the young unarmed Guinean student Amadou Diallo was shot over 40 times by New York police in 1999, Giuliani was seen as unmoved. He became a prime example of what Barbara Kellerman in her 2004 book *Bad Leadership: What It Is, How It Happens, Why It Matters* called callous leadership, understood as leadership that is uncaring and unkind, and unresponsive to the wants and needs of followers. Kellerman (2004a) views this as unethical leadership.

The fact that Giuliani announced at a press conference that he was divorcing his second wife without informing her previously, cemented the widespread perception of callousness. Still Giuliani was admired sufficiently that he was one of the celebrities on morning television on New Year's Day of the year 2000, the year that was then called Y2K, marking the start of the new millennium. Though controversial, he was the apparent front-runner for the Republican Party nomination to run against US First Lady Hillary Clinton for the US Senate seat from New York state. However, Giuliani gave up that quest after he was diagnosed with prostate cancer.

After his terms as mayor, Giuliani concentrated on his business concerns. Then in 2016 he became a political and legal adviser to Donald Trump. After Trump was elected (he won in the electoral college but lost the popular vote by three million) Giuliani hoped for a cabinet position. He was not appointed but kept on as adviser. Donald Trump's first impeachment trial in early 2020 concerned him pressuring the president of Ukraine, Volodymyr Zelenskyy, to announce that he was investigating Joe Biden and his son Hunter Biden for corrupt business practices in his country. Trump indicated he would withhold military aid from Ukraine unless Zelenskyy announced such an investigation, to harm Biden. Rudy Giuliani was at the center of these efforts for which the president was impeached.

After Trump was defeated for reelection by Joe Biden, Giuliani became a lead figure in efforts in courts around the country to overturn the election. The legal challenges almost universally flopped. Giuliani became a figure of ridicule when at one public appearance his hair dye trickled down his cheek. He was also charged with defaming election workers in Georgia, falsely accusing them of working to undermine the fair counting of ballots. But neither Trump nor Giuliani would give up. They both spoke at the rally on the morning of January 6, 2021, urging the pro-Trump crowd to march to the capital and stop the certification of Biden as president. Giuliani gave an especially inflammatory speech, calling for "trial by combat."

Giuliani's efforts on behalf of Trump before and after the 2020 election have changed the heroic image of America's mayor into the perception of a corrupt buffoon, doing Donald Trump's bidding no matter how dishonest those efforts might be. For many, one of America's true heroes has been transformed into a perceived villain.

Bill Cosby: The Fallen Hero

In our 2013 edition of this book, we highlighted Bill Cosby as a transforming hero. His list of accomplishments was extremely impressive. He had received numerous awards and honorary degrees for his artistic and humanitarian achievements, culminating in the Presidential Medal of Freedom, awarded by President George W. Bush in 2002. Yet today his status is greatly diminished after a litany of sexual harassment charges ultimately leading to Cosby being imprisoned for aggravated indecent assault. He served jail time from 2018 to 2021, when the Pennsylvania Supreme Court overruled the conviction citing due process violations. Though his rise and fall have tragic elements, we must remember the numerous women damaged by Cosby. Many of his awards have been rescinded. How did it happen?

Cosby was born to a poor family in Philadelphia, Pennsylvania, in 1937. He was a precocious athlete and wit, reveling in the role of class clown. He was president of his class and team captain in baseball and track, and he acted in school plays. But he never managed to graduate from high school. There seemed to be too many ways to spend time and excel other than academics. Cosby served several years in the US Navy and eventually got his high school equivalency diploma. But it was as an actor that he achieved success and fame.

Along with Robert Culp, Cosby starred in the detective series *I Spy* from 1965 until 1968. For his performances in that show he became the first African American to win an Emmy for Outstanding Lead Actor in a Drama Series. From 1972 through 1985, he produced the Sunday morning cartoon show *Fat Albert and the Cosby Kids*. During those years he also managed to earn a college degree from Temple University and most impressively masters and doctorate degrees from the University of Massachusetts. Still, Cosby had not reached the top as a celebrity and role model. That was attained when Cosby co-produced and starred in the immensely successful *The Cosby Show* from 1984 to 1992.

The Cosby Show was enormously popular. It was broadcast by NBC at 8:00 PM on Thursday. Many people regarded Thursdays as must-see TV night, as Cosby led off a series of network hits. In the role of physician Cliff Huxtable, the actor portrayed the father in a well-to-do middle class Black family with several children. It was modeled after Cosby's real family. It was a feel-good show dealing with typical home front issues. Race was not at all a focus of the show. It was simply about a successful American family. Soon Bill Cosby became America's Dad as he navigated with his on-screen wife and children the challenges of everyday life.

Consistent with the themes of the show, Cosby became an outspoken advocate for African Americans, especially African American boys and men, to take on more personal and social responsibility and spend more time on education rather than being tough. Some Black scholars and leaders criticized Cosby not contextualizing his advocacy in the systemic obstacles facing young Blacks. Other rose to his defense. Interestingly, his perspective was largely the same as that of US President Barack Obama. Endorsed or not, Cosby grounded his position in his own life experiences and his graduate education. While controversial, it became an important focus of discussion for American society as a whole.

In the context of Bill Cosby's remarkable status and success, his fall from grace is startling. While he entertained and inspired millions during his peak, along the way he severely harmed many others. It is a cautionary tale for hero worship and also for the naming of villains. We have seen in other transfigured heroes and villains that new information or new values can cause significant reassessments. Heroes rise and fall. Sometimes villains fall and rise. And there are instances where fallen heroes recover through efforts at redemption. One such person was long-time Massachusetts Senator Edward M. (Ted) Kennedy. An early presidential contender after the assassination of his brothers John and Robert Kennedy, Ted Kennedy's life and reputation were greatly diminished because of issues surrounding a messy divorce. But he rededicated himself to his work in the Senate, became a leading liberal politician, and was the subject of a flattering biography called *Last Lion: The Fall and Rise of Ted Kennedy* (Canellos, 2010). Unfortunately, Bill Cosby chances at redemption at this late stage of his life are remote. The good and the bad promise to endure.

Tiger Woods: The Ebb and Flow of Fame and Fortune

"Hello world." With these words, the heroic journey of a golf legend was launched. The statement was uttered at a press conference in August of 1996 by a skinny 20-year-old phenom named Tiger Woods, who had just finished shattering every meaningful amateur golf record in sight. Tiger was now announcing to the world that he was turning professional. Soon after the statement, Tiger began winning tournaments and seizing the public's attention. He showed an unprecedented mental toughness and physics-defying shot-making ability. No doubt, during the fall of 1996, Tiger Woods was a hero in the making.

At the 1997 Master's Tournament, Tiger's first major golf championship as a pro, he crushed the competition by a record 12 strokes. From 1997 to 2008, Tiger made the transition from a hero-on-the-rise to arguably the greatest golfer the world has ever seen. He appeared invincible. Opponents crumbled when they played with Tiger. The intimidation was palpable.

People once said of golfing great Jack Nicklaus that "Jack knew he was going to beat you. You knew Jack was going to beat you. And Jack knew that you knew that he was going to beat you." The same principle applied to Tiger Woods. For 12 years he was on top of the golf world, a hero to millions and one of the most recognized celebrities on the planet.

But in 2009, Tiger's world crumbled. An auto accident outside his home was revealed to stem from a domestic dispute with his wife about Tiger's extramarital affairs. His wife and children left him, precipitating a 4-month hiatus from golf and participation in a treatment program. After his return to golf in 2010, Tiger's game was the same. He no longer dominated tournaments, nor did he scare opponents. His heroism was questioned by fans who attacked his character.

But Tiger managed to make several comebacks from both his personal setbacks and his recurring physical injuries. Our research on heroes suggests that people show forgiveness to fallen sports heroes to the extent that these heroes can return to their former levels of professional success. Tiger's greatest comeback occurred in April 2019 when he unexpectedly won his last major golf tournament, The Masters. He accomplished this feat despite back fusion surgery and numerous operations to mend his shattered legs. Tiger was also 43 years old, an age that is deemed too old for success in major championships.

The hero's journey is rarely characterized by a linear trend upward in achievement and popularity. Heroes suffer setbacks, and in the case of young, privileged millionaire athletes, the public often reacts with unsympathetic venom. This pattern is seen especially in the sporting world, but it also shows up in the political arena. Richard Nixon, Eliot Spitzer, and John Edwards are all examples of politicians whose careers ended when they were caught behaving badly. Successful people, it seems, often forget the old adage that with great power comes great responsibility.

But our thirst for heroes is so great that we are often open to the idea of redemption and a return to former heroic status. Tiger Woods showed that heroes can make comebacks, atone for past ignominy, and make a positive difference. Throughout his career, Woods has made significant contributions to charitable work primarily through the TGR Foundation, which he founded in 1996. The foundation focuses on providing educational opportunities, resources, and support for underserved youth. Through initiatives like the TGR Learning Lab, Earl Woods Scholar Program, and various educational workshops and grants, the foundation has helped millions of students pursue their academic and career goals. Woods's commitment to education and youth empowerment reflects his dedication to giving back to the community and making a positive impact on future generations.

Coming to Terms with Richard Nixon

Our images of heroes and villains are so powerful that it is often difficult to change them, or even to make them a little more complicated. One fascinating case is that of Richard Nixon, the 37th President of the United States (1969–1974). Looking at historians' rankings of greatness, we see that he generally falls toward the bottom, landing in either the Failure or Below Average group. His presidency is not seen a complete disaster, but it's ranked quite low.

Nixon's poor rating doesn't come as much of a surprise. It's all about Watergate. In one of our studies, we asked students to type into a computer the first word or short phrase that came to mind when a name flashed on the screen. When they saw "Richard Nixon," nearly two-thirds typed in "Watergate" or a closely related term. Consistent with research by Dean Keith Simonton at UC Davis, scandal is highly memorable, and highly memorable information dominates impressions. And there may be good reason to grade Nixon low because of Watergate and the cover-ups. But Nixon deserves a more thorough look. The scandals that led to the country's only presidential resignation are only part of the story. Our image of Nixon, or what psychologists call our schema, needs to be more complex.

First, there were certainly times during Nixon's career when he took what we would call the high road. For example, during the 1960 debates with John F. Kennedy, he was remarkably considerate and respectful, perhaps even too deferential in what he said and how he said it. And those debates sunk his candidacy. Also, he refused to dispute the 1960 election, which was decided by very close and perhaps questionable returns from Illinois and Texas. Second, and more important, Nixon was a foreign policy visionary. His strategic thinking was inspired, and he exercised strong leadership in opening relations with China and achieving a fragile but real detente with the Soviet Union. These moves changed geopolitics, much to the benefit of the United States and arguably the whole world.

While Nixon's breakthroughs in foreign policy are well-known, though sometimes overlooked, his initiatives in domestic matters are not at all well-known. Although Nixon had his share of ethnic prejudices, he worked consistently, though quietly, toward advancing school desegregation in the South. And he also followed the lead of Daniel Patrick Moynihan in forging policies to help poor children.

The Nixon story is really a tragic one. There has been a great deal written about the childhood origins of his insecurities and hostilities. Some scholars ask whether he should be considered paranoid. Whatever the causes, Nixon was interpersonally awkward and socially uncomfortable. He was not well-liked. And in return, for the most part, Nixon didn't really like other people. These feelings created interpersonal distance, which allowed Nixon's dark side too much free rein.

We don't argue that Nixon was a hero. Some of his accomplishments could well be considered heroic, but like many real people, he was an individual of great complexity. For those who care, the good and the bad are both easy to see. Taking Nixon as a starting point, we hope that readers will move toward understanding significant public figures in at least three dimensions, and acknowledge that heroes and heroism are marked by mystery and complexity.

Oedipus the King: The Classic Tragic Hero

Human beings have long pondered whether their outcomes in life are determined by free will or by forces beyond their control. More than 2,500 years ago the ancient Greek playwright Sophocles brilliantly placed this issue in the context of heroism: To what extent is heroism chosen versus destined? And when heroes fall, how much are they responsible?

The play *Oedipus the King* tells the story of the mythical king of Thebes whose parents (Laius and Jocasta) are warned by an oracle that any son born to them would kill his father and marry his mother. After Jocasta bears a son, Laius instructs a servant to kill the young infant, but the servant takes pity on the boy and gives him to a shepherd who brings him to Corinth. The king and queen of Corinth, who are without children, adopt the young child and call him Oedipus. As a young man, Oedipus learns of the prophecy that he is to murder his father and marry his mother. To avoid fulfilling this fate, Oedipus flees Corinth and travels to Thebes.

During his journey, Oedipus encounters his true father, Laius, at a crossing of roads, and the two men have a road-rage incident. Oedipus kills Laius, unwittingly fulfilling the first part of the prophecy. Before arriving at Thebes, Oedipus correctly answers the riddle of the Sphinx, who kills herself, thus freeing Thebes from her harsh rule. Oedipus arrives at Thebes a hero, is crowned king, and is awarded the widowed Jocasta's hand in marriage, thus fulfilling the second part of the prophecy. The remainder of the play describes Oedipus' gradual recognition of how he and others tragically fulfilled the prophecy. Irony abounds – a blind prophet allows Oedipus to "see" what he has done, and when Oedipus gains full awareness, he gouges out his eyes. Throughout the play, the more that characters try to avoid their fate, the more they take actions that inadvertently guarantee its fruition.

Oedipus possesses the traits of many great heroes, most especially intelligence and courage. These traits allow him to answer the Sphinx's riddle knowing the fate of those who had failed the riddle before him. But as with all tragic heroes, Oedipus' faults are his ultimate undoing. His impulsive temper at the crossroads precipitates his deadly attack on Laius, and his thirst for ambition leads him to become the monarch of Thebes. Pride is the primary instrument of Oedipus' demise, and the Chorus in the play underscores this idea: "Pride breeds the tyrant violent pride, gorging, crammed to bursting with all that is overripe and rich with ruin . . . Can such a man, so desperate, still boast he can save his life from the flashing bolts of god?" (Sophocles, 2001; 429 BCE, p. 83).

Earlier in this, book we noted that heroic leadership requires great vision. One of the lessons of Oedipus is that true greatness in leadership requires vision combined with favorable circumstances. Oedipus' circumstances spelled doom from the start, and thus Oedipus' vision for greatness is equally doomed. After gouging his eyes, he noted, "What good were eyes to me? Nothing I could see could bring me joy" (p. 117).

6   Transposed Heroes
The Fine Line between Heroism and Villainy

Transposed heroes are individuals who undergo a complete reversal in status, either from hero to villain or from villain to hero. This status reversal is nicely illustrated in the story of basketball star LeBron James. For the first seven years of his career, James enjoyed heroic status playing in his hometown of Cleveland, Ohio, where fans adored him and statues and murals of his likeness donned the city. James was rich, famous, successful, and beloved. Just before his eighth year as a professional, he had the option of either playing the remainder of his career in his hometown or moving elsewhere, which would earn him even more tens of millions of dollars. In July 2010, in what is now infamously known as The Decision, James arranged a one-hour nationally televised show to serve as the platform for making his announcement whether to stay in Cleveland or leave for greener pastures. The show was widely viewed as ostentatious and self-aggrandizing. At the end of the hour when James announced that he was leaving Cleveland to play for the Miami Heat, the negative fallout was intense. His fans were outraged. Murals in his image were desecrated, then removed. The owner of the Cleveland team publicly denounced James as traitorous, shameful, and cowardly.

Somehow, the reaction caught LeBron James off-guard. Adapting to his new role was difficult: "During my first seven years in the NBA, I was always the liked one," he said. "To be on the other side, they call it the dark side, or the villain, whatever they call it... It was definitely challenging for myself. It was a situation I had never been in before. I took a long time to adjust to it. It didn't feel good... It basically turned me into somebody I wasn't. When you start to hear 'the villain,' now you have to be the villain. And I started to buy into it. I started to play the game of basketball at a level or in a mind state that I had never played at before. I mean angry. That's mentally, and that's not the way I play the game of basketball" (Weir, 2012, p. 1).

The second type of transposed hero is the individual who changes from villain to hero. A notable example occurs in the movie *3:10 to Yuma*. The

DOI: 10.4324/9781003328681-6

character of Ben Wade, played by Russell Crowe in the 2007 remake, is a notorious train robber. After one particularly lucrative hold-up, Wade kidnaps a father and a son from the train and notices a rift in their relationship. Revealing his tender side, Wade goes to great lengths to stage a situation in which the father is seen as a hero to the son, bringing the two close together. As the audience, we begin to see other noble traits in Wade and are led to believe that he has transposed permanently to heroism. The ending of the movie throws us another surprise. Wade is placed in a situation where his character is tested, and when he chooses to rob yet another train, we see that he has transposed back to villain status. The movie reinforces a lesson about human nature. Although transposed heroism usually refers to two types of individuals, those who transpose from good to bad and those who transpose from bad to good, these transpositions can also occur within the same individual. Most of us are, at different times in our lives, both heroes and villains.

Transposed heroism is quite common in fictional accounts of heroes, particularly in the superhero and horror genres. The story of Dr. Jekyll and Mr. Hyde is a perfect example. Ingesting a potion instantly turns the benign Dr. Jekyll into the evil Mr. Hyde. Fictional heroes not only undergo quick reversals of moral codes; they also often experience rapid, dramatic changes in power and strength. Popeye merely has to eat spinach to acquire super strength. Sinbad the Sailor tightens his belt to acquire super powers. The Incredible Hulk is unleashed any time David Banner gets angry. Writers of fiction know that people are transfixed by stories involving sudden displays of magic and supernatural power. When these powers are unleashed, heroes are either born or undergo instant transformations. The Grimms' fairy tale *The Frog Prince* features a frog who turns into prince. In *Jack and the Beanstalk*, it takes only one night for the beans that Jack plants to grow into the towering beanstalk needed for his heroism to take place. The prince in *Beauty and the Beast* experiences two magical transformations, from prince to beast and then back again to prince. Obviously, the transpositions that occur in fictional literature do not occur in the real world, yet somehow they fascinate us. We are emotionally drawn to instantaneous shifts in morality and how these shifts play a role in creating or destroying heroes.

In this section, we profile three transposed heroes: Two-Face from the Batman comic book and movie franchise; basketball great LeBron James; and college football coach Joe Paterno. Two-Face's true name is Harvey Dent, the handsome and heroic district attorney of Gotham City. After sustaining a hideous facial injury, Dent loses his sanity and becomes a villain. We then turn our attention to LeBron James, whose heroic transposition we described previously. Finally, we end with an examination of the unfortunate ending to the career, and the life, of Joe Paterno. Paterno's forced resignation from his coaching duties in 2011 fueled plenty of controversy and acrimony. The suddenness of Paterno's shift from hero to villain after a long, distinguished career makes him one of the most sad and intriguing transposed heroes of the early 21st century.

Harvey Dent as Two-Face: The Hero Turned Villain in Batman

One of the more interesting findings in our study of heroes is the tendency for fictional heroes (and villains) to be more extremely good (and extremely bad) than their nonfictional counterparts (Allison & Goethals, 2011). We suspect that creators of fiction draw from classic prototypes of good and evil when constructing their characters. While elements of these prototypes can surely be found in real-world heroes and villains, fictional prototypes are more cleanly drawn with their essential features accentuated. In this way readers of literature will be especially likely to resonate to fictional portrayals of good and evil.

The character of Two-Face in the Batman franchise represents a double dose of this tendency toward fictional exaggeration. Two-Face starts out as a hero named Harvey Dent, the clean-cut district attorney of Gotham City and a friend of Batman. At the age of 26, Dent is remarkably young to hold such a high position in law enforcement, but his unwavering commitment to the city's well-being and great success as a crime-fighter have earned him such a high rank. In fact, Dent is nicknamed "Apollo" for his perfect, virtuous image and behavior. As district attorney, he fearlessly prosecutes

Harvey Dent, Two Face

Image Source: Pat Loika

organized crime bosses and becomes the public face of law, order, and everything that is good in Gotham city.

Then Dent's life is forever altered by tragedy. He aggressively attempts to prosecute Sal Maroni, one of the toughest gangsters in Gotham City. But while in a physical altercation with Maroni, the gangster throws sulfuric acid at Dent, hideously scarring the left side of his face. As the audience, we are then witness not only to the physical transformation of the once-handsome Dent; we are also witness to his psychological unraveling. It is harrowing – the disfigured Dent develops multiple personality disorder and becomes a brutal crime boss himself.

Now known as Two-Face, Dent becomes obsessed with duality and the number 2. He begins to rob buildings with the number 2 in the address, commits crimes at 10:22 PM (22:22 in military time), and uses .22 semiautomatics and double-barreled shotguns. Two-Face becomes especially known for his terrifying method for deciding his victims' fate: He flips a coin to determine whether to kill them or not. We learn that Two-Face got his trademark coin flip routine from his abusive father, who would employ the coin flip "game" with Dent prior to physically battering him.

Why are we drawn to the tragic 180-degree transformation of Harvey Dent? Perhaps the character of Two-Face reminds us how malleable goodness and heroism can be. The research of Phil Zimbardo (2012) on the "Lucifer effect" tells us that any human being is capable of both exquisite good and horrific evil. Harvey Dent is one moment a strong, untarnished champion of justice, and in the next moment he is forever transposed into a sinister monster. Witnessing Dent's reversal of morals may illustrate the fine line between good and evil and may be a chilling reminder of how circumstances beyond our control may send any of us down a dark path at any time.

LeBron James: Hero and Sometimes Villain of the NBA

In 2023, LeBron James of the Los Angeles Lakers set the National Basketball Association all-time points record. As of this writing, he is still playing, and doing so at an extraordinary level. Along the way, James became the first player to score 30,000 points and record 10,000 rebounds and assists. It is doubtful that anyone else will match those standards. He has had an extraordinary career, entering the professional ranks right out of high school in Akron, Ohio, in 2003, at age 18. He is considered by many to be the greatest basketball player of all time, the so-called GOAT. Fans and sports watchers of different generations may disagree, arguing that Michael Jordan or even 1960s stars Bill Russell or Oscar Robertson deserve that accolade. Through all of this, James has been both a hero and a villain in the eyes of many. There are different beholders, including teammates, coaches, team executives, opponents, the sports world, the media, and the larger public. The controversies surrounding James's career have mostly been about his moves from one team to another, but also to some extent about issues of race and politics that creep into almost any intense focus on a public figure.

James was drafted out of high school by essentially his home team, the Cleveland Cavaliers, roughly 30 miles from Akron. The Cavs, as they were called, became a much better team with James but never won the NBA championship. They got to the finals in 2007 but were swept by the San Antonio Spurs. By that time James had been a three-time All Star and was twice first team All NBA. But his team had not won. When his seventh season with Cleveland ended in 2010, relations between James, the team, and the city had soured. James became a free agent. Then he orchestrated what became a public relations fiasco, leading him to be cast as a villain.

The problem was the way James handled his exit from Cleveland. James was courted by several teams, and a highly publicized announcement was arranged for an ESPN television hour called "The Decision." His choice was to go to the Miami Heat, which had also signed two other all-stars, Chris Bosh and Dwayne Wade. In finding a way to unite all three men on the same team, James had demonstrated the power that players, at least star players, could have in shaping their own futures in the league. It was an important moment of player empowerment. At the same time, many felt that James leaving his home-town team and making such an extravagant show of his choice was narcissistic and unkind.

Once James, Bosh, and Wade became a highly touted "Big Three," expectations were extremely high. Winning a championship seemed to be a must. The Heat lost in the finals in James's first year in Miami but won the next two years, in 2012 and 2013. But soon after, James was on the move again. He went back to Cleveland. To many this seemed like a kind of redemption. He had done the right thing. In his third year back with Cavaliers, the team won the NBA championship. It was the first league title for a Cleveland professional team in 52 years. With the controversy about the Decision behind hm, James was given more and more respect, as both a player and a person. Perhaps he wasn't a hero, but he was no longer the villain.

James moved on again in 2018, this time to the Los Angeles Lakers. As for other athletes before him, the star power and glitz of LA was a huge draw. Paired again with other top players, James and the Lakers won the NBA championship in 2020. James's latest achievements were leading the Lakers to the first NBA In-Season Tournament championship while winning the Most Valuable Player award. He is the oldest player in the league but going strong.

In sum, Lebron James is widely regarded as a hero for his exceptional accomplishments as a player and team leader, and for empowering other players by opening up free agency. Critics of the Decision have granted him credit for going back to Cleveland, at least for a while, and staying until the city won a championship. James's philanthropic contributions are widely respected, and his timely statements about race have generally been appreciated. While not always a popular hero, he is mostly regarded as such in what inevitably must be the twilight of his career.

Joe Paterno: Discerning the Legacy of a Transposed Hero

When Joe Paterno died on Sunday, January 22, 2012, his passing set in motion a process that is a quite natural one for human beings when contemplating another's demise: The forming of a final impression of the person and their significance. Such a cognitive task would ordinarily be a no-brainer. Death often catapults an ordinary person to heroic status, and an already established hero who dies becomes an even greater hero (Allison et al., 2009). But the case of Joe Paterno was far from ordinary. His story certainly contained many elements of the familiar tale of the man who fell from grace, but people seeking to understand its meaning were confronted with a confusing story of scandal, emotional pain, and controversy.

Coaching college football was Paterno's life, occupying about 60 of his 85 years. In 2011, Paterno was larger than life, a true legend. He won more games than any other coach and led his Penn State teams with distinction for half a century. Paterno seemed eternal, a welcome fixture in a sports world filled with so much greed and corruption. Everyone knew that Paterno's ethics were above reproach; his motto was "success with honor." Paterno was a hero in the truest sense of the word.

Then in late 2011, some horrible news emerged from State College, Pennsylvania. A former assistant coach at Penn State, Jerry Sandusky, was arrested for sexually molesting young boys. Many of the molestations took place at Penn State's football complex, where Sandusky hosted charity events for underprivileged boys. In 2002 someone witnessed Sandusky assaulting a boy and reported it to Paterno, who in turn reported the incident to his superiors at Penn State.

Those administrators, it turns out, covered up the incident in an apparent attempt to protect the school's reputation. Sandusky continued to sexually abuse boys for another nine years until his arrest. Paterno's knowledge of Sandusky's crime in 2002 came back to haunt him. People had many questions. Why didn't Paterno do more to protect those boys? After contacting his superiors, why didn't he also contact law enforcement? Paterno's lawyer, Wick Sollers, argued that Paterno fully reported what he knew to the people responsible for campus investigations. "He did what he thought was right with the information he had at the time," Sollers said.

Paterno himself expressed regret at not taking further action. No one believed that Paterno's wrongdoing was at nearly the same level of heinousness as Sandusky's alleged crimes. But we hold heroes to the highest of standards when it comes to personal conduct. People may have a great need for heroes, but people also believe that heroes must never show anything less than the best moral behavior possible.

Did Joe Paterno deserve to be forced to resign? Reasonable people disagreed. Those who supported the decision to dismiss Paterno believed that he failed to do the right thing to the fullest extent possible, and that additional children may have been molested after 2002 because of this failure. Those who opposed the decision believed that Paterno was a convenient scapegoat for the irresponsible conduct of higher-level administrators at Penn State who engineered the cover up.

Paterno's legendary career came to a sudden, shocking, and ignominious end. Days after his dismissal, statues in Paterno's likeness were taken down, awards named after him were renamed, and his reputation was forever sullied. Almost overnight he went from hero to villain. These traumatic events had to certainly take their toll on Paterno's mental and physical well-being, and they likely hastened his demise. A person's death can elevate their status in society, and we noticed that Paterno's death did briefly rehabilitate his image more than anything he could have done in life.

Nearly 15 years after the scandal surfaced, the legacy of Joe Paterno on the Penn State campus is deeply complex and polarized. He is viewed by some as a hero and by others as a villain, primarily due to his connection with the Jerry Sandusky scandal. While some continue to revere Paterno for his positive contributions, others feel that honoring him disregards the severity of the scandal and the experiences of Sandusky's victims. This divide ensures that discussions about Paterno's legacy remain contentious and emotionally charged.

7 Transparent Heroes
The Unsung Heroes among Us

A common complaint about television and online newscasts is that they seem to have a single-minded preoccupation with reporting bad news. Villainous behavior dominates the headlines, and it's been this way since the advent of media news coverage. An observer from another planet might conclude, based on our news reporting, that villains far outnumber heroes in our society. Our hypothesis about the cause of the negative news bias is based on our observation that heroic behavior occurs all around us but that it is both invisible and unexciting. These heroic actions are performed by the parents who nurture us, the teachers who educate us, the coaches who mentor us, the healthcare workers who mend us, the police and fire-fighters who protect us, and the soldiers who defend us. We call these pervasive and unappreciated individuals transparent heroes.

Why is good behavior so invisible, dreary, and unworthy of news report-ing? Psychologists have identified an important cognitive bias called the *negativity bias* (Baumeister et al., 2001). This bias refers to the human tendency to show greater sensitivity to negative information about people than to positive information. The bias manifests itself in many ways. If you are given both good and bad information about someone, you're more likely to pay attention to the bad and to remember the bad. Moreover, the bad information will carry more weight in your impression of that person. Negative experiences in our lives have more impact on us than positive ones. If you have a good and a bad experience close together in time, you'll be more likely to feel worse than if you have two neutral experiences.

To the extent that we show the negativity bias in our perceptions of the world, good behavior will always be drowned out by bad behavior even if there is a much greater preponderance of good behavior. For this reason, transparent heroes will go about doing their heroic work unnoticed and unsung. Fortunately, transparent heroes aren't motivated by fame and for-tune. They do their jobs of healing, nurturing, and protecting simply because they know it is the right thing to do. If they were motivated by

DOI: 10.4324/9781003328681-7

money or fanfare, they would most certainly pursue an alternative form of heroism. There has been very little previous research on transparent heroism, although some scholars have studied the related phenomenon of invisible heroism (e.g., Sorenson & Hickman, 2002).

In this section, we profile 13 transparent heroes. Because they are transparent, you may not have heard of many of them, but you'll discover just how important their contributions were behind the scenes. First, we profile the unsung heroic leadership of healthcare workers during the 2020 Covid-19 pandemic. Next we describe the subtle heroism of Don Quixote. Then we describe Liz Cheney's unheralded heroic leadership during and after the Trump's first term as President. Next we feature actor Drew Barrymore's quiet heroism. Then we examine the case of Montgomery Meigs, whose exemplary efforts in supplying the Union Army with food and munitions during the S\ Civil War made him indispensable to the Union cause.

Next we profile the life of basketball coach John Wooden, who won more college championships than any other coach, but that's not why he's in this book. Wooden believed that it was far more important to build character and integrity in his players than it was to win games. We then describe the hidden contributions of Marion Keisker, whose one simple action kick-started Elvis Presley's legendary career. Without Keisker, the rock'n'roll music revolution would have been delayed, or it would have unfolded differently, or both.

We then profile an unheralded group of heroes who rarely receive any attention: The prehistoric humans who first used fire to usher in the modernization of civilization. Our good friend and colleague Jesse Schultz contributed this fascinating piece on the makers of fire. Next we explore an indispensable aid to all heroes: their sidekicks. Then we offer a tribute to mothers and fathers who heroically sacrifice so much for their children. In our research, we've found that one third of all the heroes that people list are family members and that most of these family heroes are parents. We then profile the curious case of US President Woodrow Wilson's wife Edith Wilson, who may have run the country for an extended period of time while her husband lay ill recovering from a stroke. Bayard Rustin is our next hero. His name is largely unknown, but as Martin Luther King, Jr.'s sidekick his influence on the civil rights movement loomed large. Finally, we end with the remarkable story of Rick Rescorla, whose heroic planning and preparation is credited with saving the lives of thousands of people on September 11, 2001.

Healthcare Workers: Unsung Heroes of the Covid-19 Pandemic

Many of society's greatest heroes do their greatest work when people need them the most. During the Covid-19 pandemic of 2020–2022, healthcare workers faced an unprecedented crisis. Hospitals were overwhelmed with

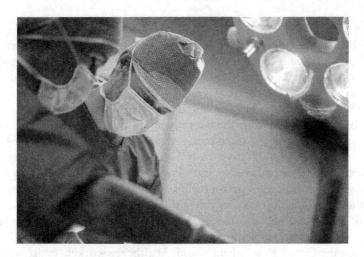

Source: Image by Peoplecreations on Freepik

a surge of Covid-19 patients, leading to a scarcity of beds, particularly in intensive care units. There was a critical shortage of personal protective equipment (PPE), which put healthcare workers at risk of infection. The pandemic also exposed and intensified existing systemic issues, such as staffing shortages, uneven resource distribution, and disparities in healthcare access, particularly affecting marginalized communities. The mental health of healthcare professionals suffered under the strain of increased workloads, emotional stress from high patient mortality, and the challenges of adapting to rapidly changing treatment protocols and guidelines.

Healthcare workers during the COVID-19 pandemic exemplified tremendous heroism by taking great risks, making great sacrifices, and working tirelessly for the greater good.

Taking Great Risks

Healthcare workers toiled in high-risk environments with a significant chance of contracting the Covid virus, especially before vaccines were available. Constantly working in close proximity to Covid-19 patients put them at high risk of infection. Early in the pandemic, there was a global shortage of PPE, forcing many healthcare workers to reuse or improvise protective gear. The novel coronavirus was not well understood initially, making treatment and prevention challenging and risky. In addition, the stress of treating a high volume of patients, witnessing mortality, and fear for their own health took a toll on their mental well-being.

Making Great Sacrifices

Many healthcare workers faced long hours, emotional stress, and separation from loved ones to reduce the risk of transmission, all while grappling with a high volume of critically ill patients. Healthcare workers made significant sacrifices during the Covid-19 pandemic, including long and exhausting work hours. Many worked extended shifts, often without adequate breaks, to cope with the overwhelming number of patients. Their commitment often meant sacrificing personal time, missing family events, and in some cases living apart from their families to reduce the risk of spreading the virus to loved ones. They endured significant stress from working in high-pressure environments, dealing with patient suffering and loss, and the constant fear of infecting themselves or their families. Beyond the risk of contracting Covid-19, the intense workloads and stress also had implications for their physical and mental health.

During the Covid-19 pandemic, some healthcare workers expressed discomfort with the "hero" label, fearing it implicitly suggested they were expendable in the face of the crisis. This label, they felt, romanticized their sacrifices and risk-taking, potentially overlooking the systemic issues such as inadequate protective equipment, staffing shortages, and lack of sufficient support. By framing them as heroes, there was a concern that it could be used to justify the extreme conditions under which they were expected to work, effectively normalizing the dire circumstances rather than addressing the fundamental problems and providing the necessary resources and support to ensure their safety and well-being.

During the pandemic, healthcare workers prioritized patient care, often going above and beyond to provide medical attention and comfort to those in isolation and to maintain public health at the cost of their own well-being. We should never take doctors, nurses, and emergency workers for granted, especially during great crises. Care should be taken to protect our heroes from harm as much as they protect us.

Don Quixote: The Idealistic but Impractical Hero

Our high school Spanish teacher used to transition from the rather boring study of grammar with an infectious enthusiasm that enlivened our whole class. With a big grin he declared "Y ahora, vamos a leer de neustro heroe Don Quixote de la Mancha, y su amigo, Sancho Panza." Translated, those words were, "And now we're going to read about our hero, Don Quixote de la Mancha, and his friend, Sancho Panza." Don Quixote was indeed a hero to us. We admired his idealism and chuckled at his foibles. Our Spanish class aside, Don Quixote is a heroic figure around the world. His heroism is of such a special kind that we have coined the term "Quixotic heroism" in our *Encyclopedia of Heroism Studies* (Allison et al., 2024.)

Who was, or is, Don Quixote? He is a fictional character created by Miguel de Cervantes in a two-volume chronicle published in two parts, in 1605 and 1615. An old man, Quixote dreams of being a knight errant, like those who fought with King Arthur. He would travel on horseback like knights of old to demonstrate his prowess and virtue for his lady. Prowess, or competence, and virtue, or morality, are key elements in the perceptions of heroes (Allison & Goethals, 2011). Quixote's chosen lady was Dulcinea del Toboso, a lady he conjures up. Her name derives from the Spanish word *dulce* for sweet, thus meaning something like sweetness or sweet one. Accompanying Quixote on his quests is his realistic but supportive side-kick, Sancho Panza, who tries to save him from disaster or death.

Quixote rides a frail old horse named Rocinante, which may have been meant to signal that he was formerly *rocin*, Spanish for nag, that is, while earlier a workhorse, he is now a worthy steed. Sancho rides on a donkey or mule. The two men and their rides are wonderfully depicted in Pablo Picasso's famous 1955 sketch. The illustration includes several windmills in the background, nodding to one of the most famous passages in *Don Quixote* where, against Sancho's pleading, he attacks the windmills with his lance, believing them to be evil giants. He is roughed up but not much the worse for wear. The chapter neatly conveys the basic idea of Don Quixote. He is a deluded old man who strives to advance morality and virtue for his lady Dulcinea. That image is captured in today's popular phrase "tilting at windmills," meaning trying to do the right thing but in a totally unrealistic and inept way. Or, equivalently we might say they are "quixotic," which means exceedingly idealistic but impractical.

Many heroes are quixotic. Though they are not competent, their idealism, and their willingness to sacrifice for those ideals, activates the hero image. Men and women who put their lives on the line, and sometimes lose their lives, for a cause are regarded as heroes. They fought the good fight. The 1960s musical *Man of La Mancha* was based on Quixote's heroic image. Its lead song, "The Impossible Dream," includes the lyrics: "To right the unrightable wrong, And to love pure and chaste from afar, To try when your arms are too weary, To reach the unreachable star" (Darion & Leigh, 1965). These words capture the essence of the quixotic hero, like Don Quixote himself, one who tries mightily albeit futilely to accomplish great deeds in the name of higher values.

Among the many, many bows to Don Quixote in popular culture is singer-songwriter Gordon Lightfoot's song and record album called *Don Quixote*. Its lyrics mention a "horseman wild and free" who "takes a battered book into his hand, standing like a prophet bold he shouts across the ocean to the shore, 'til he can shout no more." He also strikes a knightly pose and stands like a preacher, but to no avail. No one will listen. Quixote fills us with both sadness and admiration. He defines an important kind of heroism, one that the world has taken to heart.

Liz Cheney: The Hero Who Defied Trump

The daughter of Vice President Dick Cheney and Lynne Cheney, former chair of the National Endowment for the Humanities, Republican Congresswomen Liz Cheney recently became a hero to many Democrats and non-MAGA (Make American Great Again) members of the GOP. Like her parents, she is a traditional conservative. First elected to Congress from Wyoming in 2016, she rose rapidly through GOP ranks until she became chair of the House Republican Party following the 2018 midterm election. She was on a fast track to political stardom on the right. Yet when she ran for reelection in 2022, after three terms in the House of Representative, she was soundly defeated in the primary, winning less than 30 percent of her party's vote. She had become the worst kind of disloyal villain to Donald Trump's MAGA Republicans. Her sin? Serving as vice chair of the House January 6 committee and eloquently criticizing Trump for fomenting a violent attempt to overthrow the election of Joe Biden to the presidency in 2020. In today's highly polarized political United States, she became a hero to people alarmed by the January 6 insurrection and its ominous portents for the future of our way of government.

Donald Trump was impeached twice. Cheney voted against the first impeachment for withholding authorized aid for Ukraine pending an announcement from President Zelenskyy that his country would open an investigation into Joe Biden's son Hunter Biden in 2019. She was a loyal foot soldier in the world of MAGA. But in the aftermath of the 2020 election, she did not support Trump's efforts to overturn the election. He was angered enough that in his January 6 speech he said it was time to "get rid of" Liz Cheney. She was one of the few Republicans the then-president mentioned by name as weak. During the ensuing riots Cheney's father, the former vice president, called to tell her she was in danger as the mob shouted "Hang Mike Pence" and broke into the capitol. When Trump was impeached days later for his actions on January 6, Cheney was one of ten Republican members of the House of Representatives to vote with all Democrats for impeachment. She stated in part: "The President of the United States summoned this mob, assembled the mob, and lit the flame of this attack… There has never been a greater betrayal by a President of the United States of his office and his oath to the Constitution."

During the summer of 2022, as Cheney served as vice chair of the House Committee on the January 6th insurrection, she was equally forceful in her condemnation of Trump. She attempted in vain to persuade fellow Republicans to own up to Trump's responsibility for that day's chaos and violence. She eloquently stated: "Tonight, I say this to my Republican colleagues who are defending the indefensible: There will come a day when Donald Trump is gone, but your dishonor will remain." Unfortunately, very few members of her own party heeded her words.

While Cheney is still clearly on the conservative side of the political spectrum, especially on issues like support for the military (much like her father) and restraints on domestic spending, it is of interest that on one issue she has changed her mind. When Cheney explored a bid for the US Senate in 2013, she spoke out against same-sex marriage, outlining the typical Republican position. Her statement led to a public spat with her lesbian sister Mary Cheney, who shot back: "Either you think all families should be treated equally or you don't. Liz's position is to treat my family as second class citizens." The conflict played a role in Liz Cheney dropping out of the Senate race. Years later she publicly expressed regret for her position. In 2022, she was one of 47 Republicans (still a small minority within the party) who voted for a federal law recognizing same-sex marriage. Thus on a second central issue Cheney departed from conservative and Republican orthodoxy. Those deviations cost her position in Congress. She expresses no regrets.

The case of Liz Cheney underlines the key argument that heroism is in the eye of the beholder. Today that is especially true on many defining political issues. Our sense is that history will judge Liz Cheney a hero for standing up for truth and constitutional principles. However, a second Trump presidency would do all but erase her from the history books. That is a sobering reality.

Drew Barrymore: The Heroic Story of the Little Girl Lost

When we think of the obstacles that heroes must overcome, the images that usually come to mind are great physical barriers or formidable villains. For example, Batman's obstacle is the Joker; Nelson Mandela's obstacles were prison bars; Sir Edmund Hillary and Tenzing Norgay's obstacle was the sheer size of Mt. Everest. But frequently the most daunting obstacles heroes confront are unseen. They are the hero's inner traumas and demons that inflict emotional pain and trigger self-destructive behaviors. A vivid example of a hero who conquered these inner demons is the actor Drew Barrymore.

As with many people in the entertainment industry, Drew Barrymore grew up surrounded by addiction. Many of the Barrymore family members were famed actors who struggled with alcohol and drug abuse. Starting at a very young age, Drew Barrymore got caught in a whirlwind of sex, drugs, and alcohol. By the age of 11, she was a regular at the famed Studio 54, smoking cigarettes, drinking alcohol, and experimenting with marijuana and cocaine. Her mother put her in rehab when Barrymore was 13. At the age of 14, Barrymore wrote her autobiography, aptly named *Little Girl Lost*.

Drew Barrymore's story could easily have had a tragic ending, but miraculously she turned her life around and has become one of Hollywood's most successful and sought-after actors. "I've been humbled," she explained. "That makes you grateful for every day you have." Barrymore has also adopted a very healthy attitude about her troubled past. "I never regret anything," she said, "because every little detail of your life is what made you into who you are in the end."

Most impressively, Barrymore has used her fame to make the world a better place. "I don't want to sit around and hope good things happen. I want to *make* them happen," she explained. In 2005, she was devastated to learn that there are more than 100 million school-aged children around the world who don't get enough to eat. Barrymore realized that she could make a difference by becoming a United Nations World Food Program celebrity partner. Traveling to Kenya, she witnessed the tragic conditions of hunger and poverty in the children of Nairobi. "Feeding a child at school is such a simple thing," she said while serving food to Kenyan schoolchildren in 2005. "But you can tell it works miracles."

In 2007, the World Food Program appointed Barrymore as their official Ambassador Against Hunger. "I am honored and humbled to accept this challenging and rewarding assignment," she said. "I can't think of any issue that is more important than working to see that no schoolchild in this world goes hungry." In March 2008, Barrymore appeared on the Oprah Winfrey show and announced that she was donating $1 million of her own money to support World Food Program projects in Kenya. "I've seen what a difference a simple cup of nutritious porridge can make in a child's life. It helps them learn, stay healthy and sets them on track for a bright future," she said.

Barrymore's life journey is not unlike that of many heroes who are able to overcome turbulent childhoods involving parental loss or dysfunction. Typically the hero on this journey leads a life of turmoil and despair until a trigger event, or rock bottom, is reached which compels the hero to undergo a complete overhaul of their life. A big part of this overhaul involves the hero becoming a selfless and tireless advocate of positive social change. Many fictional and nonfictional heroes have followed this type of heroic journey, including Batman, Johnny Cash, Oprah Winfrey, Christina Aguilera, John Lennon, and of course, Drew Barrymore. These heroes teach us that the same strength and courage we use to overcome our inner demons can also be used to make the world better for us all.

Montgomery Meigs: A Transparent Hero of the Civil War

Very often, heroes gain their status by either achieving or sacrificing, or both, in highly dramatic fashion. But many important heroes make their marks much more quietly. On the one hand, Martin Luther King's dramatic speeches and his tragic assassination are prototypes of the hero narrative—similarly George Washington crossing the Delaware, Willie Mays making "the catch" in the 1954 World Series, or Joan of Arc defiant while burning at the stake exemplify the unforgettable images that we associate with heroes. But as Washington well knew, there's more to winning battles than courage in combat. Napoleon is often quoted as saying "an army moves on its stomach." Whether he really said that is debatable. But there is no doubt that supplying an army is an indispensable if overlooked term in the formula for military success.

From this perspective it's no surprise that George Washington had his best general, Nathanael Greene, overseeing supplies, and that Ulysses S. Grant developed his military genius serving as quartermaster in the Mexican War. And this viewpoint gives us greater appreciation for one of the Civil War's transparent heroes, Quartermaster General Montgomery Meigs. Meigs's job was to keep Union armies supplied with muskets, gun powder, shoes, leather, saddles, horses, wagons, uniforms, canteens, bullets, blankets, and beef, among other things. The armies he provisioned were scattered across a huge section of the North American continent, from Missouri to Florida, and from Virginia to Texas. It was a daunting challenge, and Meigs approached it masterfully. He successfully mobilized one of the world's largest economies in a focused effort to win the war. Meigs was honest, hard-driving, and determined. He ran the logistical operations of numerous campaigns with vision, creativity, and efficiency. One contemporary politician claimed that Meigs handled as much as "fifteen hundred million dollars" during the war and that it was "accurately vouched and accounted for it to the last cent" (McPherson, 1988).

Meigs was born in Georgia and worked closely with Robert E. Lee before the Civil War. He might have been expected to join the South. But he had sworn an oath to the Union when he entered West Point, and he regarded Lee and others as traitors. He hated the Confederacy and all it stood for. In 1864, when he was seeking a suitable burial ground for Union soldiers killed in battle, he insisted that Arlington, the grounds and mansion across the Potomac River from Washington, DC, owned by Robert E. Lee's wife, would be a good spot. He went so far as to order that remains be buried in Mrs. Lee's rose garden. Thus was born Arlington National Cemetery. A few months later one of Meigs's sons was buried there, a combat casualty of a Virginia battle.

Near the end of the war, Meigs's importance was recognized when he was included in the honor guard of Abraham Lincoln's funeral. After the conflict he served as architect of government buildings in Washington and became an early member of the National Academy of Sciences. Appropriately he was buried at Arlington.

Meigs's role isn't mentioned in most accounts of the Civil War. There is little glamour in behind-the-scenes work. But the show can't go on without it. Meigs served his country in an indispensable position with uncommon capacity. The praises of this transparent hero should be sung more often.

John Wooden: Heroic Teacher and Mentor

When we ask people to list their heroes, nearly half of the lists contain the names of teachers and coaches. The late, great John Wooden identified himself, first and foremost, as a teacher. A college basketball coach, Wooden called the gymnasium his classroom. Wooden's primary goal never wavered: His job was to teach his students how to succeed not just in basketball but in life. To him, the definition of success was simple, unique, and refreshing: "Success comes from knowing that you did your best to become the best that you are capable of becoming," he said.

Always a humble man, Wooden would recoil at any mention of his extraordinary accomplishments as a coach. But it would be criminal of us not to point out that his UCLA Bruins won more basketball champion-ships than any other NCAA Division I team in history. Stunningly, his teams won seven championships in a row from 1967 to 1973. Under Wooden's leadership, UCLA enjoyed four perfect 30–0 seasons, including an eye-popping winning streak of 88 consecutive games. In 2009, *The Sporting News* named him the Greatest Coach of All-Time. President George Bush also awarded him the Presidential Medal of Freedom, the nation's highest civilian honor.

Wooden had only a few team rules, and they were strictly enforced. Never be late. Be neat and clean. No profanity. And never criticize a team-mate. He developed a seven-point creed by which to live one's life, and he followed it to the letter: (1) Be true to yourself. (2) Make each day your masterpiece. (3) Help others. (4) Drink deeply from good books, especially the Bible. (5) Make friendship a fine art. (6) Build a shelter against a rainy day. (7) Pray for guidance and give thanks for your blessings every day. Wooden told his players to "never cease trying to be the best you could be, because that's under your control. If you get too concerned with things over which you have no control, it will adversely affect the things over which you have control."

For Wooden, success was never about winning games. Success was reaching one's full potential, and so he taught his players that the final score of a game doesn't matter. "You can lose when you outscore somebody in a game; and you can win when you're outscored," he said. "If you make an effort to do the best you can, the results will be what they should be. The score is the byproduct of doing your best and is not the end itself. The journey is better than the end. Our practices were the journey, and the game was the end. I wanted to help players attain the self-satisfaction of knowing they made the effort to be the best that they were capable of being."

With great satisfaction, Wooden recalled one player who was a mediocre shooter but whose shooting percentage was extremely high because he took intelligent shots. Another player was poor at jumping but became an excellent rebounder because he tirelessly practiced the art of positioning himself perfectly for rebounds. But Wooden's greatest pride was witnessing dozens of his players become doctors, dentists, attorneys, and teachers. "I taught them that they were there to get an education," he said. "Basketball was second."

When Wooden passed away in June of 2010 at the age of 99, his former players and colleagues were effusive in their praise for the man they all called "Coach." Kareem Abdul Jabbar recalled that Wooden "really wanted us to get our degrees and learn what it meant to be a good citizen, good parents and husbands, and responsible human beings." Dick Enberg noted that "Wooden's philosophy of teaching players lessons of life will serve as his ultimate gift." According to Keith Erickson, Wooden "was the best role model that a young man could possibly ever have." John Wooden was proof that coaches and teachers are heroes who strive to make us all better people.

Accidental Sidekicks: Marion Keisker's Moment to Help Elvis

Each August 16, the anniversary of Elvis Presley's death in 1977 is observed. Or at least most people believe he died then. But there are some who believe that Elvis went into hiding and is still alive. And some of those individuals assert that it is no mere coincidence that the word ELVIS and the word LIVES share the same letters. Several years ago Elvis was compared to Dionysus on a National Public Radio classical music show, which argued that in order to understand America, one had to understand Elvis. He was or is a hero for many, both for his music and for his overall impact on American and even world culture. On the 1999 ABC series called *The Century*, narrator Peter Jennings argued that when Elvis burst onto the scene in he 1950s, he paved the way for 1960s.

Our work on heroes has considered the role of sidekicks, such as Dr. Watson in the Sherlock Holmes stories or Sancho Panza in the two Don Quixote volumes. In Elvis's case there is a person who played a very small role in his rise to fame but a crucial and necessary one. This woman, unknown even to many of his most devoted fans, underlines a more general point – that chance and circumstance can change the course of history and make or break potential heroes.

We are talking about Marion Keisker, a woman who worked at Sam Phillips's Sun Recording Studio in Memphis, Tennessee, in the mid-1950s. Peter Guralnick relates the story in his classic 1994 Elvis biography *Last Train to Memphis*. Phillips, who also played a crucial and much larger role in the rise of Elvis, had started Sun several years before and had launched the career of a number of artists, including Howling Wolf and Ike Turner. Not long after he graduated from high school, Elvis came by the Sun studio and paid to make a record. He claimed it was for his mother's birthday, but his mother's birthday was many months away. It was clear that he wanted to be noticed. Marion Keisker was at the studio that day and handled the recording. She noted on a 3 × 5 card that Elvis was a good ballad singer. Elvis came around several more times, asking whether anyone was looking for a vocalist for any recordings. He was on the make.

In early July 1954, when Elvis was 19, a year out of high school, the pivotal moment arrived. Two young musicians, guitarist Scotty Moore and bass player Bill Black, were at the studio working with Phillips on some songs they wanted to record. They needed someone to sing. At that point, Marion Keisker asked, "How about the kid with the sideburns?" Elvis lived nearby but didn't have a telephone. Someone went to his apartment in a nearby housing project and left a message. Very soon a sweaty Elvis arrived at the studio, having run all the way over.

That night, after some desultory efforts, Elvis began strumming his rhythm guitar and singing the blues number "That's All Right, Mama." Sam Phillips said that that was the sound he'd been looking for and recorded it. "That's All Right, Mama" was a Black R&B song, and Phillips wanted a country & western (C&W) "B-side," that would have more appeal to white audiences. Pretty soon, Elvis, Scotty and Bill recorded a bouncy version of Bill Monroe's bluegrass classic "Blue Moon of Kentucky." Shortly, both sides were being played on Memphis radio stations. It wasn't long before Elvis became The King of Rock'n'Roll and a hero to millions.

Those Whom We Forgot: The Makers of Fire

There are some things in life that have become so commonplace, so normal, that we often take them for granted. One of these things is fire. The origins of the use and making of fire have been lost to history. The earliest evidence for the use of fire dates back some 1.6 million years and is often attributed to *Homo erectus*, though some believe later species of *Homo* were responsible. Whether the users of this fire actually made it or simply made use of a naturally occurring fire is not known—or even whether it was a product of one lone genius or a group through trial and error. But at some point in history fire was made, and that changed history. Humanity suddenly had a means to see in the darkness, repel predators, keep warm, and preserve and tenderize food. With it humanity spread across the globe, becoming far more cosmopolitan than any other species of primate.

We owe much of our civilization and modern world to the knowledge of combustion. Signal fires and smoke signals enabled near-instant communications over distances. The famous cave art at Lascaux was done by fire-light. Fire-stick farming, where portions of the land are purposely set on fire to create grasslands, has changed vast portions of the globe. Many European explorers seeing lands like the Americas or Australia for the first time thought that they were unspoiled wildernesses, wholly unaware that much of what they were seeing had already been altered by people.

Because of fire. Because of the people who tamed it.

Smelting gave us metals, steam engines gave us greater mobility, coal-fired power plants gave us electricity, internal combustion engines drives our industry and trade, pasteurization protects us from disease, and the burning fuel of rockets push us out to space and realms the early fire makers couldn't have even imagined. All of this would be difficult or impossible without combustion. In an era of the written word, we can now remember the names of those who gave us electricity, or plastics, the automobile, or the first airplane. The names Edison, Ford, and Wright will go down through history.

But they owe it all to people whose names we'll never know—people who lived in a world totally alien to us and were almost certainly not even members of our own species. And often modern peoples do not understand the difficulty of actually starting a fire without modern aids. Set loose in the wilderness, many of us would be helpless without lighters or some other convenience. Yet ages ago people who many would denigrate as primitive did so regularly, armed with nothing but rock, wood, and their own ingenuity. And the heroic thing about it is that those who first tended and created those early fires had to overcome their own instinctual fear. Previous contact with fire, often in the form of a wildfire, usually meant death and destruction. The taming of fire took courage, imagination, and foresight. Although their names have been lost to time, their legacy lives on with us and will do so as long as society persists. And perhaps that's all the recognition they need.

The Supporting Cast in Heroes Narratives: Sidekicks and Others

Our profile of the fictional hero Sherlock Holmes noted that Sir Arthur Conan Doyle's famous detective is revealed to us through the words of his long-suffering friend, Dr. John Watson. The Holmes–Watson team is unique in many ways, but in other ways it is typical of both fictional partners and real-life teams. In fiction, there are many other examples of what we call "hero–sidekick" pairs, starting with the memorable Cervantes characters Don Quixote and Sancho Panza. Quixote is the elderly would-be knight errant, who rides across the Spanish countryside on the broken-down Rocinante so that he can right wrongs in honor of his imagined lady, Dulcinea. He is the unrealistic, totally serious idealist who literally tilts at windmills thinking that they are evil giants. Sancho tries to impart some realism to Quixote's vision of the world, and in his bumbling attempts adds some humor to the story.

In the Holmes canon, Watson also adds some humor by deflating some of Sherlock's most self-centered and arrogant remarks. But his central role, beyond that of narrator, is to accompany Holmes on most of his adventures and occasionally to help him by bringing along his revolver on dangerous missions. Besides Watson, the Holmes stories actually have other supporting players. A familiar one for many such narratives is the villain. In this case it is Professor Moriarty, the "Napoleon of Crime." But there is an additional character in many of the Holmes stories, the Scotland Yard detective Inspector Lestrade. Holmes claims that Lestrade is the best of the lot at Scotland Yard, but even so he is portrayed as plodding and conventional. He sees himself as a practical man, in contrast to the theoretical Holmes. But he does acknowledge that Holmes's "methods" are sometimes useful. Interestingly, for the most part the two both disdain and depend on each other. In their different ways, Watson, Moriarty, and Lestrade are foils for Holmes and allow different facets of his personality to be explored.

The sidekick role was central to a number of the radio and television Westerns of the 1940s and 1950s. The Lone Ranger had his "faithful Indian companion, Tonto," and the Cisco Kid had his partner Pancho. In the Elizabeth George Inspector Lynley mysteries, Lynley's sidekick is a woman, Detective Sergeant Barbara Havers. Like Watson and Sancho Panza, one of Havers's roles is to pinprick Lynley's inflated, upper-class sense of himself. In the more recent television series *The Closer*, a woman, Deputy Chief Brenda Lee Johnson, is the hero, and her most frequent sidekick is a man, Sergeant Gabriel. Like other sidekicks, Gabriel tries to compensate for the hero's shortcomings, in this case Johnson's inability to navigate her way around Los Angeles.

Real-life sidekicks exist too, but their roles are more easily portrayed in fiction. We think that former heavyweight boxer Muhammad Ali's close friend Bundini Brown played a role very much like the sidekicks from novels, television, and the movies. He supports and relaxes the Champ but also provides some realistic grounding. Speech writer and adviser Theodore Sorensen was often described as President John F. Kennedy's "alter-ego." Clearly, Sorensen was someone JFK depended on for advice in many domains. And of course Kennedy had another important sidekick, his brother, Attorney General Robert F. Kennedy. In general, sidekicks seem to support and humanize the heroes they team up with and allow their idiosyncrasies to be seen in bold relief.

Why Our Parents Are Our Heroes

Fifteen years ago we conducted a study that underscored the importance of family members as heroes (Allison & Goethals, 2011). In the study, people of all ages and from all walks of life were asked to list their heroes. We were surprised yet pleased to see that family members were listed about a third of the time. Most importantly, over one-fourth of all people listed their mothers as their hero. Mothers were mentioned more than any other person, including fathers.

Mother's Day became a nationally recognized holiday in 1914 because of the efforts of Anna Jarvis, a West Virginian who campaigned to honor mothers after her own beloved mother passed away in 1905. Ironically, by the 1920s Jarvis became disenchanted with the commercialization of Mother's Day and began campaigning against the holiday. Still, we believe her initial sentiment was on target, and we applaud the opportunity to recognize the heroic qualities of mothers everywhere.

Many highly accomplished individuals are quick to attribute their success to their mothers. American presidents are especially likely to do so. Abraham Lincoln once noted that "all that I am, or can be, I owe to my angel mother." George Washington also observed that "all I am I owe to my mother. I attribute all my success in life to the moral, intellectual and physical education I received from her." Andrew Jackson claimed that "there never was a woman like my mother. She was as gentle as a dove and as brave as a lioness."

When the participants in our study were asked why their mothers were heroic, they generated three main reasons: generosity with time, money, and love. There are many ways that mothers gave their time to us. According to survey respondents, mothers tended to us when we were sick, accompanied us to school and soccer practice, made us dinner, and read stories to us. Our mothers made financial sacrifices, too. They wore old clothes so that we could wear new clothes; they took on part-time jobs to buy us gifts; they saved money for us to attend college; they gave us our weekly allowance; and they made sure we had food on the table. But the most important quality that distinguishes mothers from other heroes, including fathers, is the free offering of love that mothers give us. Mothers were there for us when we needed emotional support. Mothers hugged us. They comforted us and let us sit on their laps. They kissed us on our cheeks before school and at bedtime at night.

Although mothers are listed as heroes more frequently than fathers, we should emphasize that fathers are a close second. The origin of Father's Day is not entirely clear, but there are several fascinating possibilities. Babylonian scholars have discovered a message carved in clay by a young man named Elmesu roughly 4,000 years ago. In the message, Elmesu wishes his father good health and a long life. Some believe this ancient message represents evidence of an established tradition of honoring fathers, but there is little evidence to support a specially designated Father's Day until modern times.

There is some debate about the origin of the Father's Day that we celebrate today. Some claim that a West Virginian named Grace Golden Clayton deserves the credit. In 1907, Clayton was grieving the loss of her own father when a tragic mine explosion in Monongah killed 361 men, 250 of whom were fathers. Clayton requested that her church establish a day to honor these lost fathers and to help the children of the affected families heal emotionally. The date she suggested was July 8, the anniversary of her own father's death.

Still others believe that the first Father's Day was held on June 19, 1910, through the efforts of Sonora Smart Dodd of Spokane, Washington. Inspired by the newly recognized Mother's Day, Dodd felt strongly that fatherhood needed recognition as well. Her own father, William Smart, was a Civil War veteran who was left to raise his family alone when his wife died giving birth to their sixth child. Dodd was the only daughter, and she helped her father raise her younger brothers, including her new infant brother Marshall.

Whereas Mother's Day was met with instant enthusiasm, Father's Day was initially met with scorn and derision. Few people believed that fathers wanted, or needed, any acknowledgement. It wasn't until 1972 that President Richard Nixon made Father's Day an official holiday. Today the holiday is widely celebrated in the month of June by more than 52 countries.

Why are fathers heroes? The respondents in our survey listed two main reasons. First, fathers are given credit for being great teachers and mentors. They teach us how to fix a flat tire, shoot a basketball, and write a resume. Fathers tend to be less emotional than mothers, but they lead by example and devote time demonstrating life skills to us. Former governor of New York Mario Cuomo once said, "I talk and talk and talk, and I haven't taught people in 50 years what my father taught by example in one week."

Second, fathers are great providers and protectors. Our respondents told us that their fathers were heroes in their commitment to provide for their families, often at great sacrifice. Many fathers work at two or more jobs outside the home to ensure that their families have adequate food and shelter. Fathers also provide us with a sense of safety and protection. Sigmund Freud once wrote, "I cannot think of any need in childhood as strong as the need for a father's protection."

Developmental psychologists tell us that the relationship we have with our parents is the first significant relationship of our lives. It is a relationship that indelibly shapes our values, our aspirations, and our future behavior. Thus when we experience successes in our careers and in our personal lives, it is not surprising that we attribute those triumphs, at least in part, to our parents.

Edith Wilson: An Unsung Hero or Villain?

In August 1914, the same month that witnessed the world wade into what became known as the Great War, or World War I, the First Lady of the United States, Ellen Axson Wilson, passed away. President Woodrow Wilson was devastated as he tried to calm fears of US involvement in the war between Germany and Great Britain, France and Russia. Ellen had been Wilson's closest companion for nearly 30 years.

Within several months, Wilson became involved with a Washington, DC, widow, Edith Bolling Galt. The two were married in December 1915. Edith became a close and trusted adviser as well as an intimate companion. Despite Wilson's best efforts, and despite running for reelection in 1916 on the slogan "He kept us out of war," the president asked for a declaration of war against Germany in April 1917. It was clear to all parties that if the United States could mobilize quickly enough, the Allies, now including the US, could defeat Germany. But the Germans hoped that they could defeat their European enemies before the Americans could arrive in time to tip the balance. In the end, American "doughboys" got to France quickly enough for the Allies to win, but it was close.

An armistice took effect at 11:00 AM on November 11, 1918, the 11th hour of the 11th day of the 11th month. President Wilson traveled to Europe to participate in the peace negotiations, which culminated in the Treaty of Versailles in 1919. On his return from Paris, Wilson campaigned vigorously for ratification of the treaty, including American entry into the League of Nations. The president believed that the League might be able to prevent future wars. However, opposition in Congress to the League was intense. Opponents worried that the League would never work, and that it would compromise American sovereignty. Wilson went to the people on a nationwide speech making tour, arguing eloquently for treaty ratification. Already in poor health, the resident had to suspend the tour. Shortly afterward, in the fall of 1919, he suffered a stroke and was severely disabled – mentally, emotionally, and physically – for the remaining year and a half of his administration.

No other president had been as disabled as Wilson. At the time, many people believed that he should resign. Some historians hold that view today. But Edith Galt Wilson rose to defend her husband and to rigorously control access to him. Ambiguous and overly optimistic reports on the president's condition were released, and only a few close advisers and leading congressional leaders were allowed to see him. It appears that Edith made some decisions without consulting the president. She became, in effect, acting president.

Did Edith Wilson do the right thing? Did she assume more power and responsibility than she should have? It seems clear that she protected Wilson's health. She needed to save him from himself as much as from others. The president wanted to engage in national affairs much more than he was able to. Edith saw that he was not overwhelmed and that he was given the time, and the freedom from stressful demands, that he needed to regain some measure of health.

But it can be argued that Edith usurped power in a dangerous manner. It is clear that she was navigating in uncharted waters. She was a confident woman who unhesitatingly decided that she would protect Woodrow Wilson's health and his presidency. She believed that doing so was in the interests of the United States. Many students of history disagree. They think that Edith Wilson was not at all heroic. Others believe that she served the country well in a time of crisis and uncertainty. As much as anyone, Edith Wilson illustrates our belief that heroism is in the eye of the beholder.

Bayard Rustin: Peaceful Advocate of Human Rights

A number of heroes can be considered *polymaths*; these are individuals who excel in a number of different areas of life. Bayard Rustin was one such multitalented person. Rustin was an accomplished tenor vocalist, a renowned scholar, and a versatile athlete. But Rustin's most important contribution to the world may have been his life-long devotion to defending the rights of oppressed groups of people across the globe, especially in America during the civil rights movement of the mid-20th century.

As a young man in the 1940s, Rustin helped convince President Franklin Roosevelt to eliminate racial discrimination in defense industries and in federal agencies. He traveled to California to protect the property of Japanese Americans who had been wrongly imprisoned in internment camps. In the deep South, Rustin was arrested for violating segregated seating laws on buses, a crime for which he served 22 days on a chain gang. Between 1947 and 1952, Rustin made frequent trips to India and Africa to meet with practitioners of Gandhi's teachings about nonviolent protest philosophies. His subsequent influence on Martin Luther King, Jr. was unmistakable. When Rosa Parks was arrested for bravely defying Jim Crow laws in Montgomery, Alabama, Rustin was there to advise King in practicing nonviolent forms of protest, such as organizing the Montgomery Bus Boycott.

But Rustin was limited in the help that he could offer King. A gay man, Rustin lived in an era when homosexuality was unacceptable to the vast majority of Americans. During the Montgomery boycott, a reporter threatened to undermine King's cause by exposing Rustin's sexual orientation. King and Rustin agreed that their civil rights crusade would be best served if Rustin distanced himself from King. Rustin was so careful not to undermine King's work that he fled Montgomery at night in the trunk of a car. Still, Rustin continued to advise King and influence the civil rights movement in significant ways from a safe distance.

It was not just the public and the media who felt threatened by Rustin's sexuality. Many African American ministers involved in civil rights would also have nothing to do with Rustin, and some spread rumors that King was gay because of his close friendship with Rustin. Said Rustin, "Martin Luther King, with whom I worked very closely, became very distressed when a number of the ministers working for him wanted him to dismiss me from his staff because of my homosexuality. Martin set up a committee to discover what he should do. They said that, despite the fact that I had contributed tremendously to the organization. They thought I should separate myself from Dr. King" (Monroe, 2012).

As the dream of racial equality made significant headway during the 1970s and 80s, Rustin was painfully aware of the lack of social progress in the area of gay rights. In 1986, he gave a speech entitled "The New Niggers Are Gays," in which he asserted that "Blacks are no longer the litmus paper or the barometer of social change. Blacks are in every segment of society and there are laws that help to protect them from racial discrimination. The new 'niggers' are gays. It is in this sense that gay people are the new barometer for social change. The question of social change should be framed with the most vulnerable group in mind: gay people."

Rustin devoted his entire life to promoting human rights, not only in North America but in other nations such as Haiti, Poland, and Zimbabwe. When asked to summarize his philosophy, he said, "The principal factors which influenced my life are nonviolent tactics; constitutional means; democratic procedures; respect for human personality; and a belief that all people are one." As with many heroes, Bayard Rustin showed a courageous willingness to sacrifice his own well-being for the noble principle of equality. Throughout his entire life he remained a fierce advocate of civil rights for all people. "When an individual is protesting society's refusal to acknowledge his dignity as a human being, his very act of protest confers dignity on him," he said.

Rick Rescorla: The Hero Who Saved 2,700 Lives on 9/11

Some heroes perform their heroic acts in the public spotlight and are lauded immediately after displaying their courageous and selfless behavior. Other heroes perform their heroic work invisibly, outside the public view, and rarely receive the attention they deserve. Earlier we described these invisible heroes and their invaluable impact as educators, firefighters, law enforcement officers, healthcare workers, and military personnel.

We now turn our attention to one invisible hero in particular, a man named Rick Rescorla, whose behind-the-scenes work before and during the terrorist attacks of September 11, 2001, saved nearly 2,700 lives at the World Trade Center.

Rescorla was the director of security for Morgan Stanley, a large investment company headquartered at the twin towers in New York City. Rescorla was one of the few people who anticipated the possibility that terrorists might fly aircraft into the twin towers. As early as 1992, Rescorla warned the owners of the World Trade Center that a truck bomb could attack the pillars of the basement parking garage. Sure enough, in 1993, terrorists used this method, and Rescorla played a major role in evacuating the building. He was also the last man out.

Throughout the 1990s, Rescorla continued to warn authorities that the World Trade Center was a prime target for terrorists flying airplanes, and he recommended to his superiors at Morgan Stanley that the company leave Manhattan. Morgan Stanley declined to leave, as their lease at the World Trade Center did not terminate until 2006. Rescorla received permission to ensure that all employees practice emergency evacuations every three months.

On the morning of September 11, 2001, Rescorla awoke as he normally did, kissed his wife goodbye, and took the 6:10 train to Manhattan. He was at his desk on the 44th floor of the World Trade Center's South Tower by 7:30 AM. When the first hijacked plane crashed into the north tower, Rescorla ignored officials' requests to stay put. He grabbed a bullhorn and led the company's 2,700 employees down the stairwell two-by-two, singing patriotic songs such as "God Bless America" to keep them calm.

By the time the second airliner hit the south tower, most of the company's employees were out of danger. When one of his colleagues told him that he, too, needed to evacuate the World Trade Center, Rescorla replied, "As soon as I make sure everyone else is out." Rescorla and two assistants went back to look for them, never to return. He was last seen on the 10th floor of the burning tower. His remains have never been found. As a result of Rescorla's actions, all but 13 of Morgan Stanley's 2,700 employees survived.

It's important to note that Rescorla was already a hero *before* his life-saving work on 9/11. He was a highly decorated Vietnam veteran whose heroic feats in battle earned him the Silver Star, the Bronze Star with Oak Leaf Cluster, a Purple Heart, and the Vietnamese Cross of Gallantry. While serving in Vietnam, Rescorla's leadership, courage, and compassion for his troops were legendary.

Rescola's wife Susan has honored her husband's legacy by creating The Richard Rescola Memorial Foundation, with the goal of "keeping present the magnitude of Rick's life and to promote the virtues Rick lived by – duty, honor and courage." She authored a book entitled *Touched by a Hero*, which details the sacrifices Rick made to safely evacuate nearly 2,700 people from the World Trade Center on 9/11. "I am so very proud to have had him in my life," she said. "I want to have his legacy live on."

8   Traditional-Moral Heroes

A traditional hero is the prototypical hero. By "prototype," we mean the kind of person whom we usually think of when we are asked to think of a hero. The traditional hero is the individual who follows the classic hero journey as described by Campbell (1949) in his hero monomyth. The journey contains many stages, but the main ones involve the hero being cast out of their ordinary world and into a dangerous new world; the hero receiving assistance from strange and unlikely sources; the hero encountering potentially destructive temptations and father figures; the hero overcoming formidable obstacles; the hero becoming transformed in some way; and finally, the hero returning to the ordinary world with a boon that transforms it. Campbell acknowledged that not all hero stories contain every component of the monomythic journey, and that the details of the journey can vary significantly from story to story. Still, all traditional hero stories more or less follow the basic monomyth structure.

In our survey of 450 respondents, reported in Allison and Goethals (2011), we found that people generate the names of more traditional heroes than any other category. This fact explains why we this section of our book contains more hero profiles than any of the others, and it also raises some chicken-and-egg questions. Do people list so many traditional heroes because, as Campbell (1949) claims, this category of heroism taps into the Jungian hero archetype that is so deeply imbedded in our psyche? Or does the abundance of traditional hero stories found in books and movies make this hero category more deeply imbedded in us? Put differently, the abundance of traditional heroes in our cultural narratives may either reflect or be the cause of the powerful schema we have for this category of hero.

There is a fascinating contradiction with regard to our judgments about the prevalence of heroes that we would like to address. As we've mentioned, when people are asked to generate examples of specific heroes, traditional heroes come most easily to mind compared to the other hero categories in our taxonomy. Yet we've also noted in the Introduction to this book that transparent heroes are judged by people to be the most

DOI: 10.4324/9781003328681-8

abundant type of heroes in society. How do we explain this discrepancy? There are at least two possibilities. One explanation is that although transparent heroes may be judged as most abundant, their contributions are less exciting or dramatic than those of the traditional hero. Vivid instances of heroes who undertake daring and dangerous quests may be more available in memory than instances of heroes who teach history at the local high school.

Another possibility is that transparent heroes and traditional heroes are both viewed as abundant but tap into different mental hierarchies of heroes. For example, when we ask people to "list your heroes," we get different lists of heroes as compared to when we ask people to "list people who are heroes." For the former instruction, we obtain many family members, mentors, and coaches – in short, transparent heroes. For the latter instruction, we obtain the names of many traditional heroes such as Harry Potter, Mother Teresa, and Oprah Winfrey. We suggest, therefore, that when we ask people to "list your heroes," we are tapping into their vast reservoir of *personal heroes*, most of whom are Transparent. But when we ask people to "list people who are heroes," we are tapping into their large mental storehouse of *cultural heroes*, most of whom are traditional.

The traditional heroes whom we profile in Chapters 8, 9, and 10 are categorized into three subtypes: *moral, competent*, and *complete*. This carving of heroes is based on our research showing that people are judged to be heroes to the extent that they make great moral contributions, great ability-based contributions, or great contributions that require both great morality *and* great ability. Our profiles of traditional-moral heroes include Miep Gies, Eleanor Roosevelt, Pope Francis, Malala Yousafzai, Greta Thunberg, Michelle Obama, the Dalai Lama, Confucius, Pat Tillman, George Bailey, Mother Teresa, Lois Wilson, Nathan Hale, Dana Reeve, Phil Connors, Israel Spira, Irena Sendler, Rosa Parks, and Corrie ten Boom. Our profiles of traditional-competent Heroes in Chapter 9 include Jacinda Ardern, Angela Merkl, Katherine Johnson, Taylor Swift, Nancy Pelosi, J.K. Rowling, Marie Curie, Ellen DeGeneres, John Nash, Althea Gibson, Monica Seles, Dan Anderson, Humphrey Bogart, Edgar Allen Poe, Clint Eastwood, and Lucille Ball.

Finally, in Chapter 10, our profiles of traditional-complete heroes who show both great morality and great competence include Wilma Mankiller, Audrey Hepburn, Volodymyr Zelenskyy, Golda Meier, Lady Gaga, Harry Bellafonte, Terry Fox, George Marshall, Florence Nightingale, Oprah Winfrey, Winston Churchill, Roberto Clemente, George Washington Carver, Warren Spahn, George Washington, Mikhail Gorbachev, and Henry Fonda's character in the classic film *Twelve Angry Men*. We thank our good friend Jeff Green at Virginia Commonwealth University for supplying a terrific profile of Winston Churchill.

Traditional-Moral Heroes

Miep Gies: The Selfless Hero

In the shadow of a war that darkened the skies of Europe, a light of heroism shone from the actions of an ordinary secretary named Miep Gies. Gies's heroic leadership is both remarkable and inspiring. Amid the chaos and peril of Nazi-occupied Amsterdam, Miep, with quiet courage that belied the immense danger, became a guardian angel to the family of Anne Frank.

One December day, as snow gently blanketed the streets outside, Miep ascended the steps to the secret annex, her arms laden with a Christmas tree no taller than a rose bush. It was a gesture that risked much, but to her, it was a simple act of bringing festive cheer to those cloistered in shadow. This small tree, smuggled into the annex, stood as a symbol of Miep's unwavering commitment to preserve the humanity and dignity of those hiding within. Her heroism was not found in grandiose acts but in the sum of countless quiet deeds and the steadfast bravery of keeping hope alive in a time when hope was a scarce commodity.

Holocaust rescuers like Gies were beacons of moral courage, acting selflessly in an era where the stakes could not have been higher. Their bravery was not just in the grand gestures but in the everyday acts of defiance against a regime that sought to extinguish humanity. They operated with a deep sense of empathy, providing not just physical shelter but also emotional solace to those they hid. Their actions required a high degree of

Miep Gies

Source: Rob Bogaerts/Anefo

moral integrity, choosing to uphold the sanctity of human life over adherence to the draconian laws of the time. It was their unshakeable commitment to doing what was right, rather than what was easy, that truly defined their heroism.

The heroism of Holocaust rescuers also lay in their resourcefulness and persistence. They had to think on their feet, often improvising under pressure to keep one step ahead of Nazi surveillance. Their ingenuity was matched only by their perseverance, as they maintained their clandestine operations through years of war and uncertainty. Despite the constant threat of discovery, they pressed on, driven by a conviction that was as quiet as it was firm. In the aftermath, their humility stood out. Many, like Gies, did not seek accolades for their actions; they simply did what they felt any compassionate person ought to do. Their legacy is one of true altruism, marked by deeds that continue to inspire generations to value and defend human dignity.

Miep Gies was deeply transformed by her experiences during the Holocaust. Although she did not frequently speak of personal change, her actions and later reflections reveal a profound sense of responsibility and moral conviction that grew from her time spent aiding the Frank family and others. The weight of what she witnessed —the inhumanity, the suffering, and the resilience of those she helped – instilled in her a lifelong commitment to educating others about the Holocaust.

Gies became an advocate for tolerance and historical remembrance, often stating that her actions were not heroic but simply human. The enduring legacy of her involvement, including the preservation of Anne Frank's diary, indicates a deep-seated belief in the power of individual stories to effect change. Gies's experiences did not just transform her into a historical figure of compassion and bravery; they also seemed to shape her into a poignant speaker for the voiceless and an emblem of hope against despair.

Eleanor Roosevelt: The Multifaceted Hero

In the midst of the 1930s Great Depression, when the fabric of American life was fraying under economic strain and uncertainty, Eleanor Roosevelt, a first lady unlike any before her, redefined the role not just in title but in action and spirit. On one unassuming evening, she stepped into a mine pit in West Virginia not draped in the finery typical of her position but in the simple, protective garb of the miners she stood in solidarity with. Her visit was more than ceremonial; she descended into the darkened earth, a beacon of light in the depths, listening intently to the stories of the miners.

This was no mere gesture of empathy; it was a statement of her commitment to understanding the lives of those she served. Eleanor's determination to bring light to the forgotten corners of America was emblematic of her tireless advocacy for the downtrodden, a heroism born not from the battlefields of war but from the equally arduous trenches of social injustice and hardship.

Following we list several ways that Eleanor Roosevelt displayed heroism in her life:

Champion for Civil Rights

As first lady, she was a champion for civil rights, speaking out against discrimination and lynching when it was still very controversial. She supported organizations like the NAACP and advocated for antilynching legislation. In addition, she leveraged her influence as first lady to promote civil rights leaders and causes, most notably resigning from the Daughters of the American Revolution to protest their discrimination and facilitating Marian Anderson's iconic Lincoln Memorial concert. Her efforts continued post–White House as she played a key role in drafting the Universal Declaration of Human Rights, affirming her commitment to equality on a global stage.

Redefining the First Lady Role

Eleanor Roosevelt redefined the role of first lady by transforming it into a platform for activism and advocacy. She broke precedent by holding press conferences, writing a daily syndicated newspaper column, and speaking out on human rights, children's causes, and women's issues. Her hands-on approach to social issues and policy, frequent public engagements, and direct involvement in politics were pioneering at a time when first ladies were expected to remain largely ceremonial. Roosevelt's tenure marked a significant expansion of the role, turning the position into one of influence and social impact, setting a new standard for her successors.

Promoting the War Effort

During World War II, Eleanor Roosevelt displayed heroism by being an unwavering advocate for the troops and the Allied cause. She visited battlefronts to boost soldier morale, advocated for volunteerism on the home front, and tirelessly worked to ensure that the rights and needs of returning servicemen were addressed through legislation like the GI Bill. She also supported the war effort through her public communications, using her columns and speeches to unify public sentiment, champion sacrifice and service, and reinforce the democratic ideals for which the war was being fought. Her actions during the war embodied the courage and selflessness characteristic of the nation she served.

Advocate for Human Rights

After FDR's death, she fought tirelessly for human rights worldwide. Eleanor Roosevelt continued her heroic advocacy for human rights as a delegate to the United Nations, where she was instrumental in drafting the Universal Declaration of Human Rights. Her leadership in crafting this seminal document, which laid the foundation for modern human rights law, reflected her deep commitment to promoting dignity, equality, and justice worldwide. She chaired the UN Commission on Human Rights and fought tirelessly to ensure that the Declaration addressed a broad spectrum of human rights, earning her the nickname "First Lady of the World" for her international efforts in championing the causes of the oppressed and disenfranchised.

Overcoming Personal Struggles

Eleanor Roosevelt's triumph over personal struggles is a testament to her resilience and fortitude. Despite a difficult childhood marred by the loss of both parents and a rocky marriage fraught with challenges, including her husband's infidelity, she channeled her pain into public service, emerging as a voice for the voiceless and a champion for social change. She found strength in activism, authoring books, articles, and delivering speeches, thereby crafting an independent identity that transcended personal tribulations. Her ability to convert adversity into advocacy not only fortified her own spirit but also inspired a nation during some of its darkest hours.

In all of these efforts, Eleanor Roosevelt demonstrated selfless determination, strength of character, and commitment to serving others – traits that define a true hero. She broke barriers for women, redefined the role of presidential spouses, and created lasting change.

Pope Francis: Heroic Leadership by Example

On a brisk autumn morning in the heart of Vatican City, Pope Francis stepped out not clad in the traditional papal garments one might expect but in the simple, white cassock that has become his trademark. In the early days of his papacy, he visited the tiny island of Lampedusa, a beacon of hope for refugees braving the Mediterranean in search of sanctuary. There, amid the cries of the grieving and the forlorn, Pope Francis threw a wreath into the restless sea, a solemn tribute to those who had perished in its depths. It was a poignant gesture, transcending mere symbolism; it was an act of profound empathy and solidarity with the most vulnerable. This moment captured the essence of Pope Francis's heroism—a leader of the Catholic Church who embraces humility and compassion, who acts as the voice of the voiceless, and who carries the burdens of the suffering as his own.

Heroes are defined by their risk-taking, self-sacrifice, and courage (Franco et al., 2011). Here's how Pope Francis meets these criteria:

1 **Risk-taking:** Pope Francis has taken significant risks in his efforts to reform the Vatican and address controversial issues within the Church, such as financial corruption, clerical abuse, and the need for greater transparency. He has also engaged with individuals of different faiths and atheists, breaking with tradition to foster interfaith dialogue and understanding.
2 **Self-sacrifice:** Living by example, Pope Francis chose to reside in the Vatican guesthouse rather than the traditional papal apartments to remain close to the people he serves. He has also made it a hallmark of his papacy to live simply, eschewing many of the luxuries typically associated with his position and dedicating his life to the service of others, especially the poor and marginalized.
3 **Courage:** He has shown courage in addressing socio-political issues worldwide, including climate change, economic inequality, and immigration. He has not shied away from criticizing world powers on their failure to uphold the dignity and rights of every individual, regardless of the potential for political fallout.

Through these actions, Pope Francis has demonstrated that his approach to leadership is one that embodies the qualities often associated with heroism. He continue to challenge both the Church and the world to live up to higher standards of morality, inclusivity, and compassion.

Despite facing criticisms for not implementing reforms within the Catholic Church as rapidly as some may hope, Pope Francis can be considered a hero for the courage he displays in confronting deeply ingrained issues that the Church faces. His incremental yet significant steps toward transparency, accountability, and modernization – particularly in financial management and addressing the clerical abuse scandal – demonstrate a steadfast commitment to change in an institution known for its resistance to rapid transformation. Furthermore, his advocacy for social justice, environmental stewardship, and the rights of the marginalized showcase his dedication to not only leading the Church but also influencing global ethical practices. His heroism is found in his unwavering pursuit of these ideals despite internal and external resistance, exemplifying the moral fortitude that anchors his papacy.

Malala Yousafzai: The Hero of Hope and Positive Change

Malala Yousafzai is a name that resonates with courage, resilience, and hope. Her story is one of a young girl who stood up against the Taliban's ban on girls' education in Pakistan and survived a gunshot to the head.

Malala is now recognized globally for her advocacy for girls' education and women's rights, having been awarded the Nobel Peace Prize in 2014 for her efforts. Her remarkable story is one of courage and resilience.

Malala Yousafzai is considered a hero for several significant reasons, each highlighting different aspects of her impact and character:

Advocate for education: Malala's advocacy for the right to education, especially for girls in regions where such rights are denied or restricted, is perhaps her most renowned heroic aspect. She has tirelessly worked to promote education for all children worldwide.

Bravery in the face of adversity: Malala's courage in speaking out against the Taliban in Pakistan, despite the risks to her own life, demonstrates extraordinary bravery. Her survival and continued activism after being attacked for her views in 2012 further underscore her resilience.

Global influence as a young leader: As one of the youngest and most influential activists in the world, Malala has inspired millions of young people to stand up for their rights and the rights of others. Her youth combined with her wisdom and poise make her a powerful role model.

Nobel Peace Prize laureate: Malala's receipt of the Nobel Peace Prize in 2014, when she was just 17, highlights her global impact in the fight for education and children's rights, solidifying her status as a symbol of peaceful resistance and change.

Voice for the voiceless: Malala amplifies the voices of those who cannot speak for themselves. She represents marginalized and oppressed populations, particularly girls and women in developing countries who are denied educational opportunities.

Author and storyteller: Through her book *I Am Malala* and public speaking, Malala tells not just her own story but also those of other girls like her. She uses storytelling as a powerful tool for advocacy and education.

Formation of the Malala Fund: Her establishment of the Malala Fund, an organization that advocates for girls' education globally, demonstrates her commitment to long-term, sustainable change in the world.

Symbol of peace and hope: Malala has become a worldwide symbol of peace, hope, and the fight against extremism. Her story and actions offer inspiration to those fighting for justice and equality.

Malala Yousafzai's journey is a powerful testament to the strength and resilience of the human spirit in the face of adversity. Her unwavering commitment to education and equal rights, even in the face of immense danger, serves as a beacon of hope and inspiration to people around the world. Malala's story transcends cultural and geographical boundaries, highlighting the universal importance of education and the empowerment of young women.

As a Nobel Peace Prize laureate and a global advocate for education, Malala's actions and words continue to echo across the world, reminding us that one young person, armed with courage and conviction, can indeed spark a movement that changes the world. Malala's heroism is not just in the battles she has fought but in the ongoing war she leads against ignorance and inequality – a true embodiment of the power of education and the indomitable spirit of humanity. Malala summed up her life's heroic purpose: "I don't want to be thought of as the 'girl who was shot by the Taliban' but the 'girl who fought for education.' This is the cause to which I want to devote my life."

Greta Thunberg: The Courageously Outspoken Hero

In her young life, Greta Thunberg has already journeyed through many stages of the hero's cycle, effecting change and inspiring others to join her cause, demonstrating her evolving heroic narrative. Her brand of heroism, characterized by her unwavering commitment to combating climate change, has reshaped the global narrative and inspired a wave of activism. Thunberg's journey from a solitary protester to a voice that galvanizes millions underscores the power of conviction and the impact one individual can have on the collective conscience. Her story is a testament to the fact that heroism is not just about bold feats but also about sparking change through the steadfast pursuit of a just cause.

Thunberg's blunt and powerful speeches, often delivered to world leaders and policymakers, have raised awareness about environmental issues and demanded systemic change. Her moral clarity, persistence in the face of criticism, and ability to galvanize a generation toward environmental activism embody the essence of heroism—fighting for a cause greater than oneself and effecting significant impact on a global scale.

Several aspects of Greta Thunberg's life journey align with the archetypal heroic journey:

1 **Call to adventure:** Thunberg's journey began with her solitary strike outside the Swedish Parliament, which was her response to what she saw as a call to save the environment.
2 **Trials and tribulations:** Thunberg has faced and continues to face significant opposition, ridicule, and challenges from political leaders and skeptics as she advocates for climate action. She has received intense scrutiny and harsh criticism from political leaders and the public, some of whom have dismissed her concerns and efforts due to her age and straightforward approach. She has also navigated the emotional and psychological strain that comes with being a prominent public

figure, particularly as a young activist in the complex and often disheartening arena of global climate politics. Despite these challenges, Thunberg has persisted in her activism, traveling long distances by sustainable means and speaking candidly at high-profile events, all while managing the pressures of sudden fame and the weight of her critical message.

3 **Crossing the threshold:** Thunberg's decision to take her protest global, speaking at international forums and leading worldwide strikes, marked her step into a larger arena.

4 **Allies and mentors:** She has aligned with fellow activists, scientists, and environmentalists who support and amplify her message. Her allies and mentors span a diverse spectrum, from her family, who supports her lifestyle and activism, to the scientific community, whose research underpins her message. Thunberg's efforts have attracted endorsements from influential public figures and extensive media coverage, amplifying her reach.

5 **Atonement:** Thunberg's journey involves reconciling her inner conflicts about the future of the planet with her external actions.

6 **Apotheosis:** Her speeches at the UN Climate Action Summit and other high-profile venues represent moments of realization and clarity for the global audience. At the UN Summit, she not only confronted world leaders with the stark reality of the climate crisis but also embodied the collective frustration and hope of a generation demanding urgent action. This pivotal event marked a transformation in public consciousness, elevating her from a campaigner to a global symbol of environmental advocacy and youth empowerment.

7 **Return with the elixir:** Thunberg's ongoing campaign brings back to society a new awareness of the climate crisis and a call to action, which is the "elixir" she offers to help heal the planet. She has delivered a potent message of urgency and actionable knowledge to society regarding the climate crisis. This gift to society has not only mobilized a generation for environmental action but has also shifted the global discourse on climate policy, compelling both individuals and leaders to acknowledge and address the existential threat of climate change.

Greta Thunberg can be considered a hero due to her courageous advocacy for urgent action on climate change, despite her young age and initial lack of resources or traditional influence. Starting with a solitary school strike for climate in front of the Swedish Parliament, Thunberg sparked a global movement, inspiring millions of young people and adults to participate in climate protests worldwide. Her efforts are making a difference saving our planet Earth.

Michelle Obama: The Hero of Virtue and Civility

In 2010, Paul McCartney was honored at the Executive Mansion in Washington, DC. With their two daughters, President Barack Obama and First Lady Michelle Obama sat in the front row. As a warm-up, several performers sang old Lennon–McCartney Beatles songs. Finally, it was Sir Paul himself who took the stage. Looking somewhat abashed, he said, "The next song we'd like to do is a song I've been itching to do at the White House. And I hope the President will forgive me if I sing this one." Then he started in on one of the Beatles classic hits from the *Rubber Soul* album, "Michelle." The first lady seemed entranced and oblivious to her husband, as she took it all in. It was a moving and appropriate tribute to a woman regarded as a heroic leader by many. Indeed, in our university classes in recent years when we ask students to name leaders who fit their own definition of a "good leader," both Barack and Michelle Obama are often listed.

Michelle Obama is cited as a heroic leader for many reasons, importantly her principles, for example, urging young people to eat healthier food, but also for her general warmth and humanity. Though she is clearly strong, she represents a softer, kinder politics. This approach can be seen in her relationship with former President George W Bush. At various occasions when past presidents gather, the two laugh and hug. Bush simply says that she is a fun person. She laughs at his jokes. Passing cough drops to each other at otherwise solemn occasions is affectionately comical. It enacts respect for humanity across political divisions. In this divisive time, simple civility can be a heroic model.

Michelle Robinson Obama was born in the South Side of Chicago in 1964 to working-class parents, both of whom were descended from African American slaves in South Carolina. She graduated near the top of her class from a city magnet school and followed her older brother Craig, a star basketball player, to the Ivy League at Princeton. After Princeton, she attended Harvard Law School. Several years later she supervised another Harvard Law graduate as a summer intern at her Sidley & Austin firm in Chicago. His name was Barack Obama. They attended several public events together that she insisted were not dates. But in short order the two began a love affair. They were married several years later.

Although Michelle clearly understood that her husband might go into politics, she was not herself much interested in the public scrutiny that such a life would bring. Still, she joined forces with her aspiring husband and supported him in writing his keynote speech at the Democratic Convention in 2004. That speech catapulted Mr. Obama into national politics, though at that time was merely a state legislator.

Events led to Barack Obama's election as president in 2008, and Michelle Obama took the position of first lady. She surely helped him to victory with her speech at that year's party convention, when she urged people to make sure "that you work hard for what you want in life, that your word is your bond, and you do what you say you're going to do, that you treat people with dignity and respect, even if you don't know them, and even if you don't agree with them." Although often dismissively attacked, especially from the right wing, as an "angry Black woman," she persisted with her efforts for women's rights, for children's rights, for military families, and for same-sex marriage. She typically enjoyed 60 percent approval ratings from the public. Notably Ms. Obama initiated the White House Kitchen Garden, which grew organic food for both everyday and state dinners. Her *Let's Move* initiative encouraged young people to exercise and stay healthy. Besides her good works, Michelle Obama also had a winning sense of style and appeared on many best-dressed lists.

One of her most memorable speeches was for Hillary Clinton's presidential campaign in 2016. Responding to Republican lies and personal attacks, she famously declared, "when they go low, we go high." She consistently fought for a healthy world of basic morality and kindness, and she became a hero to many.

The Dalai Lama: "My Religion Is Kindness"

Although scholars have long debated whether leaders and heroes are born or made, there is no doubt a strong belief among lay people that some great heroes are born into their roles. The story of Jesus of Nazareth is the most powerful story of "the born hero" in the western world. But what about the eastern world? We would say that the greatest born hero in the east is the Dalai Lama, the head of state of Tibet and the spiritual leader of Tibetan Buddhism. The current Dalai Lama, Tenzin Gyatso, is believed to be the latest reincarnation of a series of spiritual leaders who have chosen to be reborn so as to enlighten others. There have been 14 Dalai Lamas since the year 1391.

After the 13th Dalai Lama died in December 1933, Buddhist monks prayed for guidance to find the new Dalai Lama. They consulted oracles and meditated for signs that would lead them to him. Within a few years they received a vision that the new Dalai Lama would be found in the northeast part of Tibet, and that he would be living in a house with turquoise roof tiles near a monastery. Many monks journeyed to this region of Tibet to search for this house, ultimately discovering one that fit the description in the village of Taktser. Living in the home was two-year-old Tenzin Gyatso and his parents.

The monks presented young Tenzin with a number of objects that were owned by the previous Dalai Lama, and these objects were mixed with other imitation objects. When Tenzin correctly identified the items belonging to the 13th Dalai Lama, the monks knew they had found the reincarnation of their leader. The boy and his family traveled to the city of Lhasa, where he was taken to the Drepung Monastery to study the Buddhist sutras in preparation for his role as the spiritual leader of Tibet.

The Dalai Lama's central purpose is to help people achieve enlightenment through Buddhist spiritual practices. Buddhism provides insight into the true nature of life, and Buddhists use meditation and other practices to develop the qualities of awareness, kindness, and wisdom. The Dalai Lama's job is made somewhat difficult by the fact that neighboring China has never recognized Tibet as an independent political country. When China annexed Tibet in 1959, the Dalai Lama and thousands of his supporters fled into exile. He has lived in Dharamsala, India, since 1960 and heads the Tibetan government from afar.

One of the most respected spiritual leaders in the world, the Dalai Lama embraces religious diversity. "I always believe that it is much better to have a variety of religions, a variety of philosophies, rather than one single religion or philosophy," he said "This is necessary because of the different mental dispositions of each human being. Each religion has certain unique ideas or techniques, and learning about them can only enrich one's own faith." The Dalai Lama also embraces the union of science and spirituality. Recently, he collaborated with MIT to study what role Buddhist meditation plays in human emotion and cognition. He said, "If science proves facts that conflict with Buddhist understanding, Buddhism must change accordingly. We should always adopt a view that accords with the facts."

Born heroes such as the Dalai Lama and Jesus are not revered because of their special lineage or conception. They are revered because they combine their inborn gifts with a lifetime of practicing good deeds and helping others do the same. The Dalai Lama's message is quite simply one of love. "If you want others to be happy, practice compassion. If you want to be happy, practice compassion," he said. "My religion is very simple. My religion is kindness."

Pat Tillman: The Consummate War Hero

Each Memorial Day and Veterans Day in the United States, people are encouraged to pause and remember the roughly 1.4 million Americans who have died while serving their country since 1776. Think about that number: 1.4 million. That's more people than the population of major cities around the world. It's a staggering level of human sacrifice.

While every casualty is deserving of our reverence, the loss of Corporal Patrick Daniel Tillman, a US Army Ranger, is especially noteworthy. Pat Tillman didn't start out with dreams of serving in the US military. Playing football was his passion. He was a star defensive safety for Arizona State University from 1994 to 1997, and during his time at ASU he earned a grade point average of 3.84. Believed to be too small to compete in the NFL, Tillman nevertheless made it to the Arizona Cardinals and began making headlines for his ferocious style of play. He made *Sports Illustrated*'s 2000 NFL All-Pro team. He married his high school sweetheart Marie. His future was bright indeed.

Then the September 11, 2001, attacks happened, and they forever altered Tillman's priorities. Shortly after the attacks, Tillman said, "We are such a free society, and you don't realize how great a life we have over here. In times like this you stop and think about just how good we have it and what kind of a system we live under, what freedoms we're allowed. And that wasn't built overnight."

Once the 2001 NFL season concluded, Tillman turned down a multimillion-dollar contract offer from the Arizona Cardinals. Instead of playing football, he decided to enlist in the US Army. He simply could not forget the sacrifice that others before him had made, nor could he ignore his own calling to serve. "My great grandfather was at Pearl Harbor and a lot of my family has fought in wars," he said. "I really haven't done a damn thing as far as laying myself on the line like that. So I have a great deal of respect for those who have, and for what the flag stands for."

Tillman served his country with distinction until a tragic day in April 2004, when he was killed in Afghanistan, 25 miles from the Pakistan border. At first, the US military reported that Tillman had been killed by hostile forces. He received the Silver Star, the Purple Heart, and other accolades. Every effort was made to create a powerful story of a hero gunned down by the enemy. But within weeks of his death, the true story of what happened to Pat Tillman was leaked to the press. It turns out that he had been inadvertently killed by friendly fire from his own allied forces. To this day many details about Tillman's death are not clearly understood, perhaps because of the military's desire to protect its image.

Human beings go to great lengths to remember their heroes. After his death, Pat Tillman's family established the Pat Tillman Foundation to promote Tillman's legacy of changing the world for the better. A major bridge spanning the Colorado River bears Tillman's name. A law school in San Jose established the Pat Tillman Scholarship. The Cardinals and Sun Devils retired the number he wore with those teams. The Cardinals have named the plaza surrounding their stadium the Pat Tillman Freedom Plaza. In 2006, a bronze statue was erected in his honor. Tillman's high school renamed its football field after him. The first United Service Organization (USO) center in Afghanistan was named after him.

We tell the story of Pat Tillman not to rebuke the military's questionable conduct surrounding his death but to underscore the rare nobility of character that motivated Tillman's life choices. Millions of dollars and a life of luxury were less important to him than finding Osama Bin Laden and other terrorists who brought down the World Trade Center on September 11. He was willing to die fighting for a just cause. His life, and his death, are well worth pausing to remember.

Irena Sendler: The Hero Who Stood Up to Evil

As we note in several of our hero profiles, the worst of human nature often brings out the best in human nature. The atrocities committed by the Nazis during World War II created fertile ground for heroes to emerge. Among the heroes of that terrible war were Anne Frank, George Wahlen, Israel Spira, George Marshall, Corrie ten Boom, and Winston Churchill. To this list we add the name of a Polish woman who refused to allow innocent children to die in the Warsaw Jewish Ghetto in 1942. Her name was Irena Sendler.

Our first heroes book describes many of the details of Sendler's heroism (Allison & Goethals, 2011). Here are the highlights: Using many creative means, and at great risk to her own well-being, Sendler was able to sneak 2,500 children out of the heavily guarded Warsaw Ghetto, where Jews were housed in terrible conditions before being sent to their deaths in Nazi concentration camps. Sendler was eventually caught by the Nazis, subjected to terrible torture, and sentenced to death. Miraculously, she escaped death, and after the war she attempted to reunite the children she saved with their families.

Sendler's heroic story remained largely unknown to the public until 1999, when an inspired group of high school students in Kansas learned of her heroism and later wrote a school play in her honor. The play was called *Life in a Jar*, a reference to the jar in which Sendler secretly kept the names of the thousands of children whom she saved. This play has since been performed hundreds of times all around the globe. The students and their teacher deserve great credit for bringing Sendler's amazing tale into the world's consciousness. The students were Elizabeth Cambers, Megan Stewart, Jessica Shelton, and Sabrina Coons; their teacher was Norm Conard.

Irena Sendler displayed the willingness and courage to take action rather than stand passively by while atrocities were committed against other human beings. As Edmund Burke is reputed to have said, "All that is necessary for the triumph of evil is for good men to do nothing." Most non-Jewish Polish citizens in 1942 meekly accepted the Nazis' brutality. Heroes such as Sendler do not cower from evil; they confront it, even at great peril to their own well-being.

The New York subway hero, Wesley Autrey, once said, "I did what anyone could do, and what anyone ought to do." Irena Sendler showed the same humility. She wrote, "Heroes do extraordinary things. What I did was not an extraordinary thing. It was normal." Autrey and Sendler are typical of many heroes who don't believe that their actions are exceptional, but many psychological studies point to the rareness with which average people show a willingness to risk life and limb for others. Most situations that beg for heroes feature strong social pressures that inhibit the heroic response. Heroes are somehow able to overcome these pressures and do the right thing, however difficult and dangerous it may be.

Throughout her life, Irena Sendler never claimed any credit for her actions. "I could have done more," she said. "This regret will follow me to my death." Sendler lived long enough to personally meet those four extraordinary Kansas students who told her story to the world. She passed away in 2008 at the age of 98.

George Bailey: A Hero's Wonderful Life

Sometimes great movies and great movie heroes aren't perceived as great right away. Years may go by before audiences begin to appreciate the artistic and heroic significance of the movie and its characters. A stirring example is the 1946 film *It's a Wonderful Life*, starring James Stewart and directed by Frank Capra. The lead character, George Bailey, emerges as one of the most saintly and selfless characters in movie history. As a child he saves his brother's life and stops the local pharmacist from accidentally poisoning a customer. As a young adult, he sacrifices his own life plans to save the town of Bedford Falls from falling into the hands of Mr. Potter, a greedy slumlord who is as evil as Bailey is good.

But it isn't George Bailey's heroic battle with Mr. Potter that makes him such an unforgettable hero. What moves us most about Bailey's character is the fallout from a mistake made by Bailey's uncle, who misplaces a sizeable amount of cash that Bailey owes the bank. The cash inadvertently falls into the hands of Mr. Potter, who issues a warrant for Bailey's arrest rather than return the cash.

The prospect of prison time prompts Bailey to consider suicide, but a guardian angel appears and shows Bailey what the world would be like had Bailey not existed. Bailey is stunned to learn that without him the world is a dark, grim place with thousands of lives lost or ruined. In this alternative timeline, Bailey is devastated to discover that his many friends are either dead or unrecognizably scarred, and that even his family does not exist.

The guardian angel then returns the distraught Bailey to the original timeline. Recognizing that he's had a wonderful life, Bailey rushes home a happy man despite being informed by authorities that he is under arrest for misappropriating funds. The prospect of imprisonment means far less to him that seeing his family again. At this moment, dozens of Bailey's friends and neighbors arrive to help him. Hearing that he is in financial trouble, they happily give him money of their own while joyously recounting the many times Bailey has saved them. The amount of cash given Bailey is many times the amount he owes, and so the warrant for his arrest is dismissed. In an ironic reversal of the usual hero storyline, the hero Bailey has been saved by the town's citizens.

Why does this final scene in the film pack such emotional punch? One reason is that it very powerfully portrays a community's spontaneous and selfless celebration of Bailey's heroism. In a collective act of supreme goodwill, Bailey's unsung and lifelong devotion to helping others is finally recognized and rewarded. The movie reminds us that although we need heroes, there are times when heroes need us, and that average people can – and do – perform great heroic acts of collective gratitude to deserving Samaritans among us.

Director and producer Frank Capra lived long enough to witness the burgeoning popularity of *It's a Wonderful Life* beginning in the 1970s. "It's the damnedest thing I've ever seen," Capra said in 1984. "The film has a life of its own now and I can look at it like I had nothing to do with it. I'm like a parent whose kid grows up to be president. I'm proud, but it's the kid who did the work."

Confucius: The Master Hero of Virtue

There are some heroes whose wisdom is so timeless and profound that they are able to shape the moral philosophy of an entire society for millennia. Confucius was such a hero. Born in 551 BCE in the province of Shantung in northeast China, Confucius lived in an era when China was being carved into feudal states by warlords who engaged in vicious battles, oppressed slave laborers, and heavily taxed citizens. Despite this domestic turmoil, or perhaps because of it, Confucius fashioned a philosophy of virtuous living that is embraced today by hundreds of millions of people throughout the world, especially in China, Japan, Korea, and Vietnam.

Most Confucian wisdom is contained in the *Analects of Confucius*, which was compiled by his students after his death. In the *Analects*, Confucius modestly presents himself as a "transmitter who invented nothing." He places strong emphasis on the importance of *study*; in fact, the Chinese character for *study* opens the text. For this reason, Chinese people view Confucius as the greatest of all masters. In Confucianism, people are teachable, improvable, and capable of great morality. Throughout the *Analects*, Confucius preaches honesty, hard work, and learning by example. He communicates his wisdom through conversation, by asking questions, and imploring students to find their own answers.

Confucianism also encourages the development of a humble attitude. One of his better-known aphorisms is "Real knowledge is to know the extent of one's ignorance" -- a sentiment that would be expressed by another philosopher, Socrates, more than a century later in ancient Greece. Foremost, in the *Analects* it is clear that Confucius prepares his students for public service, to develop compassion, and to respect others. His philosophy emphasizes justice, sincerity, and morality in one's personal life and in government. In the chaotic political environment of his times, he looks with a nostalgic eye to earlier times in Chinese history, when leaders treated citizens with wisdom and compassion.

Confucianism exhorts all people to strive for the ideal of the "perfect person." An apt description of perfection is combining "the qualities of saint, scholar, and gentleman." Perfect people display morality, piety, and loyalty. They cultivate humanity, or benevolence. They champion strong familial loyalty, ancestor worship, and respect of elders by their children. According to Confucius, strong family values and relationships are the key to a stable society. Mutual respect and devotion to family are central to his teachings.

Although Confucianism is often followed in a religious manner by the Chinese, it is not necessarily clear whether his teachings represent a religion per se. There are certainly a number of aphorisms that bear a resemblance to religious tenets. For example, he expressed one of the earliest versions of the Golden Rule when he wrote, "Do not do to others what you do not want done to yourself." The position adopted by most people is that Confucianism is more of a moral science or philosophy than it is a religion.

There truly is no western counterpart to Confucius. His contributions to philosophy, morality, and education have been profound and enduring. For more than 2,500 years he has remained an integral part of the Chinese cultural identity. In the People's Republic of China, Confucius is honored on October 1, the anniversary of his death. In Taiwan, he is honored on his birthday, September 28. A legal holiday in Taiwan, September 28 is referred to as Teacher's Day, honoring the greatest teacher in Chinese history.

Mother Teresa and the Call to Love

Our research has identified the "Great Eight" traits of heroes – *smart, strong, selfless, caring, charismatic, resilient, reliable,* and *inspiring* (Allison & Goethals, 2011). Which of these eight attributes is most central to heroism?

Recently we asked a group of our students to rank the Great Eight list of traits in their order of importance. The results showed that one trait emerged as the most important: *selflessness*. Heroes, it seems, are characterized by their service to others, consistently placing the welfare of other people ahead of their own well-being.

Perhaps no other individual is more strongly associated with the trait of selflessness than Mother Teresa. As a young woman, Mother Teresa felt the call to serve God. At the age of 18, she left her home in Macedonia and joined the Sisters of Loreto, a community of nuns with missions in India. In 1931, she took her vows as a nun and joined a convent in Calcutta. At that time she experienced what she later described as "the call within the call": "I was to leave the convent and help the poor while living among them," she said. "It was an order. To fail would have been to break the faith."

Mother Teresa obtained permission to leave the convent and work among the poorest of the poor in the slums of Calcutta. Her first year in the slums was painful and challenging. She had no source of income and had to beg for food and supplies. Troubled by doubt and fear, Mother Teresa was strongly tempted to return to the comfort of convent life.

But she persevered, and slowly she began to inspire a group of followers and supporters. In 1950, she founded the Missionaries of Charity to care for – in her own words – "the hungry, the naked, the homeless, the crippled, the blind, the lepers, all those people who feel unwanted, unloved, uncared for throughout society, people that have become a burden to the society and are shunned by everyone." Missionaries of Charity began with 13 members and today has 5,000 nuns running orphanages, AIDS hospices, and charity centers that care for refugees, the blind, disabled, aged, alcoholics, the poor and homeless, and victims of floods, epidemics, and famine.

During her lifetime, Mother Teresa became an international symbol of love and service to others. She appeared 18 times in Gallup's annual poll of the most admired men and women in the world, finishing first several times in the 1980s and 1990s. A Gallup poll of Americans in 1999 ranked her first among the Most Widely Admired People of the 20th Century. Much of Mother Teresa's appeal stems from her love for all people regardless of religion or ethnicity. "It is important that everyone is seen as equal before God," she observed. "I've always said we should help a Hindu become a better Hindu, a Muslim become a better Muslim, a Catholic become a better Catholic."

Although Mother Teresa championed the cause of helping the poor in India, she was deeply concerned with the emotional and spiritual well-being of people residing in the more affluent western world. "I found the poverty of the West so much more difficult to remove," she said. "The poverty in the West is a different kind of poverty – it is not only a poverty of loneliness but also of spirituality. There's a hunger for love, as there is a hunger for God. The hunger for love is much more difficult to remove than the hunger for bread."

Before her death in 1997, Mother Teresa was widely known as a "living saint." Since her death, she has progressed rapidly toward attaining actual sainthood, an honor the church will bestow upon her in a few short years. The overarching theme of her life was simply loving others. "Not all of us can do great things," she said. "But we can do small things with great love. Love is a fruit in season at all times, and within reach of every hand."

Lois Wilson: The Hero Who Helped Families of Alcoholics

Heroes of great causes don't necessarily start out as exceptional people. In fact, it's not unusual for heroes to be everyday people who experience a life-changing calamity that transforms them into champions of a social movement. Examples include John Walsh, who established the TV program *America's Most Wanted* after his five-year-old son was murdered, and Candice Lightner, who founded Mothers Against Drunk Driving after her 13-year-old daughter was killed by a hit-and-run driver. To this list we add Lois Wilson, who created the Al-Anon Family Groups after experiencing many years of emotional heartache and financial ruin while living with her alcoholic husband, Bill. Lois was among the first to recognize that alcoholism is a family disease that has adverse emotional effects on every member of the alcoholic's family.

The story of Lois and Bill is quite poignant. After marrying Bill in 1918, Lois witnessed him and their marriage spiral downhill due to the ravages of the disease of alcoholism. During the 1920s and 30s, Bill's drinking problem destroyed his career, his relationships, and his health. Lois tried, but there was nothing she could do to stop him from drinking. Desperate for children, they were turned down by adoption agencies when they discovered Bill's problem. They lost their home. Bill checked in and out of alcoholic sanitariums as he neared the point of either insanity or death.

Miraculously, in 1934 Bill had a spiritual awakening, stopped drinking, and co-founded Alcoholics Anonymous. While her husband attended AA meetings, Lois would socialize with family members of other alcoholics and became aware of the devastating effects of the disease on spouses and children. In 1951, she established the Al-Anon Family Groups, a program of recovery for families and friends of alcoholics. Today there are over 25,000 Al-Anon groups worldwide, with a membership close to 400,000.

What are the core tenets of Al-Anon? First, it is promoting the idea that no one but the alcoholic can stop the drinking. In Al-Anon, family members beaten down by the disease learn that they can be as sick as the alcoholic, even if they don't drink. Al-Anon members focus on two main goals:

Enriching their own moral and spiritual lives, and not contributing further to the alcoholic's disease. During the early years of Al-Anon, Lois spoke to many groups, sharing her wisdom and inspiring tens of thousands of people. She was instrumental in helping develop Al-Anon books, pamphlets, manuals, and guidelines. The program grew and became a healthy, widely respected organization.

As with many heroes, Lois had parents who taught her generosity and service to others. She always gave Bill unconditional love, even during the worst moments of their marriage. Lois exuded a positive attitude, which has its imprint all over Al-Anon's principles of recovery. "The world seems to me excruciatingly, almost painfully beautiful at times," she said, adding that "the goodness and kindness of people often exceed that which even I expect."

In conclusion, Lois Wilson's heroism lies in her compassionate response to the silent suffering of families affected by alcoholism. By founding Al-Anon, she provided a lifeline of support and understanding, transforming personal adversity into a movement that has helped millions worldwide. Her dedication to creating a safe space for sharing and healing has not only empowered countless individuals but also underscored the profound impact of community and empathy in overcoming life's challenges. Lois Wilson's legacy continues to inspire and offer hope to those facing the struggles of addiction within their families.

Nathan Hale and the Powerful Heroic Script

Heroes are often known through a particular image or association. When we hear their names, something specific springs to mind. While most school children know almost nothing about early American hero Nathan Hale, they are most likely to know what he supposedly said when he was hung for spying: "I only regret that I have but one life to lose for my country." But this quote actually sheds light on a deeper aspect of the way people think about heroes and heroism.

Nathan Hale was a young Revolutionary War soldier from Connecticut. A Yale graduate and a teacher, in 1776 he undertook a dangerous assignment during the battle for New York. He would go undercover and pretend to be a loyalist to the British crown. His mission was to collect information about General William Howe's deployment of British and Hessian troops in and around the city. Before long, Hale was recognized and captured. There was no doubt that he was guilty of spying. Hanging was a certainty. But Hale was offered the chance to speak before his sentence of death was carried out. He gave what many witnesses said was an eloquent speech, with the most memorable passage expressing his regret at not being able to give more than one life.

What is most interesting about that statement is that it was almost surely based on lines from fiction that Hale, like most educated citizens of the time, knew well. They come from a climactic scene in Joseph Addison's famous 1712 play *Cato*, where the hero, facing death like Hale, proclaims, "How beautiful is death, when earn'd by virtue? Who would not be that youth? What pity is it that we can die but once to serve our country."

What is the significance of Hale basing his own last words on those of a fictional hero? Fictional heroes are molded to reflect popular conceptions, or images, of courageous and altruistic behavior. But they not only reflect those popular conceptions, they also shape them. The playwright wants to do more than create characters and scenes that are familiar to the public. More important is putting an original stamp or interpretation on ideals such as heroism. In *Cato*, Addison certainly did that. He created a powerful script for heroic young men facing death.

Nathan Hale wanted to leave behind an eloquent and moving statement, both to claim honor for himself and to provide inspiration for others. The war would be long and difficult, and fashioning a heroic model might contribute as much or more than detailing the movements of enemy combatants. Surely the example of a brave young soldier willingly dying for the cause would provide a needed morale boost to General Washington's weary army. Hale crafted carefully a powerful expression of his unwavering commitment to the cause. Joseph Addison's words helped him create one that Americans remember many, many years later.

In conclusion, Nathan Hale's heroism is immortalized by his unwavering commitment to the cause of American independence and his profound courage in the face of death. His famous last words, "I only regret that I have but one life to lose for my country," epitomize the selflessness and patriotism that define true heroism. Hale's sacrifice serves as an enduring inspiration, reminding us of the profound impact that individual bravery and dedication can have in shaping the course of history. His legacy continues to be a testament to the spirit of American resilience and freedom.

Dana Reeve: The Unsung Selfless Hero

It is not unusual for heroes to emerge from crisis and suffering. At these times, the hero truly separates themself from others by rising to the occasion, displaying uncommon selflessness, courage, and grace. In 1995, when her husband Christopher Reeve was paralyzed from the neck down after a horse-riding accident, Dana Reeve seized the heroic moment and became one of the most selfless and inspiring individuals that we've heard about in many years.

Prior to the accident, Dana and Christopher Reeve led a charmed life. They were talented, attractive, successful, and happy. He was an accomplished actor known especially for his film role as Superman during the 1970s and 1980s. Dana herself was a successful actress and singer. She graduated cum laude from Middlebury College in 1984, met Christopher in 1987, and married him in 1992. They soon had a son. Life was good.

Then came the horrific accident that shattered Christopher's uppermost vertebrae. At first, things looked bleak and hopeless. But Dana was the source of support and love that fueled his determination to survive and live a life that would become an inspiration to millions. A pivotal moment came just days after the accident. After assessing his dire situation, Christopher considered suicide. He mouthed the words to Dana, "maybe we should let me go." In tears, she replied, "I am only going to say this once: I will support whatever you want to do, because this is your life, and your decision. But I want you to know that I'll be with you for the long haul, no matter what. You're still you. And I love you." Hearing these words, he never considered ending his life again.

Christopher insisted that Dana resume her singing and acting career. She remained busy but rarely left Christopher's side. She bristled at the media label of her as "Saint Dana" and "Superwoman": "I felt very uncomfortable with that. There was nothing superhuman about standing by Chris. That compliment always felt a little false. What's so saintly about that? Lucky me. I'm with him! Really, my job here is to be the voice for the many, many spouses who are caregivers, who don't have the advantage of the world patting them on the back every day."

When Christopher died in 2004, Dana felt compelled to continue her efforts to seek better treatments for paralysis. For her, there was no choice. "I have to carry on his mission," she said. She was unanimously elected as head of the Christopher Reeve Foundation, which eventually changed its name to the Christopher and Dana Reeve Foundation.

Sadly, within a year of Christopher's death, Dana was diagnosed with lung cancer. "Now, more than ever, I feel Chris with me as I face this challenge," she announced. "As always, I look to him as the ultimate example of defying the odds with strength, courage, and hope in the face of life's adversities." Dana underwent aggressive treatments but lost her battle with cancer on March 6, 2006. Her good friend, actor Robin Williams, best summed up the loss: "The brightest light has gone out."

We can learn several things from the Dana Reeve story. First is that tragic circumstances often beget heroes who seize the heroic moment. The worst of times can bring out the best in people. A second lesson is that heroes need social support. The heroic journey of Christopher Reeve might not have happened at all without the continuous loving support of Dana. Throughout Christopher's recovery, she remained a beacon of hope. "We have become accustomed to living our life with joy amidst pain and challenges," she said, while telling Christopher that "I still you love you; I will continue to love you. We will get through this together, and I promise to keep you challenged and not to pity you."

Groundhog Day's Phil Connors and the Heroic Theme of Redemption

One of the most compelling actions that a hero can perform is an act of redemption. A redeeming act is any behavior that corrects a previous misstep or wrongdoing. Redemptive acts are common occurrences in athletic competitions, as when a football placekicker boots the winning field goal after botching a kick the previous week. Especially powerful instances of redemption are great acts of morality that follow prior moral transgressions. This type of moral redemption is portrayed in a most poignant way in *Groundhog Day*, a movie released in 1993 starring Bill Murray and produced by Harold Ramis.

In *Groundhog Day*, the lead character Phil Connors is a television weatherman who is arrogant, nasty, and utterly self-absorbed. Connors spends February 2 covering the Groundhog Day festivities in Punxsutawney, Pennsylvania, a place he despises. But when he wakes up the following morning, he discovers that it is February 2 in Punxsutawney all over again. To his horror, this day continues to repeat itself, and Connors is trapped in Punxsutawney in a seemingly endless time loop.

At first, Connors uses the repetition of the day to steal money and to manipulate women to sleep with him. Yet the one woman he grows to love, his producer Rita, won't succumb to his advances. Connors grows depressed when he realizes that his methods will never allow him to achieve real intimacy with Rita. He becomes suicidal, believing he is stuck, alone forever, in a dull town on an endlessly cold winter day.

Connors' road to redemption begins when he honestly confides to Rita what is happening to him. She shows him great empathy, suggests that his plight may actually be a gift, and for the first time spends the entire day with him. When Connors awakes to repeat yet another February 2, he is a new man. He takes piano and ice-sculpting lessons. He helps a poor homeless man. He saves a boy from a bad fall, performs the Heimlich maneuver on a choking victim, and fixes an old woman's flat tire.

Rita witnesses the change in Connors and falls in love with him. The arrogance and selfishness that once characterized him have been replaced by kindness, enlightenment, and a drive to make the best out of one's circumstances. At the end of the day, they fall asleep, in love and in his bed. And when Connors awakes, she is still there, it is finally February 3, and the cycle has been broken. Connors' long redemptive journey has been completed.

Over the years, *Groundhog Day* has received high acclaim from both critics and audiences. The movie has found its way onto Roger Ebert's Great Movies series. In 2009, the American literary theorist and legal scholar Stanley Fish named the film one of America's all-time greatest movies. In 2006, the film was added to the United States National Film Registry for being "culturally, historically, and aesthetically significant."

Groundhog Day's story of redemption moves many people deeply, a reaction that caught director and producer Harold Ramis by surprise. "This movie spoke to people on a lot of levels," said Ramis. "The spiritual community responded to this film in an unprecedented way. Hasidic Jews held up signs outside of theaters asking, 'Are you living the same day over and over again?' Then I started getting letters from the Zen Buddhist community, the Yoga community, the Christian fundamentalist community, the psychoanalytic community, and everyone claiming that this was their philosophy and that I must be one of them for having made this movie."

The story of a hero's redemptive journey has universal appeal and touches something powerful inside the human psyche. To legions of people, there is great spiritual significance in Bill Murray's unforgettable portrayal of the hero Phil Connors. *Groundhog Day* suggests that all of us, whatever our flaws or circumstances, can redeem ourselves.

Rabbi Israel Spira: A Hero of the Holocaust

Sometimes unimaginably terrible circumstances produce the most inspirational stories of human heroism. The Nazi concentration camps of World War II housed Jews, gypsies, gays, the disabled, and other groups deemed "undesirable" by the Nazis. Conditions at the camps were nightmarish. Prisoners were subjected to starvation diets, forced into slave labor, and routinely beaten. Millions died in the gas chambers or from firing squads, starvation, overcrowding, disease, or exposure to cold.

In 1982, Yaffa Eliach authored an important book called *Hasidic Tales of the Holocaust*, in which Jewish survivors of the concentration camps told their harrowing stories of survival. One of the most moving tales was that of Israel Spira, a rabbi who suffered horribly in the camps yet survived to become one of the great spiritual leaders of the Jewish community in Brooklyn, New York, after the war. His wife and children were not so fortunate; all of them were murdered by the Nazis.

Spira recalled one particular incident that took place during his imprisonment in the Janowska concentration camp in Poland. On a cold winter night, a German voice over the loudspeaker barked out the following order: "You are all to evacuate the barracks immediately and report to the vacant lot. Anyone remaining inside will be shot on the spot!" Exhausted and emaciated, the prisoners stumbled to the vacant field and saw before them a large open pit. The voice commanded, "Each of you dogs who values his miserable life must jump over the pit and land on the other side. Those who miss will get what they rightfully deserve – ra-ta-ta-ta-ta." The voice imitated the sound of a machine gun.

According to Spira, jumping over the pit would have been nearly impossible even under the best of circumstances. The prisoners were "skeletons," feverish from disease and physically exhausted from their daily labors. Spira himself suffered from bruised and swollen feet. Awaiting their turn to jump, he and a close friend watched prisoners die in a hail of bullets with each unsuccessful attempt. The bodies began to pile up in the pit. Spira's friend recommended that they not bother trying and simply accept death, but Spira encouraged him to jump.

They leapt into the darkness and found themselves alive on the other side of the pit. Incredulous at their success, Spira's friend asked him how he did it. "I was holding on to my ancestral merit," said Spira. "I was holding on to the coattails of my father, and my grandfather and my great-grandfather, of blessed memory."

Spira then asked his friend how he reached the other side of the pit. "I was holding on to you," he said.

Spira miraculously survived several years in the camps. During that time, he buoyed the spirits of his fellow Jews by secretly performing important Jewish rituals and ceremonies, such as lighting the menorah, saying blessings, and obtaining matzah. To acquire materials for these observances, Spira would establish a rapport with the camp commandant or guards. When asked why he bothered to recite the Hanukah blessing amid such suffering and death, Spira noted that he saw "faith" and "devotion" in the faces of the prisoners all around him. "If, indeed, I was blessed to see such a people with faith and fervor, then I am under special obligation to recite the blessing," he said.

Heroes help people even under the most grim of circumstances. Spira witnessed the horrors of the Holocaust unfolding right before him, but it didn't deter him from doing everything he could to lift the spirits and faith of those around him. Six million people perished in the camps, but Spira lived to become a highly revered religious figure for many years before passing away peacefully in 1989. He once said, "There are events of such overbearing magnitude that one ought not to remember them all the time, but one must not forget them either. Such an event is the Holocaust."

Rosa Parks's Transforming Act of Civil Disobedience

Heroism can take a lot of time to achieve, or it can happen in a split second. In this book we profile many heroes who devote their entire lives to doing heroic deeds, accumulating an impressive body of work over many decades. Examples of this type of heroism achieved across the lifespan include Mahatma Gandhi, Nelson Mandela, and Martin Luther King, Jr. But we also give ample coverage to heroes who perform a single bold action that instantly catapults them to heroic status. New York subway hero Wesley Autrey is a vivid example of this type of instantaneous heroism.

Perhaps once in a generation we are witness to a rare and extraordinary individual who assumes the characteristics of both kinds of heroes. Rosa Parks was one such person. Her single act of civil disobedience on December 1, 1955, forever transformed the American racial and political landscape. And her lifelong commitment to promoting racial equality paved the way for sweeping changes in American culture and helped bring about the Civil Rights Act of 1964.

Before 1964, Jim Crow laws enacted during the post–Civil War Reconstruction required racial separation in buses, restaurants, and public transportation. Those laws also legally sanctioned racial discrimination that prevented Black people from pursuing many careers and from residing in certain neighborhoods. Rosa Parks lived and worked under such conditions. One rainy day in 1943, a bus driver demanded that she give up her seat for a white passenger. While changing seats she dropped her purse, and to retrieve her spilled belongings she had to take a moment to use a seat reserved for white riders. The bus driver became enraged and barely let her step off the bus before speeding off.

Years of this kind of subjugation eventually took their toll on Parks. On December 1, 1955, after working a long day, she headed to the bus to make her way home. On this day she once again complied with the rules, which required Black passengers to enter the front of the bus to pay the fare, then exit and reenter the back of the bus where Black people were required to sit. When the bus became full, Parks was asked by the driver to give up her seat for a white passenger. This time she refused. Later she recalled that although she was tired from working a long day, more importantly she was "tired of giving in."

Police arrested her, and four days later Parks was convicted of disorderly conduct. A 26-year-old Baptist minister, the Rev. Martin Luther King, Jr, heard of her arrest and organized a boycott of Montgomery buses. Tens of thousands of Black people were galvanized by Parks's simple act of defiance. She had single-handedly triggered an unstoppable flood of protest and legislative work geared toward bringing about long overdue social change. A year after Parks's arrest, the Supreme Court ruled that Alabama's laws requiring segregation on buses were illegal, and eight years later the landmark 1964 Civil Rights Act was signed into law by President Lyndon B. Johnson.

Some heroes are ordinary human beings who perform a single heroic act in response to a situation that requires immediate action. These heroes are everyday people who encounter a *heroic moment*, and they rise to the occasion by doing the right thing in that moment. Rosa Parks is remembered as a quiet woman whose simple act on a bus helped spark what was arguably the greatest social movement in American history.

Parks was voted by *Time* magazine as one of the 100 most influential people of the 20th century. Long after that fateful day on the bus, Parks remained a quiet crusader for equal rights for all human beings. "I would like to be known as a person who is concerned about freedom and equality and justice and prosperity for all people," she said.

Corrie ten Boom: The Holocaust Hero with a Hiding Place

People are moved by powerful tales of heroism in defiance of Nazi Germany's eradication of Jews during World War II. For this reason, we have written about the life of Israel Spira, and now we focus on another remarkable story of selflessness and courage during this tragic period of human history. The hero to which we now turn is Corrie ten Boom of the Netherlands.

ten Boom was one of the leaders of the Dutch resistance during the Nazi occupation of the Netherlands. It is estimated that Corrie ten Boom helped 800 Jews avoid being shipped to Nazi concentration camps during the war. ten Boom's father, Casper ten Boom, played a critical role in shaping her values and worldview. The ten Booms were devout Christians who lent a helping hand to people of all faiths. When Casper was asked if he knew he could die if he were caught helping Jews, he replied, "It would be an honor to give my life for God's chosen people."

To hide Jews in their home, the ten Booms built a secret room in Corrie's bedroom, located on the top floor of the building. The hidden room was behind a false wall that the ten Booms secretly constructed. The room was tiny, about the size of a medium-sized closet. To enter the room, people had to crawl on their hands and knees through a small panel in a lower cupboard. An electronic buzzer was installed to give the home's residents warning of a raid. When the Nazis raided the ten Boom house in 1944, six people used the hidden room to avoid detection.

Eventually, though, an informant reported the ten Booms' activities to the authorities, and the entire ten Boom family was shipped to concentration camps. Corrie and her sister Betsie were sent to the Vught concentration camp and later to the notorious Ravensbruck camp in Germany. It was here that Betsie died on December 16, 1944. Before she died, Betsie reassured Corrie that God and love would triumph over the evil that surrounded them. "There is no pit so deep that God's love is not deeper still," Betsie told her.

To her surprise, Corrie was released from Ravensbruck on New Year's Eve, December 1944. She later learned that her discharge was due to a clerical error. She also learned that one week after her release all the women her age were sent to the gas chamber. After the war, in 1947, Corrie was approached one day by one of the cruelest former Ravensbruck camp guards. "Will you forgive me?" he asked and held out his hand. Ten Boom recalled the moment: "I stood there and could not. Betsie had died in that place. Could he erase her slow terrible death simply for the asking? It could not have been many seconds that he stood there, hand held out, but to me it seemed hours as I wrestled with the most difficult thing I had ever had to do. We then grasped each other's hands, the former guard and the former prisoner. I had never known God's love so intensely as I did then."

Heroes rarely choose the easy path in life. It would have been easy, and safe, for Corrie ten Boom and her family to turn away Jews who asked for sanctuary from Nazi oppression. But the ten Booms recognized that they would be accomplices to evil if they had condoned Hitler's genocidal Final Solution at work in their community. The ten Booms put their lives in danger, and some of them did ultimately lose their lives, trying to protect the innocent. There are no better heroes among us.

9 Traditional-Competent Heroes

Jacinda Ardern: Hero of Compassionate Crisis Management

Sometimes the shelf-life of one's hero status is remarkably brief. In 2019 and 2020, New Zealand Prime Minister Jacinda Ardern was widely recognized as a hero both for her response to the terrorist killings at Christchurch in early 2019 and for her actions during the Covid crisis the next year. She was praised often both internationally and within her own country. Yet she quickly lost political support in the next few years and resigned as leader of her Labour Party in early 2023. It seems that great but unrealistic expectations were set by her fast rise to political prominence, her charisma, and her heroic handling of two very different but equally challenging crises.

Jacinda Ardern, prime minister of New Zealand (2017–2023)

Source: Newzild

DOI: 10.4324/9781003328681-9

In 1980 Ardern was born into a family of modest means but one that had political connections and aspirations. Her aunt Marie Ardern was a Labour Party member. She asked Jacinda to help her campaign while she was still a teenager. During her college years, she also studied for a semester in the United States at Arizona State University. At age 21 she was hired as a researcher for Prime Minister Helen Clark.

Her years in government started in 2008 when she was elected a member of parliament, or MP. By 2017 she had become head of her Labour Party. Certainly her charisma helped. She was regarded as a celebrity by many, and the press referred to the "Jacinda effect" or "Jacindamania" as she generated markedly increased support for Labour. An election was held in her first year as leader, and Labour won enough votes to form a governing coalition with the Green and New Zealand First parties. Ardern became prime minister in October 2017. She promised that her party would be "focused, energetic and strong." Her politics were reliably progressive. She was opposed to US President Donald Trump and generally advocated policies designed to reduce poverty and support women and families, such as supporting minimum wage legislation and parental leave. One critic referred to her as a "pretty communist."

On the personal level things, changed quickly for Ardern. A few months into her terms as prime minister she announced that she was pregnant, and that she and her partner Clarke Gayford would become parents the next summer. She appointed an acting prime minister during her six-week maternity leave in the summer of 2018. But she continued to do her job with energy and effectiveness.

Ardern's mettle was tested after a shocking terrorist attack on two mosques in Christchurch killed over 50 people. She immediately met with first responders and family members, appearing modestly empathetic. She rallied the nation against hate and introduced gun control legislation that significantly controlled firearms. The bills passed. Part of her success was simply showing up and demonstrating her, and thereby her country's, sympathy and support.

Even more challenging was the Covid pandemic of 2020 and 2021. Ardern immediately required people entering the country to quarantine for 14 days and then closed the borders to all but citizens or permanent residents. One estimate of the effectiveness of her policies put the number of lives she saved at close to 80,000. Though there was some pushback against the restrictions she put in place, overall her approach was persuasive and effective. She communicated often and openly. As with the Christchurch massacre, she showed up. One appraisal stated that she offered a "master class in crisis communication." She became a hero.

However, within about two years her popularity and her party's decreased sharply. In some respects her loss of authority is reminiscent of that of US President George H.W. Bush's drop in popularity following historically high approval ratings after the Desert Storm Gulf War of 1991. In Ardern's case she was the victim of unrealistic expectations. Seeing the writing on the wall, she announced in early 2023 that she would step down as party leader and prime minister.

Angela Merkl: Heroic Leadership During Crises

In the midst of a global crisis, when leadership can become either a beacon of hope or despair, Angela Merkel stood before her nation not as a distant politician but as a scientist, a leader, and, most importantly, a fellow citizen. It was March 2020, and the world was grappling with the unprecedented challenges of the Covid-19 pandemic. Merkel addressed Germany with a calm yet firm resolve, emphasizing the seriousness of the situation while calling for unity and collective responsibility.

What made this moment stand out wasn't just the content of her speech but the manner in which she delivered it. Merkel, a trained physicist, approached the crisis with a logical and factual demeanor, a stark contrast to the panic, madness, and denial seen in other nations. She laid out the facts, presented the projected models, and made a heartfelt plea to the German people: to follow social distancing measures, to look out for one another, and to understand the gravity of the pandemic.

This wasn't a leader hiding behind rhetoric or downplaying fears. This was a leader confronting reality head-on, armed with data, empathy, and a deep sense of duty. Merkel's leadership style—marked by her unassuming demeanor, her reliance on expertise, and her unwavering commitment to her country's welfare—shone brightly in a moment of global darkness.

Angela Merkel's tenure as chancellor of Germany, spanning from 2005 to 2021, was marked by numerous challenges, including global financial crises, the European sovereign debt crisis, and significant geopolitical tensions. Her effectiveness and heroic leadership can be attributed to several qualities and decisions, but two stand out in particular.

First, Merkel showed mastery of crisis management and commitment to European unity. Merkel's leadership during the European sovereign debt crisis underscored her role not just as a national leader but as a central figure in European politics. Faced with the potential collapse of the eurozone, Merkel advocated for stringent fiscal discipline combined with solidarity among EU member states. Her insistence on austerity measures was controversial but underscored her commitment to the stability and integrity of the European Union. Merkel's ability to navigate the delicate balance between national interests and European cohesion, particularly during negotiations with Greece, helped prevent a catastrophic unraveling of the eurozone. Her actions demonstrated a deep commitment to the

European project, earning her respect as a stabilizing force in European and global politics.

Second, Merkel demonstrated a pragmatic and ethical approach to the refugee crisis. In 2015, as millions of refugees fled conflict in Syria, Afghanistan, and other regions, Merkel made a bold and humanitarian decision to open Germany's borders, welcoming over one million asylum seekers. This decision was not only a significant logistical and political challenge but also a highly contentious move within Germany and across Europe. Merkel's mantra during this period, "Wir schaffen das" ("We can do this"), became a symbol of her optimistic and moral approach to governance. By prioritizing human rights and offering protection to those in dire need, Merkel demonstrated a leadership style that went beyond pragmatic policy-making to encompass ethical responsibility. This stance, despite facing criticism and political backlash, highlighted her commitment to humanitarian principles, reinforcing her legacy as a leader who dared to make difficult decisions in the face of humanitarian crises.

Angela Merkel's leadership style—characterized by pragmatism, a deep sense of duty, and an ability to maintain calm and decisive action in times of crisis—cemented her status as one of the most effective and heroic leaders of her generation, both for Germany and the global stage.

Katherine Johnson: Brilliant Scientist and Barrier-Breaker

Katherine Johnson, born on August 26, 1918, in White Sulphur Springs, West Virginia, was an extraordinary American mathematician whose contributions to space exploration were nothing short of heroic. Johnson's story is a testament to courage, intellect, and perseverance. She not only helped humanity reach the stars but also shattered barriers for women and people of color in STEM fields. Her brilliance and perseverance in the face of adversity established her as a true American hero. Her critical contributions to aeronautics and spaceflight helped the United States lead the space race, and her determination as a woman and person of color broke barriers in the name of exploration.

Here are some remarkable aspects of her life and work:

1 **Early brilliance:** Katherine Coleman's intelligence and numerical prowess became evident at a young age. By the time she was 10 years old, she was already attending high school. In 1937, at the age of 18, she graduated with highest honors from West Virginia State College (now West Virginia State University), earning bachelor's degrees in mathematics and French. Her academic achievements were exceptional.
2 **Breaking barriers:** In 1939, Katherine was selected as one of the first three African American students to enroll in a graduate program at West Virginia University. Although she studied mathematics there, she

left after marrying James Goble and deciding to start a family. Later, she married James Johnson. Her determination and resilience were evident even in a society marked by racial and gender discrimination.

3 **NASA career:** In 1953, Katherine Johnson began working at the National Advisory Committee for Aeronautics (NACA), specifically in the West Area Computing unit. This group of African American women, known as the West Computers, manually performed complex mathematical calculations for the program's engineers. Their work was crucial to the success of the early US space program. Despite facing segregation, Katherine and her colleagues analyzed test data and provided essential computations.

4 **Space task group:** When NACA merged into the newly formed National Aeronautics and Space Administration (NASA) in 1958, Katherine Johnson continued her groundbreaking work. She became a member of the Space Task Group, where her mathematical expertise played a pivotal role. She co-authored a paper in 1960 with one of the group's engineers, focusing on calculations for placing a spacecraft into orbit.

5 **Moon missions:** Katherine's most significant contributions were during the Apollo era. She calculated and analyzed the flight paths of numerous spacecraft, including those that eventually carried astronauts to the Moon. Her precise calculations ensured the safety and success of these missions.

6 **Presidential Medal of Freedom:** In recognition of her exceptional achievements, Katherine Johnson received the Presidential Medal of Freedom in 2015. Her legacy extends beyond mathematics; she became an inspiration for generations, proving that determination, skills, and talent can propel anyone to great heights.

Katherine Johnson's technical achievements and her courage in shattering expectations redefined what was possible for mathematicians, African Americans, and women. Her legacy of hard-won progress continues to inspire generations of scientists, students, and all who struggle against prejudice. Johnson proved that one need not be the loudest voice or hold the highest position to dramatically advance humanity's greatest adventures. Through her quiet competence, confidence, and character, Katherine Johnson changed the course of history.

Taylor Swift: The Wise and Gifted Hero

In 2017, during her "1989 World Tour," Taylor Swift took a moment to address her audience, sharing a deeply personal story. She spoke about the emotional toll of her very public battle against a former radio DJ who had sexually assaulted her. Instead of remaining silent, Taylor chose to take the issue to court not for financial gain but to make a powerful statement about standing up to abuse and protecting others from similar experiences. She won the case and was awarded a symbolic $1, which she had asked for to signify that it was never about the money but about principle and justice. This courageous act resonated with countless fans and victims of abuse, showcasing her heroism and commitment to using her platform for positive change.

This story not only highlights Taylor Swift's personal bravery but also her dedication to advocacy and the empowerment of others, setting the stage for a discussion on her heroism and the impact she has had beyond her music career. Throughout her career, Swift has exemplified unwavering commitment to her values. Her song "Anti-Hero" provides a candid exploration of self-acceptance, acknowledging both strengths and flaws. Through her music and actions, Swift inspires fans to persevere and embrace their authentic selves.

Taylor Swift's cultural impact extends beyond her music, resonating deeply with fans and moving them to show resilience and accept their true selves. Here are some ways she achieves this:

1 **Empowering lyrics:** Many of Taylor Swift's songs carry themes of empowerment and resilience. Anthems like "Shake It Off" and "Blank Space" encourage listeners to embrace their individuality and bounce back from life's challenges.
2 **Unity and acceptance:** Through her lyrics, Swift urges women to unite and break down societal barriers. She fosters an environment where unity and understanding prevail over judgment and division, inspiring her audience to lift each other up.
3 **Interaction with fans:** Taylor Swift interacts with her fans in a unique way. She has cultivated a devoted fan base through social media platforms, inviting fans to her house for album listening sessions and hosting meet-and-greets after her shows. This personal connection helps cultivate passion and loyalty among her fans.
4 **Authentic expression:** Swift explores themes of love, heartbreak, empowerment, and personal growth in her music. Her authentic expression of these emotions resonates deeply with millennials, who see themselves in her songs and find inspiration in her journey.

To argue that Taylor Swift is a legitimate hero, one could consider her cultural impact. Swift has influenced and inspired millions of fans worldwide, particularly young women, through her music and personal journey. Swift's music has resonated with millions of people around the world, providing comfort, inspiration, and a sense of connection. Her music has also helped to shape popular culture, influencing other artists and creating a community of dedicated fans.

Swift has used her platform to raise awareness and advocate for important social and political issues, such as LGBTQ+ rights, women's rights, and the rights of artists. Her activism has helped to start important conversations and drive change. Swift's music and public persona have inspired and empowered many people, particularly young women, to be confident in themselves, pursue their dreams, and speak up for what they believe in.

In addition, Swift's charitable work has helped to support important causes, such as education, disaster relief, and music education. Her philanthropy has helped to make a positive difference in the lives of many people. She has used her platform to speak out on social and political issues, voter registration, and gender equality in the music industry. Swift has made significant charitable donations to various causes, including education, disaster relief, and support for sexual assault survivors. She has taken a stand against unfair practices in the music industry, advocating for better treatment and compensation for artists. Swift has overcome public scrutiny, cyberbullying, and industry challenges, serving as an example of perseverance. Swift has proven that gifted artists can rise to the status of "hero" when they use their talents to make a significant and enduring positive impact on society.

Nancy Pelosi: Heroic Leader of Legislative Justice

Nancy Pelosi has been regarded as an important hero by those in the United States who support the initiatives of the Democratic Party. She was the leader of the House of Representatives caucus for her party from 2005 to 2023. During those years she was twice speaker of the House, second in line for presidential succession, the first woman in American history to hold such high office. Republican John Boehner, who succeeded Pelosi after the 2010 mid-term selections, called her the most powerful speaker in history. Her time in the House has been turbulent. She has for many years been a convenient GOP punching bag, mocked as a radical from far-out liberal San Francisco. But at critical moments she got landmark bills passed. She even prevailed when many moderate Democrats who won seats in 2018, during the middle of Donald Trump's first administration, vowed to oust the overly progressive Pelosi as speaker. She was masterful both within her party and in Congress as a whole.

Nancy Pelosi was born into a political family in Baltimore, Maryland. Her father was a US congressman and mayor of Baltimore. Later her brother was elected mayor. She married after college and moved with her family to San Francisco in her late twenties. Rising steadily through the ranks of the Democratic Party in California, she first won a seat in Congress in a special election in 1987. She became increasingly influential and eventually became party leader in 2004. Just over two years later she was warmly introduced as the nation's first "Madam Speaker" by President George W. Bush.

Pelosi's most visible moments came during the Trump's first administration, when she led the House to impeach the president twice. There were two especially notable events during those months. In early 2020, after Mr. Trump gave a State of the Union address that she regarded as larded with untruths, Pelosi ostentatiously tore up her official copy. Responding to criticism, she said, "it was a courteous thing to do given the alternatives. It was such a dirty speech." She also drew attention during a televised negotiating meeting with Trump when she admonished him for saying that she was limited within her own caucus. She replied, "Mr. President, please don't characterize the strength that I bring to this meeting as the leader of the House Democrats." She jabbed at the president on a number of occasions, once calling him "morbidly obese" or claiming that he had cognitive disorders.

Her tiffs with Trump aside, her most important, indeed heroic, work was done with slim Democratic majorities during the first two years of the Barack Obama administration and the first two years of the Joe Biden administration. When President Obama sent the Affordable Care Act (ACA) to Congress early in 2009, his Democratic Party controlled the House of Representatives and had a filibuster-proof margin in the Senate. Then in early 2010, a special election in Massachusetts to replace the deceased long-time Senator Ted Kennedy unexpectedly went to a Republican. Then the Democrats didn't have the votes in the Senate to stop a filibuster. The Obama administration decided to abandon overall healthcare reform and try instead to pass piecemeal modifications. Pelosi derided the new proposals as Kiddie Care and tirelessly rallied Democrats in both houses to pass the landmark ACA, better known as Obamacare. It was an act of legislative genius reminiscent of the best days of Lyndon Johnson as "Master of the Senate."

Equally impressive was her work to get President Joe Biden's infrastructure and CHIPs bills through the House so that they could then be passed by the Senate in 2021 and 2022. She had an extremely small majority in the House during those early years of the Biden administration, but she managed to keep her often fractious caucus together to pass these and other important bills. In contrast, the narrow Republican House majority in the next Congress has been historically ineffective.

Pelosi was also effective in opposition. After George W Bush was re-elected in 2004, as leader of the minority Democratic Party she made quick work of Bush's efforts to partially privatize social security. They went nowhere. As a trail-blazing combative woman political leader Nancy Pelosi did heroic work on behalf of the American people. She enabled the two Democratic presidents she served with to pass foundational progressive legislation.

Marie Curie: Trailblazing Scientist Who Paid the Ultimate Price

In one of the other profiles in this book, we describe the heroism displayed by technicians working to repair Japan's damaged nuclear power plants. This remarkable sacrifice gives us pause to look back at the history of nuclear energy and our evaluations of the people who first harnessed it. Robert Oppenheimer, for example, served as the scientific director of the Manhattan Project that developed the first nuclear weapons during World War II. Oppenheimer's work was made possible by the innovative discoveries of many scientists before him, most notably the person who first discovered radioactivity, Marie Curie.

People are judged to be heroic to the extent that they overcome formidable obstacles to achieve great things. Albert Einstein once said that Marie Curie faced "the most unheard-of difficulties which have seldom been encountered in the history of experimental science." She lived in an era when women were denied opportunities to pursue professional careers. Curie's scientific brilliance and steadfast determination propelled her to success. She was also fortunate to have progressive parents who supported her educational pursuits, and a husband Pierre, also a scientist, who valued her as an intellectual equal.

Marie and Pierre Curie were the first to recognize the special properties of pitchblende waste left over from uranium mining operations in Austria. The dangers of radiation were unknown at that time, and while extracting this residue the Curies unknowingly exposed themselves to radioactive fumes. For years they carried out much of their work without proper safety measures in place. Curie herself often carried test tubes containing radioactive isotopes in her pocket and stored them in her desk drawer, noting the attractive blue-green light that the substances emitted in the dark. These exposures to the hidden toxicity of radiation samples were likely responsible for the leukemia that killed her in 1934.

Curie's career accomplishments as a scientist were substantial and enduring. She was the first person to coin the term *radiation* and to develop a theory of radiation. Curie was also the first female professor at the University of Paris, and the first recipient of two Nobel Prizes, one in physics and one in chemistry. She developed important techniques for isolating radioactive isotopes and was responsible for identifying two new elements, polonium and radium. When she died, she became the first woman to be buried under the famous dome of the Panthéon in Paris in recognition of her own accomplishments rather than being the wife of a famous man.

"We must believe that we are gifted for something," Curie once said, "and that this thing, at whatever cost, must be attained." She most certainly lived and died by those words. Although Curie's contributions to science were remarkable, she and others who helped usher in the nuclear age have been criticized by some for making weapons of mass destruction possible. We argue that these criticisms are misplaced. Curie opened up an entire new frontier of science that has benefited the human race much more than it has harmed it. We applaud her courage in overcoming the gender biases of her day to become one of the greatest scientists in human history.

Ellen DeGeneres: Heroic Comedienne and Underdog Advocate

People not only love an underdog who prevails; they also revere the supportive people who help underdogs prevail. Ellen DeGeneres is a vivid example of an individual who has used her celebrity status to advocate for members of society who traditionally have not had a voice. After establishing herself as one of America's best comic talents, DeGeneres has dedicated her life to improving the lives of disadvantaged children, animals, and cancer survivors.

Raised in Louisiana, DeGeneres started her career as a stand-up comic at small local clubs. Audiences loved her, and she soon began touring nationally. Her big break came when she appeared on the *Johnny Carson Show* in 1986. In 1997, during an episode of her highly acclaimed television sitcom *Ellen*, DeGeneres made her homosexuality public. Since that time she has become a tireless advocate of gay rights. As host of her Emmy Award winning *Ellen DeGeneres Show*, she has strongly condemned the recent trend of teenage boys committing suicide after being bullied about their sexual orientation. "Something must be done," said DeGeneres. "This needs to be a wake up call to everyone that teenage bullying and teasing is an epidemic in this country, and the death rate is climbing. We have an obligation to change this."

DeGeneres has also been heavily involved in causes that protect animal rights. She recently teamed up with the US Postal Service to promote a campaign aimed at increasing animal adoption from local shelters. "This is a subject I am extremely passionate about," DeGeneres said. "By working together, we can find good homes for millions of adoptable, homeless and abandoned pets." DeGeneres was named PETA's 2009 Woman of the Year for her effective role in promoting the welfare of animals.

As befitting a hero, the list of charities that DeGeneres supports with her time and money is lengthy. She helped launch the Small Change Campaign to support and benefit the organization Feeding America, which distributes food to hungry Americans. DeGeneres has been a strong promoter of Breast Cancer Awareness Month on her show, and she has also supported the Children's Health Fund, the Society for Animal Protective Legislation, St. Jude Children's Research Hospital, the American Wild Horse Preservation Campaign, and the Humane Society.

DeGeneres has contributed significantly to the Hurricane Katrina Relief Fund through the American Red Cross. In 2009, she received the Tulane University President's Medal. Tulane President Scott Cowen said, "She never forgot New Orleans, especially after Katrina."

Our research on heroes reveals that people view heroes as either extremely competent, extremely moral, or both. Ellen DeGeneres falls into this latter category. Her comic genius has been compared to that of Jerry Seinfeld, Woody Allen, and Steve Martin, and her television shows have earned dozens of Emmy Awards. Most impressively, she has used her stature in the entertainment industry to fight for the rights of disadvantaged people and animals. In the eyes of millions, her advocacy of numerous underdog causes has elevated Ellen DeGeneres to the status of a heroic leader.

John Nash: A Hero's Brilliant Triumph over Mental Illness

Our studies of heroes reveal that people are quick to assign heroic status to those who successfully overcome daunting obstacles. Sometimes these obstacles are external and physically imposing, as when Sir Edmund Hillary and Tenzing Norgay reached the summit of Mt. Everest in 1953. But sometimes these obstacles are internal and psychologically formidable. John Forbes Nash, the groundbreaking mathematician, is a striking example of a person who courageously battled, and overcame, the demon of severe mental illness that gripped him through much of his life.

From a very young age, Nash displayed a natural genius for mathematics. The only signs of the paranoid schizophrenia that would debilitate him later in life were his tendencies toward acerbic isolation and aloofness. Because of his mathematical brilliance, people overlooked his quirkiness. Nash was admitted to Princeton University's doctoral program at the tender age of 20, and he was offered a faculty position at MIT at the astonishingly young age of 23.

Throughout his 20s, Nash made landmark contributions to the fields of economics and mathematics. In his 27-page doctoral dissertation, written at the age of 21, he formulated his now-famous solution, called the Nash equilibrium, to vexing two-person noncooperative games. Nash also enhanced our understanding of differential geometry and partial differential equations. His contributions have made a significant and enduring impact on evolutionary biology, artificial intelligence, military strategy, and market economics.

But by the age of 30, Nash began having auditory hallucinations that completely incapacitated him. He believed that an organization composed of men wearing red ties was placing him in danger, and he began inventing individual characters, some of them extraterrestrials, who he believed were after him. Nash left his tenured position at MIT, was admitted to a series of mental hospitals in America and in Europe, and received numerous therapies, including drug and insulin shock therapies.

None of these treatments provided long-term relief, and for years Nash led a disgraced and solitary life as an outcast of society. But miraculously, by the age of 60, Nash's symptoms abated, and he slowly regained his sanity. His friends were contacted by Stockholm's Nobel Prize committee, who wanted to know if Nash was lucid enough to receive the award. They assured the committee that he was now fine. And so in 1994, Nash received the highest acclaim that a scientist can receive, the Nobel Prize for his groundbreaking contributions to economics. Shortly afterward, an Academy Award–winning movie was made about his life, called *A Beautiful Mind*, starring Russell Crowe as Nash.

Someone once asked Nash, "How could you, a mathematician, believe that extraterrestrials were sending you messages?" Nash replied, "Because the ideas I had about supernatural beings came to me the same way my mathematical ideas did. So I took them seriously." Scientists who study paranoid schizophrenia claim that it is virtually impossible for a person to overcome the illness without treatment. That Nash was able to conquer his inner demons on his own may have been every bit as remarkable as any mathematical discoveries he made.

Althea Gibson: Barrier Breaker and Way Paver

African Americans have had to break numerous barriers in US society. For a brief period after the Civil War, Black people in this country seemed on the verge of genuine political equality and an uneasy but real social equality. However, with the end of Reconstruction in 1877, African American advances were stopped cold. Conditions became worse and worse during the early 1900s Jim Crow era. When Al Smith received the nomination for president at the Democratic Party convention in Houston, Texas, in 1928, African Americans were separated from white people in the convention hall by chicken wire.

During the administrations of Franklin Roosevelt (1933–1945), some forward progress was achieved, but racial segregation in the South and other parts of the United States was firmly implanted, and southern Black people were almost completely disenfranchised. The late 1940s saw two major breakthroughs. In 1947 Jackie Robinson broke the color line in major league baseball with the Brooklyn Dodgers, and in 1948 President Harry Truman desegregated the armed forces of the United States by executive order. But individual African Americans had to put themselves on the line to chip away at one obstacle after another. One such person was the tennis player Althea Gibson. Gibson was born in South Carolina and brought up in Harlem. She won table tennis tournaments in the Police Athletic Leagues and attracted the attention of people who thought she could excel in the game of tennis.

One of her sponsors was Dr. Walter Johnson from Lynchburg, Virginia, who later assisted Arthur Ashe to develop his tennis career. With the help of Johnson and other patrons, Gibson finally was able to graduate from college and break into a highly segregated tennis circuit.

Finally in 1950, after white tennis player Alice Marble wrote in a magazine article that only "bigotry" prevented Gibson from playing in major tournaments, Gibson became the first African American, male or female, to play at Forest Hills in New York, home of the US Open tennis championships. The next year she became the first Black person to play in the prestigious Wimbledon tournament in England.

Her performances improved steadily, and in 1956 she won the French Open. In 1957, she won both the singles and doubles championships at Wimbledon. That year and the next she triumphed in the US Open. The Associated Press named her Female Athlete of the Year in 1957. Turning professional, she won the women's singles title in 1960.

Later, Gibson took a turn at a professional golfing career but had only modest success. She returned to tennis and eventually became a valued instructor. In 1975 she was named Commissioner of Athletics in New Jersey and stayed in that position for 10 years. Later Gibson suffered a stroke and endured multiple health and financial problems. She went on welfare and contemplated suicide. Tennis great Billy Jean King, among others, helped her through some of the most difficult times. However, her health continued to decline. She died in 2003 at the age of 76.

Gibson was helped by many people throughout her life -- before, during, and after her career. At the same time, as the "Jackie Robinson of tennis," she blazed the trail for others, including Arthur Ashe. Gibson was one of the individuals who both gave and received aid in helping African Americans advance in one significant sector of American society. To many, that qualifies her as a genuine if largely unrecognized hero.

Monica Seles: Tennis Hero and Tragedienne

Athletic heroism rarely occurs without years of preparation, hard work, and sacrifice. Achieving great success as an athlete requires arduous training to perfect skills and to attain world-class conditioning. A young hero-to-be starts out as a fresh upstart, an underdog who slowly begins building a resume of successes. He or she is said to be *trending* toward heroism. Eventually the young phenom overtakes the older established stars and achieves the status of hero.

Monica Seles is an example of an individual who was not just trending toward heroism; she was trending toward being the greatest female tennis player of all-time. Born and raised in Yugoslavia, Seles began winning professional tennis tournaments as a young teen. At the age of 16, she won her first Grand Slam singles title at the 1990 French Open, defeating World No. 1 Steffi Graf in the final match.

Seles absolutely dominated the women's tennis scene in 1991 and 1992. During those two years she replaced Graf as the world's best player by winning 22 titles and reaching 33 finals out of the 34 tournaments in which she played. Virtually unstoppable, Seles compiled a 159–12 win-loss record, which included winning 55 of 56 matches in Grand Slam tournaments. At the tender age of 19 she was on top of the tennis world and seemed destined to obliterate all of tennis's records.

Then tragedy struck. On April 3, 1993, during a quarterfinal match at the Citizen Cup tournament in Hamburg, Germany, a man named Günter Parche ran onto the tennis court and stabbed Seles with a boning knife between her shoulder blades. Parche later said that he did it because he wanted Steffi Graf to become the number one ranked player again. Seles's stab wound was serious but took only a few weeks to heal. The incident, however, shattered her emotionally.

Parche was charged following the incident but was only given a two-year suspended sentence. Seles was devastated at the news and vowed never to play tennis in Germany again. "What people seem to be forgetting is that this man stabbed me intentionally and he did not serve any sort of punishment for it. I would not feel comfortable going back. I don't foresee that happening."

Although Seles was fit to play tennis throughout much of 1993 and 1994, she became clinically depressed in the aftermath of both the stabbing incident and her father's cancer diagnosis. Seles soon developed a food addiction and put on weight. Although she returned to tennis in 1995, she was never again the dominant player that she had been previously. In 2009, Seles released a book entitled *Getting a Grip: On My Body, My Mind, My Self*, which chronicled her bout with depression and food addiction, her journey back to the game, and her new life beyond tennis.

When Seles retired in 2008, she was adored by fans who sympathized with her tragic story and admired her courage in overcoming many obstacles. Today Seles says that despite everything that she's been through, she is happy with her life. "The 'what ifs,' they are there. But I think the difficult years made me who I am today," she said. "And I think I'm a much happier person than I used to be."

The heroic journey is rarely predictable. Just as no one could have predicted Tiger Woods's fall from grace in 2009, no one anticipated Monica Seles's tragic encounter with a deranged man with a knife. Yet somehow the knife attack allowed Seles to become an unsurpassed hero of a different type. *Sports Illustrated*'s Jon Wertheim summed it up best in 2008: "Transformed from champion to tragedienne, Seles became far more popular than she was while winning all those titles. It became impossible to root against her. At first, out of sympathy. Then because she revealed herself to be so thoroughly thoughtful, graceful, dignified. When she quietly announced her retirement last week at age 34, she exited as perhaps the most adored figure in the sport's history. As happy endings go, one could do worse."

Daniel Anderson: The Hero Who Redefined Alcoholism

One significant contribution of heroes is their ability to change the way we think about the world. Heroes challenge conventional thinking or traditional ways of conceiving everyday phenomena, and they do so in a way that improves the quality of people's lives. Daniel Anderson is a striking example of a hero who completely defied the conventional wisdom about the causes and treatment of alcoholism.

In the early 1950s, while working as a psychologist at Willmar State Hospital in Minnesota, Anderson began to question the prevailing view that alcoholism was caused by poor willpower and a weakness of character. At that time alcoholism carried with it a severe social stigma, with alcoholics receiving the same degree of disdain as common thieves and pedophiles. But Anderson hypothesized that drug and alcohol addiction wasn't caused by poor character or corrupt morals. He proposed that chemical addiction was a complex disease characterized by psychological, physical, social, and spiritual deficits.

With the goal of improving treatment for alcoholics, Anderson developed what is now known all around the world as the Minnesota model. The central elements of the Minnesota model are (1) the recognition that addiction is an illness with multiple components; (2) the idea that improved mental and physical health is achieved through total abstinence; (3) the notion that education about the nature of chemical dependency helps people maintain sobriety; (4) the importance of having a trained interdisciplinary staff to aid addicts in recovery; (5) the recognition that the duration of treatment is highly individualized; (6) the importance of living in a therapeutic community that includes attending lectures, participating in support groups, and receiving individual therapy; (7) an emphasis on preparing and credentialing the recovered alcoholic to work in the field and become an important of the multidisciplinary treatment team; and (8) the idea that recovering addicts should be treated with dignity and respect by a caring, concerned staff.

Anderson's Minnesota model represented a radical departure from previous treatment programs. Most significant was the model's emphasis on removing the stigma associated with alcoholism. "Anderson's most heroic quality was what he gave the struggling alcoholic: The gift of respect," said Marcia J. Lawton, founder of Virginia Commonwealth University's Alcohol and Drug Education and Rehabilitation program in the Department of Rehab Counseling. "He believed strongly that treatment should involve preserving the dignity of recovering alcoholics and giving them unconditional love."

Anderson was instrumental in creating the Hazelden Foundation treatment center in Minnesota, which has served as a model for alcohol and drug treatment facilities around the world. Throughout his career, Anderson was applauded for his selflessness. Shortly after establishing Hazelden, he became a highly sought-after consultant as other treatment programs grew in number. Anderson "always had the bests interests of patients at heart in his work," said John Schwarzlose, president of the Betty Ford Center in Rancho Mirage, California. "Some in Dan's position would have seen the Betty Ford Center as a potential threat to Hazelden's preeminence. Dan's reaction, however, was not only to graciously agree to help, but to encourage our center to improve on what Hazelden had done."

Our research on heroic work has shown how heroes have developed new ways of looking at old situations. In 16th-century Europe, Copernicus challenged the medieval view of the earth being the center of the universe. In ancient China, Confucius challenged the moral philosophies of Taoism and Legalism. In more modern times, the Dalai Lama, Martin Luther King, Jr., Gandhi, and other spiritual leaders have all challenged conventional thinking by advocating peaceful solutions to difficult conflicts. We argue that Dan Anderson's revolutionary contributions to our understanding of alcoholism and addiction have been no less significant. Tens of thousands of recovered individuals owe a tremendous debt of gratitude – and perhaps even their lives – to Anderson for his wisdom, compassion, and heroism.

Tough Without a Gun: Heroic Portrayals by Humphrey Bogart

It is somewhat ironic that the title of Stefan Kanfer's new biography of Humphrey Bogart borrows Raymond Chandler's comment that "Bogart can be tough without a gun." Bogart uses a gun in some of his most iconic roles, including in the climactic scene in *Casablanca*, where he shoots the Nazi Major Strasser (but only after Strasser shoots first).

But there is a special brand of unarmed toughness to Bogart in many of his films. That quality has come to define a certain kind of male hero: powerful, self-contained and independent, but ultimately kind, decisive, and moral.

One distinctive characteristic of powerful people is their self-control, their ability to direct their own behavior rather than let others manipulate them or "push their buttons." They know how to be patient and how to wait out others so that they can take their own course of action. Ralph Waldo Emerson is often quoted as saying, "A man is a hero not because he is braver than anyone else, but because he is brave for 10 minutes longer." Abraham Lincoln, as an example, is credited with incredible patience and an ability to keep his temper and his poise. He could not be rushed into action, but when he sensed the time was right, he acted forcefully and without hesitation.

Perhaps Bogart illustrates this kind of controlled heroism most power-fully in the climactic scene of the 1948 film *Key Largo*. His character appears at a hotel on the Florida Keys run by the father and widow of a slain war buddy. He has come to pay respects to both. While he is there, the hotel has to endure not only a hurricane but also a group of ruthless gangsters. Their leader is the notorious outlaw Johnny Rocco, played tensely by Edward G. Robinson. Initially the gangsters push Bogart around, along with the others. The audience hopes that he is simply biding his time, but it begins to look like he doesn't have the courage to confront them. Perhaps he is waiting for the right moment, but maybe he'll just let the thugs run over him.

Eventually the gang forces Bogart to pilot a motor boat to Cuba. There are four of them, but they don't know that Bogart has a gun. Underway at sea, Bogart causes one of the outlaws to fall overboard and then shoots two more. Finally, only Bogart and Johnny Rocco remain. Bogart is lying over the hatch overseeing the passageway to below decks. He waits for Rocco to come out. Rocco repeatedly calls out "Soldier!" in an attempt to get Bogart to reveal where he is. He offers Bogart a share of the money his gang has stolen. He gets increasingly angry and anxious as nothing he says or does draws a response from Bogart.

Finally, Rocco pretends that he is unarmed and slowly comes into view, with a hidden gun. Of course, Bogart prevails in the shootout and returns to Key Largo as a hero. He was tough with his gun but even tougher before he had to shoot. His patience and composure directed the action. He was brave for a few minutes longer.

Edgar Allan Poe: American Literary Giant

Heroes are often indirect leaders who influence others through what they have done, how they have acted, what they have produced, or what they have fashioned. Heroes who are admired because of their artistic or liter-ary works, or musical or theatrical performances, probably appeal to fewer people than transforming heroes such as Nelson Mandela or Martin Luther King, Jr. Still, their contributions have enriched the lives and cultures of many. One such hero is the writer Edgar Allan Poe.

A number of elements have made Poe's writings so influential and moving. First, his stories of death and the supernatural have thrilled many. A chilling example is one of Poe's briefest stories, "The Tell-Tale Heart." It has been said that Poe often tried to establish the mood of a story in the first sentence. "The Tell-Tale Heart" offers a perfect illustration: "True! Nervous, very, very dreadfully nervous I had been and am; but why *will* you say that I am mad?" The narrator's madness becomes more apparent from there. He murders an old man, buries his heart under the floor boards, and imagines that its beating can be heard by the police. In a fit of nervous agony, he confesses to the crime that none suspected.

Second, Poe's wrenching poems about lost women are heartbreaking, from "the beautiful Annabel Lee" to "the lost Lenore." It is not clear whether such poems were inspired by his dead mother, his dead wife, or some unattainable woman Poe had encountered. Third, Poe's work is widely credited with the invention of the detective story through the character C. Auguste Dupin. Dupin appears in three of Poe's most famous tales. Sir Arthur Conan Doyle paid tribute to Poe's character, who undoubtedly shaped Doyle's own literary hero, Sherlock Holmes.

Edgar Poe was born in Boston in 1809, the same year as Abraham Lincoln. His father abandoned him the next year, and his mother died soon after. Poe was taken in by the couple John and Frances Allan of Richmond, Virginia. He was educated as a young boy in Scotland and England but returned to America and attended the University of Virginia. He left the university after a short time, possibly because of financial constraints. By that time he was completely alienated from his foster parents, the Allans. Poe then joined the army and eventually won an appointment to West Point. He didn't last long there, either.

When he was 26, Poe married his 13-year-old first cousin, Virginia Clemm. By that time his literary career was well underway. The couple moved between New York, Philadelphia, and Baltimore, as Poe tried to find a steady position as editor or literary critic. In the meantime, he continued his prolific writing and in 1845 published his best-known poem, "The Raven." In this classic piece he ends up asking the mysterious bird, standing "on the pallid bust of Pallas just above my chamber door" whether in the afterlife he will find "a rare and radiant maiden, whom the angels named Lenore?" The unforgettable reply, "Quoth the raven, 'Nevermore.'"

Go Ahead, Make My Day: Clint Eastwood as Contemporary Hero

In 2014, Clint Eastwood demonstrated quick thinking and bravery in a real-life situation that showcased his heroism beyond the silver screen. While attending a party during the AT&T Pebble Beach National Pro-Am golf tournament, Eastwood noticed the tournament director, Steve John, choking on a piece of cheese. Without hesitation, Eastwood rushed to John's side and performed the Heimlich maneuver, successfully dislodging the obstruction and saving John's life. This act of heroism was a powerful reminder that Eastwood's courage and decisiveness are not confined to his roles in films but are qualities he embodies in his everyday life. This incident underscores the true nature of heroism, where swift and selfless action can make all the difference. Clint Eastwood is a hero both on and off the screen.

Arguably, Eastwood did his best professional work in the years after he qualified for Social Security and Medicare. After age 70, between 2000 and 2024, he directed or starred in at least a dozen important films. The quality of Eastwood's work makes him a hero to many, both insiders in the film-making industry and the general public. But during his career he has also had many harsh critics among reviewers and in the general public.

Eastwood's early career took off in the late 1950s with his role in the so-called "adult Western" television series *Rawhide*. There he played a young cowhand named Rowdy Yates. While the part paid the rent, Eastwood felt confined by having to play a younger man without much depth. He jumped at the chance to portray the "Man With No Name" in Sergio Leone's *Fistful of Dollars*, the first of the "spaghetti Westerns" that Eastwood starred in during the 1960s. In the late 1960s, Eastwood starred as a rogue New York City policeman in the film *Coogan's Bluff*. It made good money but was criticized, as were many of his films, for glorifying both violence and macho law enforcement that exceeded legal boundaries. More important, it provided the template for Eastwood's *Dirty Harry* films, a series of four that spanned the 1970s and early 1980s. The last of those films, *Sudden Impact*, contained the iconic line, "Go ahead, make my day," which Harry says to a bad guy, threatening to shoot a hostage. President Ronald Reagan used the phrase in 1985 when he threatened to veto a tax increase.

Although the Man With No Name and Dirty Harry characters defined Eastwood's persona for much of the 1980s and 1990s, he also starred in several other genres and began a directing career with the film *Play Misty for Me*. Slowly he gained recognition from the critics, and in 1992 his film *Unforgiven*, a Western, won Eastwood Academy Awards for best director and best picture. He was also nominated for best actor. Eastwood felt the acclaim was overdue.

As impressive as these accomplishments were, Eastwood's work over the last quarter century has gained him respect bordering on awe and qualifies him as a hero to many. In 2003, he directed *Mystic River*, a tense police drama set in Boston. It won Academy Awards for best actor Sean Penn and best supporting actor Tim Robbins, as well as best picture and best director nominations for Eastwood. In 2004, *Million Dollar Baby* won Academy

Awards for best director and best picture and a nomination for Eastwood as best actor. It also won best actress and est supporting actor awards for Hillary Swank and Morgan Freeman. In the next few years, Eastwood directed two films about the World War II battle of Iwo Jima, *Flags of Our Fathers* and *Letters from Iwo Jima*. The latter was nominated for best picture and best director.

Since then, Eastwood directed *Changeling* with Angelina Jolie; *Gran Torino*, in which he also acted; and *Invictus*, an inspiring film starring Morgan Freeman and Matt Damon about Nelson Mandela and South Africa's victory in the 1995 World Cup rugby championship. Eastwood also received well-deserved acclaim for directing the movies *Richard Jewell, Sully*, and *American Sniper*. Only a director of Eastwood's stature would have won support from a major studio to produce the Iwo Jima films, and only one so skilled would have been chosen by Freeman, who had obtained the film rights to *Invictus*, to direct that film. Eastwood's accomplishments in his 70s and 80s are noteworthy and remind us all that heroism is available to people of all ages.

Lucille Ball: A Heroic Comic Genius

Very few of us possess exceptional talent in one area of life, and still fewer have talent in multiple areas. Throughout her career, Lucille Ball proved herself to be the most gifted comedian of her generation as well as a pioneering businesswoman who reshaped the Hollywood studio landscape. Her wildly popular television shows broke new artistic ground and provided raucous entertainment to millions of her adoring fans each week.

Surprisingly, as a young woman Lucille Ball struggled to break into show business. At age 16, she enrolled in the John Murray Anderson School for the Dramatic Arts in New York City. She was sent home a few weeks later after her drama coaches told her that she "had no future at all as a performer." As a young aspiring actress, Ball was hired to play a role in the Broadway show *Vanities* but was quickly fired. Later, she was briefly hired, then let go, from the production of *Stepping Stones*.

Undeterred, Ball was able to play many small movie roles in the 1930s as a contract player for RKO Radio Pictures. She soon acquired the ignominious reputation as Hollywood's "Queen of the B's." But a life-changing event occurred in 1940 when Ball met and fell in love with Cuban-born band leader Desi Arnaz. They married, but their relationship was strained by the fact that each had a hectic performing schedule that often kept them apart. When CBS wanted Lucy to star in a television series, she insisted that Desi play her husband, believing that working together with him would help their marriage. But the network executives balked, arguing that the public would never accept an all-American redhead and a Cuban as a couple.

Eventually, CBS agreed to produce the show on Lucy's terms, and the *I Love Lucy* show was born. The series was the beginning of television's first dynasty, and it broke new ground in several areas. Ball was among the first women to star in her own show and the first to be shown pregnant with her and Desi's baby. *I Love Lucy* pioneered a number of methods still in use in television production today. Shooting long shots, medium shots, and close-ups before a live audience, using multiple cameras, required discipline, technique, and skilled choreography. Ball eventually became the first woman in television to become head of a production company, which she and Desi named Desilu.

Airing from 1951 to 1960, *I Love Lucy* was the perfect forum for Lucille Ball to showcase her comic genius. She perfected the art of physical comedy while also demonstrating impeccable comedic timing. Audiences roared at her wide range of facial and vocal expressions in response to the many outlandish situations scripted for her. The on-screen chemistry between her and Desi was palpable, and there were consistent comic sparks between them and their loving yet insufferable neighbors, Fred and Ethel Mertz. *I Love Lucy* dominated the weekly TV ratings in the United States for most of its run. The series garnered more than 200 awards, including 5 Emmys. After the show ended, Ball starred in two other successful sitcoms, *The Lucy Show* and *Here's Lucy*.

Lucille Ball's professional triumphs, unique comedic gifts, and uncommon business acumen made her a true hero. The US Postal Service honored her with a commemorative postage stamp. She appeared on the cover of *TV Guide* more than any other person and was voted as the "Greatest TV Star of All Time." *TV Guide* also named *I Love Lucy* the second best television program in American history, after *Seinfeld*. Lucille Ball was chosen as the second out of the "50 Greatest TV Icons," after Johnny Carson. In a public poll, however, she was chosen as the greatest TV icon ever. We certainly agree with the public on this one.

10 Traditional-Complete Heroes

Wilma Mankiller: Heroic Commitment to the Cherokee Nation

Wilma Mankiller, a Native American activist and the first woman elected to serve as principal chief of the Cherokee Nation, embodies heroism that transcends adversity and culminates in empowerment. Her remarkable journey intertwines resilience and service, exemplified by her recovery and community engagement after a life-threatening accident in 1979. Despite formidable personal obstacles and an extended healing process, Mankiller harnessed her energy to forge a visionary leadership style that would later define her tenure as principal chief. Her heroism extends beyond shattering the glass ceiling; it is deeply rooted in her unwavering commitment to rejuvenating her community.

Wilma Mankiller, photographed with President Clinton as she is awarded the Presidential Medal of Freedom in 1998

Source: White House Television (WHTV) uploaded by Clinton Presidential Library

DOI: 10.4324/9781003328681-10

Under her guidance, the Cherokee Nation experienced a remarkable revival across economic, educational, and health systems, rekindling a sense of autonomy and prosperity among its people. Mankiller's transformation from convalescent to change catalyst epitomizes the quintessential qualities of a hero: The ability to rise above personal trials and lead a collective resurgence, echoing the resilient spirit of the Cherokee Nation itself.

Wilma Mankiller is considered a hero for several reasons:

1 She was the first female principal chief of the Cherokee Nation (1985–1995), breaking barriers and paving the way for other Native American women leaders. Her election was groundbreaking in a traditionally patriarchal society.

2 As principal chief, she revitalized the Cherokee Nation's economy and community development. She improved housing, education, healthcare, and children's programs benefiting thousands of Cherokee families. Her initiatives helped reduce Cherokee households below the poverty line by over 60 percent.

3 She was a strong activist for Native American rights and sovereignty. She advocated for tribal self-governance, the revision of discriminatory laws, and the protection of Cherokee language and culture.

4 Mankiller played a pivotal role in improving the image and political power of Native Americans. She raised national awareness of tribal issues and empowered Native communities across the United States.

5 She overcame many personal adversities including poverty, violence, and health issues like myasthenia gravis and lymphoma. Her resilience in the face of challenges was inspirational.

6 Mankiller championed women's rights and served as a role model for young Native American women. She proved women could be influential leaders in Indigenous communities.

Through her pioneering leadership, policy achievements, activism, and perseverance, Wilma Mankiller helped revolutionize the Cherokee Nation and Native American communities across the United States. Her heroic life story demonstrated courage, compassion, and trailblazing spirit.

As with most heroes, Wilma Mankiller faced criticism, though more so earlier in her career than later on. In the 1970s, she was among a group of activists who occupied the Cherokee Nation tribal headquarters to protest the administration and demand more accountability and services for communities in need. This activism was seen as radical by some at the time. Her 1983 autobiography *Mankiller: A Chief and Her People* was candid about social dysfunctions like alcoholism and domestic violence in Native communities, which made some uncomfortable.

When first elected principal chief in 1985, her gender, activist background, and progressive policies sparked backlash from more traditional Cherokee factions resistant to change. Her push for self-determination and reducing federal oversight of tribal affairs was criticized by some in the US government who feared a loss of control. A few fellow tribal leaders felt she focused too much on building the Cherokee Nation's autonomy versus pan-Indian unity across tribes.

However, by the end of her terms as principal chief in 1995, Mankiller had largely won over her critics through her effective leadership, economic successes, and restoration of pride among the Cherokee people. While controversial stances earlier on, her heroic accomplishments eventually overshadowed any objections to her approach and values. She left office with an 85 percent popularity rating among Cherokees.

Audrey Hepburn: Hero of Compassion, Grace, and Humility

Do people become heroes just because they are famous or because they are beautiful or highly talented? There is evidence that mere exposure or familiarity can lead to increased liking, despite the adage that familiarity breeds contempt. While some heroes, such as Sherlock Holmes, are mostly admired for their talent rather than their ethics, for many of those heroes there is also a component of morality. In the case of Sherlock Holmes, he almost always did what readers considered the right thing, even if it was not entirely legal. An interesting example of fame and beauty is the actress Audrey Hepburn. A compelling performer, she achieved hero status for endearing beauty but most importantly for her work for the greater good, particularly her efforts with UNICEF (originally the United Nations International Children's Emergency Fund, now simply United Nations Children's Fund).

Although she appeared in a range of movies, Hepburn is best known for her roles in *Roman Holiday, Breakfast at Tiffany's,* and *My Fair Lady.* The 1953 *Roman Holiday,* playing opposite Gregory Peck, introduced Hepburn for the first time in a starring role. She won the 1954 Academy Award for best actress and that same year won a Tony for her leading Broadway performance in the play *Ondine.* Peck deserves credit for insisting that Hepburn equal billing in *Roman Holiday,* though he was far better-known.

In the next several years she performed brilliantly in films such as *Funny Face* and *The Nun's Story.* One of her most luminous roles was as Eliza Doolittle in *My Fair Lady.* Sadly, casting Hepburn in that part caused some difficult controversy. Julie Andrews had played the role in the stage version, and many thought she deserved to star in the film. Any hard feelings were largely assuaged by the success Andrews had with the film *Mary Poppins,* which was released the same year. Hepburn played in selected films after 1964, but she more and more focused on family and the world's needy.

Hepburn's awareness of and contributions to the common good began during and after World War II. She was born in 1929 in Belgium and spent time in England and the Netherlands as well as her home country. Before the outbreak of World War II, she attended British schools. Her family returned to the Netherlands at the start of the war, and Hepburn developed skill as singer and ballet dancer. At age 15, she danced to raise money for resistance to Nazi Germany. She had vivid memories of the trauma of war, including watching other children shipped off to death in concentration camps. Both during and after the war she suffered from malnutrition, as did many others, and its potentially fatal effects. She eventually received aid from a former British officer. Those life-threatening experiences were unforgettable. Throughout her adult years she worked to give back.

Starting in the 1950s, Hepburn recorded children's stories for UNICEF. In her later years she became especially active with the fund. Starting in the late 1980s, she traveled for UNICEF to Ethiopia, Turkey, and countries in Central America. She was appointed a UNICEF Good Will Ambassador in 1989. Remembering her own traumas from the world war and its aftermath, she never forgot the support she received. And she reciprocated.

Audrey Hepburn was honored both for her work in the arts and for humanity. She was one of the very few performers to win an Oscar alongside a Tony, Grammy, and Emmy. Perhaps her most visible honor was receiving the Presidential Medal of Freedom from George H.W. Bush in 1992, shortly before her death from cancer in 1993 at age 63. But even more meaningful perhaps was the dedication of the statue "The Spirit of Audrey" at New York's UNICEF headquarters. She died a hero for work on behalf of children everywhere but also for luminous screen performances.

Volodymyr Zelenskyy: The Tenacious Underdog Hero

In 2022 Volodymyr Zelenskyy, the president of Ukraine, was named *Time* magazine's "Person of the Year." He had achieved heroic status for his bravery in leading his nation against the supposedly overwhelming power of the Russia military. Despite years of diplomatic efforts to avoid armed conflict, by both Ukraine and the United States, Russian president Vladimir Putin launched an invasion of Ukraine in February 2022. As of this writing the tides of battle were moving in favor of the Russians, partly because the US Congress was blocking a resumption of aid to Ukraine. But Zelenskyy continues to rally his country. His spirit, and the reality he faces, were proclaimed early the war when both Turkey and the United States urged him to evacuate and offered him assistance in leaving his country. His legendary reply was, "the fight is here; I need ammunition, not a ride." Today Ukraine still needs ammunition, and we can hope that the United States and NATO will have the will and the wit to supply it.

Zelenskyy's brave stance reminds us of even better-known words of an earlier recipient of *Time's* Person of the Year award, Winston Churchill. That was in 1940, following Churchill's leadership in resisting Nazi Germany during World War II. Then the British prime minister pledged, "We shall fight on the beaches, we shall fight on the landing grounds, we shall fight in the fields and in the streets, we shall fight in the hills; we shall never surrender." Zelenskyy's resilience and determination are no less inspiring than Churchill's.

In some ways, Zelenskyy's rise to the presidency is surprising, but on reflection it is not so strange. Born in 1978 of Jewish parents, Zelenskyy grew up speaking Russian as his first language. He was educated at university and received a law degree. But he was drawn to comedy and acting and founded the broadcast company Kvartal in 1995. From 2015 to 2019, he starred in the highly successful series called *Servant of the People*, in which Zelenskyy portrayed the president of Ukraine. For an actor to become president of a country may appear anomalous until we recall that US President Franklin Roosevelt aspired to be an actor and that Ronald Reagan actually was one. In Zelenskyy's case, he ran for the position of actual president shortly after playing the role on television. He was elected in a landslide.

Two of the biggest challenges for Zelenskyy's administration were resolving conflict in the Donbas region of eastern Ukraine, where many separatist Russian nationals reside, and tackling long entrenched corruption at the highest levels of the government. These two concerns intersected in a much-discussed and analyzed telephone conversation with US President Donald Trump during July 2019. The US Congress had allocated funds for Ukraine's defense, to strengthen that country as it faced increasing Russian threat. In a phone call between Zelenskyy and Trump that summer, the US president indicated that the release of financial support was conditional. Trump said, according to White House transcripts, "I would like you to do us a favor though," specifically to launch investigations into the company that had linked Russia to the Trump campaign in 2016 and into the Ukraine business dealings of Joe Biden's son Hunter Biden. Joe Biden was seen as a threat to Trump's reelection, and the mere announcement of an investigation into his son's foreign business dealings would hurt the potential Democratic nominee. In the end, Zelenskyy did not respond to the pressure, but news of Trump's attempt to leverage his cooperation in US political affairs led to Trump's first impeachment trial. It turned out that Trump was right to fear Biden's candidacy. He defeated Trump in the 2020 presidential election.

It remains to be seen whether Zelenskyy and Ukraine can hold out against vicious Russian attacks. After Donald Trump's reelection, their chances seem remote, as Trump seems enthralled by Vladimir Putin and is unlikely to oppose his interests. Still, Volodymyr Zelenskyy will always be a Churchillian figure of courageous heroic resistance to the world's dark forces.

Golda Meir: Heroic Founding Mother of Israel

In the fall of 2023, the 50th anniversary of the Yom Kippur War in the Middle East, the film *Golda* streamed on several video platforms. Starring Helen Mirren, it portrayed rather sympathetically the woman who was prime minister of Israel during that conflict, Golda Meir. While her leadership in that momentous war has long been questioned, we have long regarded her as a hero, such that she graces the first edition of this book.

Meir was born Golda Mabovitch in what is now Ukraine in 1898. Her parents brought her to the United States as a child, first to New York City and then to Milwaukee. There she attended elementary school and became a precocious leader and a top student. In high school, she fell in love with Morris Myerson and married him once he agreed to move with her to Palestine after they wed. After World War I, they emigrated to the land that was then a British Mandate.

In Palestine, Meir was constantly involved in political and labor affairs and frequently rose to leadership positions. One of her many abilities was being a prodigious fund-raiser. While she also had great political skill, she was often pushed aside on the basis of her sex. Still, she became the Jewish observer to the 1938 Evian conference in France, which struggled with issues of Jewish persecution by the Nazis in Europe. Later she was one of the signatories of the 1948 Israel Declaration of Independence.

After the new country was established, Meir served first as labor minister and then foreign minister. She consistently raised much-needed funds. She became prime minister in 1969 when her predecessor Levi Eshkol died. She became visible to the world during the Yom Kippur War, named for the day that Egyptian President Anwar Sadat launched an attack on Israel. Prior to the outbreak of conflict, Israeli intelligence sources gave conflicting appraisals of whether the Arabs really intended to attack. Her most trusted adviser, Moshe Dayan, hero of the 1967 Six Day War, believed that they would not. However, in the final hours it became clear that Sadat and his allies were serious; they would go to war. Then Meir faced the choice of launching or not launching a preemptive strike. Her bet was that doing so would sacrifice US and international support. She stood down.

When the conflict actually started, Sadat's hope was to defeat Israel quickly and regain the losses from the 1967 war, a conflict in which Israeli armies and air forces soundly defeated the armies of Egypt, Syria, and Jordan. While for a time Israel was on the brink of destruction, in just a few days Israeli counterattacks crossed the Suez Canal to threaten Cairo. An invasion there would most likely have caused a much wider war involving the United States and the Soviet Union.

The film *Golda* shows Meir talking to US Secretary of State Henry Kissinger and telling him that there was "trouble with the neighbors." She used her personal relationship with Kissinger to gain his support for finding a way out that would not lead to a wider war. Eventually a cease-fire was arranged with Israeli combat units in the outskirts of the Egyptian capital. Escalation was avoided.

After the war, there was much criticism of Meir. However, Kissinger agreed that a preemptive Israeli attack would have cost the country dearly in international support. An investigative commission in Israel found that Meir "acted wisely, with common sense," and largely agreed that she had done the right thing. Four years later, Anwar Sadat launched an unprecedented effort to make peace with Israel by going to Israel and speaking to the Knesset. One Egyptian diplomat said it seemed like a biblical vision. Many Israelis were ecstatic at the initiative. At the Ben-Gurion airport in Jerusalem, Sadat met Meir. They both said that they had hoped to make contact much earlier. But now that the time had come, Meir looked at Sadat and said, "Shalom, Welcome."

Meir died of lung cancer shortly after Sadat's visit to Jerusalem but before the 1978 Camp David Accords led to a peace treaty between Israel and Egypt. Her restraint during the Yom Kippur War paved the way for both. For us she is a hero for her lifelong leadership efforts to establish and support the state of Israel, despite the burdens of sexism, and for making decisions during the Yom Kippur war that made peace between Egypt and Israel possible just a few years later.

Lady Gaga: Heroic Singer, Actor, and Activist

In the early 2010s, we surveyed our students for their opinions about Lady Gaga and whether she had earned the status of hero. At the time, she was a brash new phenomenon, and the jury was definitely still out. While very few of our students were willing to assign the label "hero" to her, they did concede that she was a great talent and a role model to many people. Several also said that Gaga could become a hero over time. These latter students were very much correct.

Lady Gaga is considered a hero for her unwavering advocacy for mental health and LGBTQ+ rights, and her efforts to combat bullying. Through her Born This Way Foundation, she has worked tirelessly to create a kinder and braver world, promoting mental wellness and empowering young people to create positive change. Her openness about her own struggles with mental health and trauma have helped to destigmatize these issues, offering support and encouragement to many who face similar challenges. Additionally, her bold and inclusive artistry has provided a powerful platform for marginalized communities, making her a symbol of acceptance and resilience.

The responses from our students years ago raise the question of what Lady Gaga, or any rising entertainment star for that matter, would have to do to be perceived as a hero. Possessing a great and unique talent certainly helps. In 2008, Lady Gaga's debut album *Fame* reached number one in the UK, Canada, Austria, Germany, and Ireland, and it peaked at number two in the United States. Since then, she has produced many excellent musical compilations and has even excelled as an award-winning actor in the acclaimed 2018 movie *A Star Is Born*. Her musical style is said to combine the elements of many legendary rock icons, including Madonna, Gwen Stefani, David Bowie, and Freddy Mercury. The latter singer's classic piece "Radio Gaga" was the inspiration for Lady Gaga's own moniker.

Following are several ways that Lady Gaga has garnered heroic admiration and acclaim:

1 **Advocacy for equal rights:** Lady Gaga has used her fame to promote equal rights, particularly for the LGBTQ+ community. Her efforts in this area have positioned her as a champion of social justice and inclusivity.
2 **Humanitarian efforts and activism:** She engages in humanitarian work and activism, advocating for causes such as mental health awareness, antibullying campaigns, and disaster relief efforts. Her commitment to making a positive impact on society has resonated with many people.
3 **Talent and creativity:** Lady Gaga's immense talent as a singer, songwriter, and performer has captivated audiences worldwide. Her unique blend of music, fashion, and artistry has set her apart and inspired countless fans.
4 **Overcoming adversity:** She has faced personal struggles, including health challenges and industry pressures. Her resilience and ability to overcome adversity have made her a relatable figure for those navigating their own difficulties.
5 **Self-confidence and authenticity:** Lady Gaga's unapologetic self-expression and authenticity have empowered others to embrace their true selves. Her journey from Stefani Germanotta to Lady Gaga exemplifies the power of staying true to one's identity.

In summary, Lady Gaga's impact extends beyond her music; she has become a hero through her advocacy, creativity, and ability to connect with people on a profound level.

Harry Belafonte: Hero of the Arts and Social Justice

The late Harry Belafonte always used his visibility as a unique musical and acting talent to speak out for and push for what he believed was right. His political views were often controversial, and perhaps cynical, but he consistently spoke with courage and authenticity, mainly for Black people in America and Africa. He backed his beliefs with financial support for people and organizations that needed help in their struggle for justice, notably including Dr. Martin Luther King, Jr.

Belafonte was born in New York City's Harlem in 1927 to Jamaican immigrants. He lived for eight years as a child in Jamaica with one of his grandmothers before returning to high school in the United States. But he joined the Navy rather than graduate and served during World War II. After the war he attended the American Negro Theatre and fell in love with acting. He befriended actor Sydney Poitier, a lifelong friend. An important mentor was the Black singer Paul Robeson, who was an active participant in Black political circles.

One of Belafonte's early breakthroughs was as the solider Joe in the 1954 musical *Carmen Jones* opposite Dorothy Dandridge and other African American actors. Despite that success, what brought him instant fame was his breakthrough 1956 RCA album *Calypso*. It featured perhaps Belafonte's most memorable hit, "The Banana Boat Song," widely known simply as "Day-O," from the song's opening line. *Calypso* was the first LP to sell one million copies in one year. It was a remarkable achievement for a Black artist in the United States. Belafonte kept recording and performing, notably on several occasions at Carnegie Hall in New York. The record of one of those appearances included the signature number "Matilda," one that is sung interactively with the audience. Belafonte was clearly a star, one who shone for many years after his initial breakthroughs.

While some individuals are regarded as heroes simply for their competence and achievements based on extraordinary abilities, Belafonte was more than an entertainer. From his earliest days as actor and singer he was involved in political struggle. He befriended Martin Luther King, Jr. shortly after Rosa Parks's refusal to move to the back of the bus in 1955 led to the Montgomery bus boycott. Among other things, King needed funds to continue his civil rights work around the country. Belafonte was in a position to help, and he did so. During this time he had a healthy skepticism about conventional white politicians, including the 1960 Democratic presidential candidate, John F. Kennedy. During the campaign, the Republican candidate Richard M. Nixon received support from one of the country's most famous Black athletes, baseball player Jackie Robinson. Robinson questioned the depth of Kennedy's commitment to civil rights. Kennedy reached out to Belafonte, but the latter was initially unimpressed. But he did suggest that Kennedy engage Martin Luther King, Jr. In the end, both King and Belafonte signed on to support Kennedy after he and his brother Robert Kennedy made phone calls to King's wife Coretta and worked with a judge to get King freed from jail in Georgia. Belafonte then played an active part in mobilizing other Black entertainers for the Democrat.

Belafonte also worked toward anti-apartheid policies in South Africa and generally opposed European colonization on the African continent. His commitment to such issues was lifelong. He became an outspoken critic of President George W. Bush's invasion of Iraq, an invasion involving thousands of Black soldiers. He had a fundamentally positive perspective on President Barack Obama but still expressed skepticism about how far Obama would push for unpopular policies, especially if they seemed to overly favor African Americans.

In all his political engagements, Belafonte was decidedly independent in his judgments and his actions. He is regarded as a hero for his enduring commitment to high quality entertainment and for his work toward civil rights and racial equality. And he was a beautiful person, in appearance and in performance, in and out of the realm of popular entertainment. He died an esteemed national figure in 2023 at age 96.

Terry Fox: The Audacious Modern-Day Pheidippides

The ancient Greek story of Pheidippides is familiar to many people. You may recall that Pheidippides was the Athenian messenger who ran 26 miles from the town of Marathon to the city of Athens to announce the Greek victory over Persia in the Battle of Marathon. He died from exhaustion immediately after delivering his message, and his story inspired the creation of today's 26-mile marathon race.

Recently, Canadian entertainer Sook-Yin Lee made a convincing argument that a heroic young man named Terry Fox is our modern-day Pheidippides. In 1979, Terry Fox was just an average Canadian college student working toward a degree at Simon Fraser University. He went to see a doctor after experiencing a lingering pain in his right knee. To his shock, the doctor diagnosed him with osteosarcoma, a rare form of bone cancer. As Fox underwent painful treatments, including a leg amputation, he was disheartened to learn how little money was dedicated to cancer research. After Fox was fitted for a prosthetic leg, he decided to do something extraordinary to raise awareness and money for research. He would run across Canada, a distance of 5,000 miles.

Fox vowed to do everything in his power to complete his run, even if he had to "crawl every last mile." When Fox informed his mother of his plans to run across Canada, she asked him why he couldn't just run through

British Columbia with a start at the Alberta border. Fox answered, "because not only do people in B.C. get cancer, people all across the country do, too, and that's why I've got to run across the country." Fox recognized the magnitude of the challenge. Very few people with two good legs have been able to run 5,000 miles. Fox, with only one natural leg, was undeterred. "I was determined to take myself to the limit for this cause," he said.

On the morning that he began his run on the coast of Newfoundland, only a tiny crowd of well-wishers were there to support him. During the first few weeks of his run, he received scant attention from the media. On more than one occasion, annoyed drivers almost ran him off the road. But Fox, a fine natural athlete, ran with remarkable determination. Stunningly, he averaged 26 miles per day, the equivalent of a daily marathon. The physical demands took its toll on Fox's body. He suffered shin splints, an inflamed knee, cysts on his stump, and dizzy spells.

It soon became clear that Fox was accomplishing his goal. As the weeks went by, his incredible run began to capture Canadians' attention. Large crowds were now greeting him at each town, and generous donations to his cause began pouring in. People were awed by Fox's courage, audacity, and gritty tolerance of pain to achieve his dream of finding a cure for cancer. As Fox passed the halfway point across Canada, it appeared that nothing would stop him from making it to British Columbia.

Unfortunately, the spread of cancer in Fox's body did stop him. Fox had run for 143 days and traveled 3,339 miles. But he was simply in too much pain to complete his journey. After conferring with doctors, he held a tear-ful press conference at which he announced that his cancer had spread to his lungs. He died a few short months later at the age of 22.

By the time of Fox's passing, his extraordinary story had galvanized Canada. Tens of millions of dollars were raised to fight cancer, and the contributions continued to stream in. Shortly after Fox's death, Canadian Prime Minister Pierre Trudeau addressed the nation: "It occurs very rarely in the life of a nation that the courageous spirit of one person unites all people in the celebration of his life and in the mourning of his death . . . We do not think of him as one who was defeated by misfortune but as one who inspired us with the example of the triumph of the human spirit over adversity."

Today, Fox's heroic status in Canada is unquestioned. Recent surveys and polls highlight that Terry Fox continues to be recognized as one of Canada's greatest heroes. For instance, in recent years, various polls and public opinion surveys have consistently placed him at the top. Notably, his legacy was celebrated during Canada's 150th anniversary, where he was frequently mentioned as one of the most admired Canadians. The annual Terry Fox Run, involving millions of participants, raises millions of additional dollars for cancer research. The story of Terry Fox reveals an important lesson about our most courageous heroes: They leave an indelible imprint on us. "He gave, gave and gave until he had nothing more to give but his life," said one fan. Fox's legacy of audacity and perseverance is forever sealed.

George Marshall: The Hero with a Plan

As we've noted before, leaders exert their impact either directly, through face-to-face interactions with their followers, or indirectly by exerting impact through the works that they create (Gardner, 1995). George C. Marshall was one of those rare individuals whose exemplary leadership was both direct and indirect. As a US Army General, he inspired his subordinates and fellow officers through direct contact with them. And later, as Harry Truman's postwar secretary of state, he influenced millions by devising a plan that helped Europe recover from the ravages of war.

Marshall's leadership skills were first tested shortly after he was appointed in 1939 to the nation's highest military rank, the Army chief of staff, by President Franklin D. Roosevelt. At that time the US Army consisted of 189,000 poorly trained and ill-equipped men. Anticipating America's involvement in World War II, Marshall coordinated a large-scale expansion and modernization that grew the army to eight million strong by 1942. Marshall proved to be a skilled planner, organizer, and delegator. He was also an inspiration to his fellow officers.

Not surprisingly, Marshall's role in planning the 1944 invasion of Normandy was pivotal. But when D-Day arrived, Roosevelt placed General Dwight D. Eisenhower in command of the operation, telling Marshall, "I didn't feel I could sleep at ease with you out of Washington." Throughout the war, Marshall was the central coordinator of Allied operations in Europe and the Pacific. Winston Churchill later credited Marshall as the "organizer" of the Allied victory.

After the war, as secretary of state, Marshall was deeply concerned about the condition of war-torn Europe, which was gripped by famine, poverty, and social ruin. He was also very much aware that Soviet Russia stood to benefit from a European collapse. On June 5, 1947, at Harvard University's commencement ceremonies, Marshall gave a speech in which he outlined a plan for the United States to provide massive assistance, in the form of money and materials, to ensure Europe's economic recovery. He referred to this plan as the European Recovery Program, but it soon became commonly known as the Marshall Plan. For his efforts to bring about world peace, he was awarded the Nobel Peace Prize in 1953.

After leaving office in 1953, Harry Truman was asked which American had made the greatest contribution in the last 30 years. Without hesitating, Truman chose Marshall. "I don't think in this age in which I have lived, that there has been a man who has been a greater administrator; a man with a knowledge of military affairs equal to General Marshall," said Truman. In an interview with Dick Cavett, Orson Welles called Marshall "the greatest human being who was also a great man . . . He was a tremendous gentlemen, an old fashioned institution which isn't with us anymore."

Sir Winston Churchill once offered this tribute to Marshall: "During my long and close association with successive American administrations, there are few men whose qualities of mind and character have impressed me so deeply. He was a great American, wise in war, understanding in council, resolute in action. In peace he was the architect who planned the restoration of the battered European economy. He always fought victoriously against defeatism, discouragement and disillusion. Succeeding generations must not forget his achievements and his example."

Florence Nightingale: The Heroic Lady with the Lamp

Great leaders and heroes are often associated with memorable nicknames. John F. Kennedy was the "King of Camelot"; the Beatles were the "Fab Four"; Babe Ruth was the "Sultan of Swat"; Charles Lindbergh was the "Lone Eagle"; Michael Jordan was "Air Jordan"; Harry Truman was "Give 'Em Hell Harry." These nicknames or phrases serve several purposes. They evoke a powerful image while capturing the most central defining feature of a hero. They also tend to be enduring expressions of endearment and respect that help preserve the memory of a person's greatness.

Florence Nightingale was nicknamed the "Lady with the Lamp" for her tireless efforts to nurse wounded British soldiers back to health during the Crimean War in the 1850s. The nickname has its origins in an article that appeared during the war in *The Times* of London. According to the article, Nightingale was "a ministering angel without any exaggeration in these hospitals, and as her slender form glides quietly along each corridor, every poor fellow's face softens with gratitude at the sight of her. When all the medical officers have retired for the night and silence and darkness have settled down upon those miles of prostrate sick, she may be observed alone, with a little lamp in her hand, making her solitary rounds" (Cook, 2012, p. 236).

Prior to the Crimean War, hospital conditions were nightmarish. Sanitary practices were poor or nonexistent, and it was common for patients to be either neglected or mistreated. Nightingale was intent on making sweeping changes to hospitals and to the practice of nursing, particularly during wartime. While assigned to a military hospital during the war, she realized that her first challenge was simply getting the military doctors to accept her and the other nurses. Once this was accomplished, Nightingale restored order to the hospital, improving patient care to the point where the death rate among patients fell by 67 percent.

But Nightingale was far more than an extraordinary leader of the nursing profession. She pioneered the use of new techniques of statistical analysis, developing the polar-area diagram, which mathematically demonstrated the rate of needless deaths as a function of unsanitary conditions. Nightingale was an innovator in developing and using sophisticated data-analytic tools, techniques, and graphical analysis to illuminate the causes and treatments of many social problems, including famine, irrigation, and healthcare.

After the war, Nightingale founded the Nightingale School for the training of nurses at St. Thomas's Hospital in London, England. She began to acquire international fame as the leading expert on military and civilian sanitation and its effects on mortality rates. In 1860, Nightingale wrote *Notes on Nursing*, a landmark book that became required reading for all nursing students at the Nightingale School and other schools of nursing throughout the world.

As with many heroes, Nightingale devoted her life to helping make the world a better place. Her career was extraordinary when one considers the fact that most Victorian women of her era did not attend universities or pursue professional vocations. She established herself as a great leader in a world dominated by men, earning the respect of both male and female subordinates and coworkers. In 1883, Queen Victoria awarded Nightingale the Royal Red Cross for her work. She also became the first woman to receive the Order of Merit from Edward VII in 1907.

Nightingale saw herself as the spiritual mother of all the men of the British army whom she had saved. "Nursing is an art," she once said, "and if it is to be made an art, it requires an exclusive devotion as hard a preparation, as any painter's or sculptor's work; for what is the having to do with dead canvas or dead marble, compared with having to do with the living body, the temple of God's spirit? It is one of the Fine Arts: I had almost said, the finest of Fine Arts."

Oprah Winfrey: The Hero with Talent, Resilience, and Charisma

By the time you've reached this point in our book, you've no doubt noticed a general pattern in the lives of many of our most treasured heroes. Great heroes often grow up in impoverished or tumultuous households (e.g., Drew Barrymore, Johnny Cash, Bill Wilson, John Lennon, etc.). Great heroic leaders confront and overcome daunting obstacles that would defeat most ordinary people (e.g., Israel Spira, Dana Reeve, Winston Churchill, Lois Wilson, and John Nash). And they show extraordinary generosity and selflessness, endowing society with many gifts and boons (e.g., John Wooden, George Bailey, Reed Richards, and Mahatma Gandhi).

Seldom does any one hero show all of these characteristics. But one contemporary hero who comes very close to fitting the ideal mold is none other than television host and philanthropist Oprah Winfrey. Fans of Oprah know her poignant history quite well. She grew up in extreme poverty and was subjected to sexual abuse by family and friends. As a 14-year-old she became pregnant but lost the baby soon after its birth. She never let her race or gender stop her from succeeding in the white-male-dominated profession of television broadcasting. And once a success, she became a tireless advocate of many humanitarian causes.

We believe that Oprah possesses one trait of leadership and heroism that has especially helped her on the road to heroism: *charisma*. When we've asked people to name the most important qualities that heroes possess, charisma is one of the most frequently listed traits. The dictionary defines charisma as "a personal quality attributed to those who arouse fervent popular devotion and enthusiasm." For the past 25 years, Oprah's magnetic personality has helped her attract legions of devoted fans. The telltale signs of Oprah's charisma are quite evident. She exudes confidence and intelligence. She is also extremely likeable, humorous, and socially skilled.

Oprah has been credited with revolutionizing the television talk show format. When she interviewed guests on her popular show, they were made to feel so utterly safe and comfortable that Oprah was able to extract highly personal information from them. The *Wall Street Journal* coined the term "Oprahfication" to describe public confession as a form of therapy. We believe that Oprah's skills as an interviewer stem largely from her charismatic personality. Devotion for Oprah was on full display during her annual "Favorite Things" episode, during which pandemonium erupted as Oprah gave away prizes to ecstatic audience members. Oprah-mania today is, in many ways, not unlike Beatlemania of the 1960s.

As with most charismatic people, Oprah has been able to wield tremendous influence over people. Two University of Maryland economists conducted a study to determine Winfrey's impact on Barack Obama's successful run for president in 2008. The study showed that Oprah's endorsement of Barack Obama was worth one million votes to him in the Democratic primary elections. Sure enough, if Winfrey hadn't endorsed him, Hillary Clinton would have earned the Democratic Party's nomination for president. In short, Oprah Winfrey was responsible for Obama's election victory and thus forever changed the world.

At a more personal level, Oprah's greatest legacy resides in way she has modeled the trait of resilience during times of adversity. She has inspired millions by teaching them the following life lessons: "Where there is no struggle, there is no strength." "The only people who never tumble are those who never mount the high wire. This is your moment – Own it." "Don't back down just to keep the peace. Standing up for your beliefs builds self-confidence and self-esteem." "The big secret in life is that there is no big secret – whatever your goal, you can get there if you're willing to work."

Winston Churchill: The Resilient Hero

Winston Churchill epitomizes one of the most important of the Great Eight traits of heroes: resilience. On the surface, Winston Churchill seems like a poor choice for a hero, particularly a 21st-century hero. He was portly, unattractive, had a slight lisp, and constantly smoked cigars. He could be surly and condescending to friends and foes alike. As a privileged member of the British aristocracy, he would seem to be particularly unattractive to Americans, who gravitate to underdog heroes. But Churchill is a hero of ours and gets our vote for being among the most important heroic leaders of the 20th century.

Churchill possesses several of the Great Eight traits. His strength and charisma while Germany was bombing England in preparation for an invasion helped inspire Great Britain to literally soldier on. (If England had fallen, Hitler arguably might have ruled Europe for decades.) Churchill's incredible speeches energized and inspired the British people. For example, one speech ended with, "We shall fight on the beaches, we shall fight on the landing grounds, we shall fight in the fields and in the streets, we shall fight in the hills; we shall never surrender."

Churchill possessed a fierce wit, a characteristic of many heroes. When Lady Astor exclaimed, "If you were my husband, I'd poison your tea!" Churchill immediately replied, "If I were your husband, I'd drink it." When another woman confronted him with, "Winston, you're drunk," he retorted, "Madam, you are ugly. In the morning I shall be sober." He described a fellow politician as a "modest man who has much to be modest about."

But Churchill's greatest strength may have been his resilience. Without his ability to overcome obstacles, health problems, and political catastrophe, he may have been out of politics when Hitler started conquering Europe. Would anyone else have been prepared to oppose and defeat Hitler?

Churchill's political career had nine lives. He became a celebrity at age 25 after escaping from a prisoner-of-war camp in South Africa during the second Boer War. He was elected to Parliament the next year. When he was 41 (in 1915), Churchill was named first lord of the admiralty and helped plan the Gallipoli campaign in the Dardanelles. It was a bold attempt to hasten the end of the first world war, but it ended in disaster, and Churchill was demoted and marginalized. He eventually was given cabinet positions again, but he damaged his political career when he opposed independence for India in the 1930s.

Hours before Germany invaded France, when it was painfully clear that Hitler would not be appeased, Churchill became prime minister. The politician who had been mocked and isolated for his obsession with Hitler's rearming of Germany suddenly was the hope of Great Britain and the world.

Whereas his political resilience was necessary to get him to this position, physical and emotional resilience was necessary to successfully prosecute the war. He suffered from depression (which he called "black dog") throughout his life, but he successfully hid it. He also had two mild heart attacks (one while visiting the White House) and pneumonia during the war. But he pressed on relentlessly, buoyed the spirits of the British people, and tirelessly and effectively devised war plans to oppose Germany. He traveled over 100,000 miles during the war years. In the end, he saw Germany and Japan surrender, though he was defeated in the 1945 election as the populace quickly turned to domestic concerns.

We respect heroes and admire them for their ability to overcome adversity. The greater the adversity, the greater the heroism required to prevail. But resilience shows us another side of a hero: The ability to triumph despite a past marred with previous failures. Churchill was just such a hero. His lengthy service to his beloved Great Britain was marked by a string of successes, but also missteps that left him relegated to the political sidelines—washed up—a has-been. Yet when an epic struggle loomed, his nation turned to him as the sole person capable of leading it to victory.

Roberto Clemente and the Night the Happiness Died

What is the recipe for heroism? Because heroism is in the eye of the beholder, there is no definitive list of ingredients. But our research reveals that especially powerful heroes often possess the following four characteristics: (1) They have an exceptional talent; (2) they have a strong moral compass; (3) they overcome significant adversity; and (4) they die in the process of helping others.

Roberto Clemente was one of those rare and extraordinary individuals who beautifully, and tragically, fit this mold of a great hero. Today, nearly four decades after his untimely death, Clemente's accomplishments, selflessness, and charisma make him an unforgettable hero. Former major league baseball commissioner Bowie Kuhn once said of Clemente, "He had about him the touch of royalty." Dozens of schools, hospitals, parks, and baseball fields bear his name today.

We won't delve into many details of Clemente's genius on the baseball field. We will say that while playing for the Pittsburgh Pirates from 1955 to 1972, he won multiple batting titles, Gold Glove awards, world championships, and most valuable player awards. He hit for average, and he hit for power. He possessed great speed and a rocket of a throwing arm. Los Angeles Dodgers announcer Vin Scully once said, "Clemente could field a ball in New York and throw out a guy in Pennsylvania."

People who knew Clemente argue that as great as he was a player, he was an even better human being. When traveling from city to city as a player, he routinely visited sick children in local hospitals. According to author David Maraniss, Clemente spent significant time in Latin American cities, where he would often walk the streets with a large bag of coins, searching out poor people. Wrote Maraniss: "To the needy strangers he encountered in Managua he asked, What's your name? How many in your family? Then he handed them coins, two or three or four, until his bag was empty." Clemente once said, "Any time you have an opportunity to make things better and you don't, then you are wasting your time on this Earth."

Clemente, a native Puerto Rican, also overcame significant adversity. He grew up in poverty. He faced discrimination, living in an era that tended to be intolerant of nonwhite, non-English-speaking people. Because baseball at the time was dominated by Willie Mays, Mickey Mantle, and Hank Aaron, Clemente was often overlooked in discussions of great athletes. Clemente was also hampered throughout his career by chronic back and neck problems. Yet he still managed to accumulate an exemplary record of achievement on the field.

To this day, the manner in which Clemente died still brings people to tears. In late December 1972, he heard that Managua, Nicaragua, had been devastated by a massive earthquake. Clemente immediately began arranging emergency relief flights from Puerto Rico. He soon learned, however, that the aid packages on the first three flights never reached victims of the quake. Apparently, corrupt officials had diverted those flights. Clemente decided to accompany the fourth relief flight to ensure that the relief supplies would be delivered to the survivors. The airplane he chartered for a New Year's Eve flight, a Douglas DC-7, had a history of mechanical problems and was overloaded by 5,000 pounds. Shortly after takeoff, the plane crashed into the ocean off the coast of Puerto Rico, killing the 38-year-old Clemente and three others.

News of Clemente's death spread quickly. In Puerto Rico, New Year's Eve celebrations ground to a halt. "The streets were empty, the radios silent, except for news about Roberto," said long-time friend Rudy Hernandez. "Traffic? Except for the road near Punta Maldonado, forget it. All of us cried. All of us who knew him and even those who didn't wept that week."

Nick Acosta, another friend, summed up the fateful night that Clemente died. "It was the night the happiness died," he said.

George Washington Carver: The Humble and Ingenious Hero

Heroes are sometimes born into dire circumstances. Their very survival while young may be in doubt, and yet somehow they endure and craft a lifetime of great heroic accomplishment. George Carver came into this world in Missouri in 1864, one year before slavery was abolished in that state. While an infant, Carver was stolen by a group of raiders who traded him back to his owners in exchange for a horse. A frail and sickly child, Carver was unable to work in the fields, but he did show an aptitude for studying plants. Little did anyone know that Carver was destined to become one of America's greatest botanists, educators, and inventors.

George Carver witnessed firsthand how the American South had been economically ravaged by the Civil War. As director of the Department of Agriculture at Alabama's Tuskegee Institute, Carver worked with another heroic African American educator, Booker T. Washington, to improve the quality of Black Americans' lives through education, skill acquisition, and economic development. Carver noticed that the farming soil of the South had been depleted by many decades of growing only cotton and tobacco. Carver urged southern farmers to diversify by planting peanuts, pecans, sweet potatoes, and soybeans – crops that would restore nitrogen to the soil while also adding protein to southerners' diets. When farmers found little demand for these new crops on the market, Carver began exploring the commercial possibilities of peanuts and sweet potatoes by embarking on an ingenious program of laboratory research.

Carver used his creative gifts to invent hundreds of new uses for peanuts, pecans, and other new crops that he helped introduce. Among the items that Carver developed were adhesives, axle grease, bleach, buttermilk, chili sauce, fuel briquettes, ink, instant coffee, wood stain, talcum powder, synthetic rubber, shoe polish, shaving cream, pavement, plastic, paper, metal polish, meat tenderizer, mayonnaise, and linoleum. These products energized the southern economy and turned Carver into a national hero.

Carver's creative output was astonishing, as was his selflessness. He did not patent or profit from most of his discoveries; he freely gave his inventions to humankind. In 1940, Carver donated his life savings to the establishment of the Carver Research Foundation at Tuskegee. He is also credited for improving race relations, mentoring children, and composing fine poetry and artwork. He exemplified the virtues of hard work, optimism, humility, and service to others.

A gifted educator, Carver was also devoted to developing character in his students. He compiled a list of eight virtues for his students to embody: (1) Be clean both inside and out. (2) Neither look up to the rich nor down on the poor. (3) Lose, if need be, without squealing. (4) Win without bragging. (5) Always be considerate of women, children, and older people. (6) Be too brave to lie. (7) Be too generous to cheat. (8) Take your share of the world and let others take theirs.

In 1939, Carver received the Theodore Roosevelt medal for restoring southern agriculture. In 1941, *Time* magazine compared Carver to the Renaissance Italian artist and inventor Leonardo da Vinci. In 1943, US President Franklin Roosevelt honored Carver with a national monument dedicated to his accomplishments. After Carver died, it was only appropriate that he receive this stirring epitaph: "He could have added fortune to fame, but caring for neither, he found happiness and honor in being helpful to the world."

Warren Spahn: The Greatest Left Hander Ever

In February 2011, President Barack Obama awarded the Medal of Freedom to over a dozen distinguished Americans, most poignantly perhaps one of his predecessors, the 41st president of the United States, George Herbert Walker Bush. Those honored included two distinguished professional athletes, baseball player Stan Musial and Boston Celtics center Bill Russell.

There is nothing wrong with Obama having recognized Musial and Russell. Musial was a true gentleman, when that accolade is hardly ever appropriate today, and he was a baseball superstar equal to his more visible contemporaries, Joe DiMaggio and Ted Williams. Bill Russell's role in the 1960s civil rights struggles deserved commendation. But other players were perhaps more worthy, including some who were war heroes from America's "greatest generation." One of the most interesting and inspiring for us is Warren Spahn of the Boston then Milwaukee Braves.

Spahn is a particularly interesting sports hero. For one, he holds the record for most career wins for a left-handed pitcher, 363, and most wins by any pitcher since the live-ball era started in the 1920s. He led the major leagues in strikeouts four times, innings pitched four times, wins eight times, and shutouts nine times. These feats are even more remarkable when we consider the trajectory of Spahn's career. He played in the majors briefly as a 21-year-old in 1942, but then served in the US Army for the next three years. He didn't win his first game until he was 25 years old, in 1946. If he had been able to pitch during the war years, he probably would have won another 50 games and would have been one of only three pitchers to win 400 games (the others being Walter Johnson, 417 wins, and Cy Young, 511).

Be that as it may, his war record is of some note. He fought in the Battle of Bulge and at the Ludendorff Bridge, and he won Purple Heart and Bronze Star medals. Early in his career, manager Casey Stengel thought Spahn didn't have enough courage and aggressiveness to succeed as a major league pitcher. He cited that judgment as one of his biggest gaffes: "I said 'no guts' to a kid who went on to be a war hero and one of the greatest" pitchers of all time.

For his achievements as a war veteran and as perhaps the most durable and effective pitchers of all time, Spahn is included in our list of heroes. And there is another reason he deserves recognition. He was one of baseball's greatest wits. Baseball buffs know that Willie Mays's first hit was a dramatic home run off Warren Spahn in 1951. Spahn reminisced about the moment. First, he said, "I'll never forgive myself. We might have gotten rid of Willie forever if I'd only struck him out." He added that the pitcher's mound is 60 feet, 6 inches from home plate, and that for 60 feet it looked like "a helluva pitch." (Mays tormented Spahn, hitting 18 home runs off him, a career record for a hitter against a pitcher.) Most notably, during the 1957 World Series, which the Braves won, a sports columnist asked Spahn whether that was the most pressure he'd ever faced. Spahn deadpanned, "Well, there was the Battle of the Bulge."

Warren Spahn, on several counts, was a great American hero.

George Washington: The Indispensable Man

As President's Day in February is celebrated in the United States each year, Americans honor one of the most important heroes in their history, the person called the "Indispensable Man" by definitive biographer James Thomas Flexner. Although most Americans know that Washington was the first president and led the Continental Army to victory in the long Revolutionary War, he is something of a plaster saint. He kept his contemporaries at a distance and maintained a dignified and elevated persona for most of his public life. What was Washington like, and what is *most* but also *least* heroic about him?

The biographical sketch is familiar. Washington became a wealthy landowner in Virginia in the mid-1700s. As a young man, he served bravely but not always brilliantly in the Virginia militia, but well enough to be an obvious choice to lead the first Continental Army starting in 1775 at the age of 43. He won the war mostly by not losing decisively and by not letting the British destroy his army. Quite remarkably, he resigned from the army after the war, though he easily could have become a military dictator or even king.

The British monarch, George III, asked what Washington would do after the war. When told that he would simply go back to his farms, the king said that if he did that, he would be the greatest man in the world. After just a few years back at Mount Vernon, Washington was convinced to attend the constitutional convention in Philadelphia in 1787, and he served as its president. When the executive branch of the new government was created, many of its specific duties were left unclear. Everyone knew that Washington would be the first president and that he would conduct the office honorably and effectively. He was elected unanimously for two terms, the only man to be so chosen. He left office exhausted two years before his death but succeeded in firmly establishing our system of government.

Washington was highly emotional but very tightly controlled. He was thin-skinned and extremely sensitive to slights. Nevertheless, he could arise above the hurt and anger that went with his responsibilities and almost always do the right thing.

Perhaps the most interesting and complex aspect of Washington's life, both personally and professionally, is what he did and did not do regarding slavery. When he took command of the armies in 1775, no African Americans, even those who were free, were allowed to fight. But war challenged national prejudices. Manpower requirements led Washington to recruit Black people and even to promise freedom to some of those who fought. By the end of the war, perhaps 15 percent of the Continental Army, including the most effective units, was Black.

At the same time, Washington developed deepening doubts about the morality of slavery. Some of the young men who influenced him most, including the French general Lafayette, urged Washington to act to move the new nation toward emancipation. They refused to let Washington ignore the glaring contradictions between the lofty republican principles of equality on which the nation was founded and the institution of slavery. Still, Washington did little to free slaves at Mount Vernon or to support early abolition proposals from Benjamin Franklin and others. Political and economic considerations, both public and private, led Washington to back away from what he knew clearly was right.

However, in his last act Washington did all that he could to steer the country in the right direction. He freed his own slaves in his will. Unfortunately, few others followed. It would take another great president, Abraham Lincoln, to oversee the end of American slavery.

Mikhail Gorbachev: A Revolutionary Hero in the Kremlin

On Christmas Day 1991, the United States and its allies in what was known as "the free world" received a holiday present that had been "devoutly wished for" for nearly four decades. Mikhail Gorbachev resigned the presidency of the Soviet Union, and its government went out of existence. Gorbachev was immediately replaced by Russian President Boris Yeltsin. The Americans had won the Cold War.

Mikhail Gorbachev behaved heroically in taking a series of steps that produced a peaceful revolution, one that changed not only the states within the former Soviet Union, but the whole world. Gorbachev came to power in the Soviet system as a minister of agriculture and by the early 1980s was overseer of the Soviet economy. In 1985, he became general secretary of the Communist Party when his three elderly predecessors – Leonid Brezhnev, Yuri Andropov, and Konstantin Chernenko – died, one after the other, in the course of three years.

Gorbachev was only 54 years old and sought to breathe new life into a sclerotic system with a repressive government and a floundering economy. His leadership was marked by two departures that would have been unheard of under earlier Soviet rulers: *Perestroika*, meaning restructuring, and *glasnost*, meaning openness. Under *perestroika*, Gorbachev tried to open up the governmental structure to make it more adept in keeping up with changes in the global economy. Under *glasnost* he attempted to make more room for divergent political opinion and even press criticism of the Communist Party. Gorbachev went so far as to allow other political parties to field candidates in elections.

On the international front, Gorbachev cultivated improved relations with the west and managed to build constructive bridges to both the United States and the United Kingdom, even though they were both led at the time by outspoken anticommunists, President Ronald Reagan and Prime Minister Margaret Thatcher. Famously, Thatcher once told Reagan that Gorbachev was someone they could do business with.

The most important events in Gorbachev's time in office centered around the decline of Communist dictatorships in the Soviet satellite states of East Germany, Hungary, Czechoslovakia, and Romania. In each case, opposition groups within the country began to challenge party orthodoxy and official repression. In each case, observers wondered whether the Soviets would intervene and crush liberalization as they had in Hungary in 1956 and Czechoslovakia in 1968. On a critical October night in 1989, Gorbachev made it clear he was not going to send in Russian troops to crush protesters at the Berlin Wall, and in a wave of euphoria citizens crossed from East to West Berlin and back. The wall was literally chipped away in the ensuing days and weeks.

Despite all the reforms, the Soviet economy could not make the progress needed to legitimize Gorbachev's approaches, and he was forced out of office. But by that time the creaking, repressive regime had fallen apart. Soviet republics gained their independence and a promising new era began. Like many such revolutionary movements led by a true hero, many of the achievements were rolled back. But Mikhail Gorbachev was a heroic leader for world peace and an easing of international tensions. Fittingly, he was awarded the Nobel Peace Prize in 1990.

Twelve Angry Men: A Most Unlikely Hero

In his classic text *Social Psychology*, Roger Brown argued that the character played by Henry Fonda in the 1957 film *Twelve Angry Men* is a special kind of hero. Fonda's character combines intelligence and virtue, or as we have framed it in our book *Heroes*, competence and morality. Those personal qualities allow the lead character in the movie based on Reginald Rose's play to achieve something that we know almost never takes place. That is, he convinces a jury of 11 other men who all vote "guilty" to switch their vote to "not guilty." In real life, the majority position, especially an 11-1 majority, almost always wins. How does Henry Fonda pull off this near-miracle, and why does the action of the play make the outcome seem so plausible?

The research on group polarization shows that group decisions generally reflect whatever outcome the majority of information and arguments in a situation actually favors. Therefore, in a trial, the verdict typically reflects the evidence and argument that emerge during the trial. But in the case of *Twelve Angry Men*, Henry Fonda is able to show that much of the trial evidence and testimony that pointed toward a guilty verdict is flawed or misleading. He is even able to discredit the testimony of an eyewitness. While this is quite clever, in a real trial the defense lawyer would have done what Fonda does during the jury deliberation. Roger Brown argues that in this case the jury deliberation is, in effect, a retrial. So Fonda becomes a hero on the basis of his intelligence. He is insightful and well-reasoned.

But morality is also built into his character. He is a good guy. He wears a white suit. He is calm and kind. He establishes warm relationships with other apparently good people in the room and maintains a polite distance from those who are bullying, bigoted, bored or bombastic. He shows respect for an old man, an immigrant, a young man from the slums, and a meek middle-aged man whom everyone else ignores. As one person after another is persuaded, either by information and argument or because they identify with Fonda and want to be on his side, we find that the good guys vote "not guilty" and the villains hold out for a conviction. The latter are all revealed to be biased or just plain too preoccupied to care about the defendant's life. There is, Brown argues, a correlation between verdict and virtue in Rose's play.

It is common for fictional heroes to combine morality and competence. Two examples from our earlier book are Randle Patrick McMurphy from the novel *One Flew Over the Cuckoo's Nest* and Rick Blaine, Humphrey Bogart's character in the classic movie *Casablanca*. In their case, and in many others, the competence is established early, and the question is whether their morality will rise to the top. In Henry Fonda's case, the sequencing goes the other way. His morality, his "good guy-ness," is clear from the outset. The drama of the play and movie centers around whether he will have the ability to persuade others to do the right thing. When he does, however unlikely such an achievement may be in real life, the script makes it seem perfectly plausible. We leave the movie feeling quite satisfied.

Importance of the First Follower

There is one important and often overlooked aspect of heroic leadership. It is the essential truth that *the first follower makes heroic leadership possible*. We all know that heroes can't do their heroic work alone. Sometimes a hero standing alone, expressing an unpopular message, is seen as a dangerous lunatic. This scenario describes what happened to Henry Fonda's character at the beginning of *12 Angry Men*.

Fonda needs at least one follower, or else he and his heroic ideals will be squashed. Sitting next to him, Juror 9 takes a chance and steps up joins Fonda, not necessarily because Juror 9 agrees with Fonda, but because he believes that with a life at stake all voices should be heard. Juror 9 is keeping an open mind to a possible truth.

Fonda's character endures some ridicule and pressure to change his vote to guilty, and when Juror 9 joins Fonda, he is also at the receiving end of derision and anger. Juror 9's courage and risk-taking is arguably as heroic as Juror 8's. By stepping up to support our lone heroic leader, Juror 9 allows time for the jury to reconsider some of the evidence in the case. During the ensuing jury discussion, one piece of crucial evidence loses credibility, leading to another juror, Juror 5, to change his vote to not guilty.

At this point our hero, Henry Fonda, has a solid backing, a critical mass of followers. There are now two legitimate factions in the group rather than one lone nut against the world. Juror 9 made this possible and also opened the door to Juror 5 and others to be receptive to a different interpretation of the facts of the case. The movie *12 Angry Men* is a compelling story of heroism at several levels. It showcases the courage needed to be the only dissenter in a group, and the equal courage to be the first follower of that dissenter.

Heroism is not the monopoly of great leaders; it is also a central characteristic of great followers.

11 Transfigured Heroes
The Cognitive Construction of Greatness

The Jungian concept of archetype implies that we are motivated to notice objects, events, or people who correspond to our evolutionarily based unconscious latent images. For example, Jung (1969) wrote about the *demon* archetype. Human beings have a readiness to perceive human or animal creatures as demons and to react to them accordingly. They might be repelled by them, or maybe held in fascination. Archetypes seem to follow the rules of schematic perception such that when there is enough similarity between an object and an archetype, the object will be seen as an exemplar of the archetype. In accordance with Piaget's (1952) principles of assimilation and accommodation, objects that are reasonably similar to schemas or archetypes will be misperceived or misremembered slightly so that they actually do fit the schema. This is the process of assimilation. Also, perceptions that are assimilated to schemas can, by varying from the schema in small ways, actually change the schema. Piaget referred to this process as accommodation. The schema changes to accommodate the perception of the object.

Some of our favorite examples, described in this chapter, are iconic lines from movies. Often the line is so good and so appropriate, it is recalled exactly. For example, Roy Scheider in the movie *Jaws* famously tells actor Robert Shaw, "You're going to need a bigger boat" after seeing the huge shark that has terrorized the town of Amity. Sometimes, however, the line is altered, or "transfigured," to make it more fitting and expressive. People remember Clint Eastwood in the movie *Dirty Harry* asking the villain, "Do you feel lucky?" as the bad guy thinks about reaching for his gun. Of course, the actual line is, "You've got to ask yourself a question. Do *I* feel lucky?" Similarly, we think of Kevin Costner in *Field of Dreams* standing in his corn field hearing a voice saying "If you build it, they will come." People use that phrase frequently to express the idea that people will be drawn to attractions that are constructed for them. If they utter those words, it's another example of misremembering and misquoting. Costner hears "If you build it, *he* will come," referring to

DOI: 10.4324/9781003328681-11

Shoeless Joe Jackson. But "if you build it, they will come" is a handier phrase in everyday conversation. Similarly, people combine phrases from the famous Sherlock Holmes stories and recall him saying, "Elementary, my dear Watson." But those exact words never appear in Sir Arthur Conan Doyle's stories or novels. There are variations, but the misremembered line best summarizes our sense of the way Holmes talked to Watson.

Just like quotes from movies or stories, heroes are misperceived and misremembered to make them more heroic. We transform them to make them fit the *hero* archetype or schema more perfectly. Individuals so misperceived fall into the category we called transfigured heroes. As the following profiles illustrate, transfigured heroes can be created from either real people or fictional ones. For example, we will discuss Marty Robbins's classic country song "Big Iron." Its lyrics tell relate how the mysterious rider who suddenly appears in town is transformed from a threatening stranger ("no one dared to ask his business, no one dared to make a slip") to the handsome Arizona Ranger come to capture the outlaw Texas Red, dead or alive. Woody Guthrie's song "Pretty Boy Floyd" transforms a real, fairly ruthless fugitive from the law into a well-meaning folk hero resisting the corrupt establishment.

Another of our sketches profiles Betsy Ross, lionized for sewing the first American flag in Philadelphia to help General George Washington inspire the dispirited Continental Army. It is not at all clear that she did that. But the heroic myth lives on. Our need for inspiring figures who help the noble cause shaped the persona of Betsy Ross until she was converted into a transfigured hero.

Some of our research work has emphasized the *death positivity bias* (Allison & Eylon, 2005; Allison & Goethals, 2008; Allison et al., 2009). We often evaluate people who have died more positively after their death. This is especially true when they are young and when they were killed violently. The so-called Kennedy myth sprang up almost immediately after the charismatic President John F. Kennedy was assassinated in 1963. Kennedy was not only suave and good-looking, he was the youngest man elected to the presidency, at age 43, and the youngest to die, at age 46. His life and death were such that he became an ideal candidate for becoming a transfigured hero.

Our other transfigured heroes include Merlin, legendary wizard from King Arthur's court. We are grateful to Jesse Shultz for contributing this piece. We also profile the famed aviator Amelia Earhart, the Chilean miners who were rescued after being trapped underground for more than two months in 2010, St. Patrick, and the legendary Robin Hood, who we are told, robbed from the rich and gave to the poor. In each case we find the story of a person who demonstrated unquestioned heroism transfigured so that he or she fits the hero schema even better than before.

Robin Hood: The Thief Who Became a Hero

One of the most enduring heroic figures in western legend is that of Robin Hood. Yet we don't even know whether he was a real person. He might have been a yeoman farmer and an authority-defying outlaw back in 13th-century England. But real or not, through court records, ballads, plays, and poems, the supposed hero emerged. We call Robin Hood an amalgamated hero (Allison & Hutchins 2024). An amalgamated hero is a legendary cultural hero who consists of a complex blending of similar historical figures and our own cognitive embellishments of those figures.

Robin Hood's heroism is based on his mission to steal from the rich and give to the poor. His enemies and allies make his story compelling: Maid Marion; John Little, or Little John; Friar Tuck. And then there are the villains, the Sheriff of Nottingham and the wicked Prince John, brother to the noble King Richard the Lion Hearted.

In 2010, Robin Hood was back in the movies, this time portrayed by Russell Crowe. Through what evolving narrative did he get there? Let's work backward, starting with Crowe, bearded and scowling, returning from war in the Middle East. Nearly 20 years earlier, we encounter Kevin Costner, also returning from war in the Middle East, but this time clean-shaven. Rewinding further back through dozens of appearances in films and television to Errol Flynn's definitive 1938 portrayal, we encounter a moustache and goatee taken directly from the lip and chin of Douglas Fairbanks's 1922 silent film. We can easily push back another five hundred

Robin Hood, Robin Hood statue outside of Nottingham Castle
Source: Photograph by Mike Peel (www.mikepeel.net)

years through the aforementioned novels, plays, and poems to Robin's earliest appearances in popular ballads.

Starting with the earliest conceptions, we see a typical evolution of the heroic legend with the times. For example, in the 16th century, the folk hero, the yeoman, the bandit, and the enemy of the prince is suddenly granted an earldom. And soon the narrative has him going along with Richard to fight in the crusades.

How might the story have grown? Robin is a common enough diminutive of Robert, one of medieval England's most popular names. Hood simply signals that he wore a hood, as bandits were commonly supposed to do. Since the earliest appearances of the name are in court records, we are tempted to suppose that the name Robin Hood was simply applied to any unnamed bandit. Then the saga evolved until various outlaw stories were conflated into the mythical bandit prince we now call Robin Hood.

Over the centuries, Robin Hood would fill many roles. He may have begun as a story told around the campfire, where his first job was to defy authority, perhaps any authority, but certainly illegitimate authority. He does this admirably. As he looms larger, he is assigned a number of other jobs. As an emerging hero, he must be more than a murderer and a thief. His moral development must happen quickly. He soon learns to rob only from the rich. This strategy may reflect common sense more than ethics, because the rich tend to have more worth stealing. So fairly soon he learns not only to rob from the rich but also to give to the poor.

Robin Hood thus becomes a quite perfect hero. He fights the good fight, for the common good, against the privileged forces of evil. He is wise, competent, and ethical. He is charismatic enough to become a leader of men and dashing enough to be an object of affection for women. And his legend becomes a model for many others, including Jesse James and Pretty Boy Floyd. Russell Crowe put his own gloss on the story, but its basic elements have been present for centuries.

Big Iron: A Western Hero Narrative

Fiction not only provides us with examples of heroes – from Sherlock Holmes to Superman, from Wonder Woman to detective Brenda Lee Johnson in the television series *The Closer* – it also illustrates familiar hero narratives. One kind of fiction rich in hero narratives is popular songs. In our society, songs about the old West, like comic books, pulp fiction, and movies about that time and place, have given us some wonderful poetry depicting hero narratives. One in particular stands out: "Big Iron," by country & western singer Marty Robins.

The song opens describing a mysterious stranger who rides into town and may be up to no good. Because of his large gun, the "big iron," he is a potential threat to society. Because he keeps his own counsel ("Hardly spoke to folks around him, didn't have too much to say"), he is clearly scary: "No one dared to ask his business, no one dared to make a slip, for the stranger there amongst them had a big iron on his hip." As long as his silence continues, the belief that he is a bad guy intensifies and spreads: "He's an outlaw loose and running came the whisper from each lip, and he's here to do some business with the big iron on his hip." But as it turns out, there are worse people in town, especially "an outlaw by the name of Texas Red," who had already gunned down 20 men.

Soon the strange rider lets it be known that he is an Arizona ranger whose sole mission is to eliminate Red, one way or another: "He came here to take an outlaw back alive or maybe dead, he said it didn't matter he was after Texas Red."

As events unfold, Texas Red learns that the ranger is after him, and they meet in the center of town for a gunfight. The song reveals that the scary stranger has now become a good-looking hero, but he is also the clear underdog: "Folks were watching from their windows, everybody held their breath, they knew this handsome ranger was about to meet his death." But of course the stranger (now hero) prevails, in some of the most famous lines from country & western music: "And the swiftness of the ranger is still talked about today. Texas Red had not cleared leather 'fore a bullet fairly ripped, and the ranger's aim was deadly with the big iron on his hip."

The arc of the narrative in this case is typical. Dramatic tension is created by a mysterious and possibly sinister individual who represents a potential threat to a community. But this town already has a villain, and the stranger gets transformed in the locals' minds when they discover that he represents good rather than evil. He becomes the "handsome ranger" with the stunning skills needed to defeat a seemingly unbeatable foe.

Villains should avoid hubris. In the most common narratives, the good guys finally win. In the case of Texas Red, though "vicious and killer," "he made one fatal slip, when he tried to match the ranger with the big iron on his hip."

Willie Mays's Catch: The Iconic Image of a Hero

James Hirsch's biography *Willie Mays: The Life, The Legend* brings back memories of heroic greatness for those old enough to have watched or read about "The Say Hey Kid" during the 1950s and 1960s. It also creates a new hero for those too young to have followed baseball in those storied decades. One reviewer of this account of Mays's career is moved to ask whether perhaps Mays really was the greatest who ever lived. While not the hitter that Babe Ruth and Ted Williams were, Mays did hit 660 life-time home runs, trailing only Hank Aaron and Ruth from the pre-steroids era, and posted a career batting average over .300.

But as Hirsch makes clear, Mays the batsman was eclipsed by Mays the fielder and Mays the base runner. And while it's been said that Mays's glove was where triples go to die, his throws overshadowed his catches. In 1951, when Mays was rookie of the year, a teammate said that it was dangerous to cut off his throws back to the infield. You might get your head taken off. A ball thrown by Willie Mays from the outfield still had plenty of heat on it when the catcher nabbed it for a putout at the plate.

Heroes are situated in time and place, and Mays was no exception. Jackie Robinson and Larry Doby broke the color lines in the National and American leagues, respectively, in 1947. But they were mature, comparatively well-educated men when they reached the majors. Willie Mays was barely 20 in his first year, and his exuberance, his innocence, and his all-out effort on every play lit up New York and other major league cities as few players ever had. The game had become plodding, as teams waited for one of their sluggers to hit game-winning homes runs. Mays charged ground balls that got through the infield and even threw out a casual runner at first base. Only the reckless few tried to take the extra base on Mays's arm.

Not only was Mays lucky to be one of few African American players to reach the majors as a comparative youngster, he was fortunate to play in one of the oddest shaped ballparks in the big leagues. New York's Polo Grounds had the deepest center field in baseball and provided the perfect stage for Mays to demonstrate his glove and his arm.

Heroes are often known through specific images or associations. Most Americans know almost nothing about Nathan Hale but can recite what they've been taught are his famous last words, "I only regret that I have but one life to give for my country." In Willie Mays's case, there is the "Say Hey" association, but trumping that is a visual image, called simply "the Catch." In the first game of the 1954 World Series, the heavily favored Cleveland Indians had runners on first and second with no outs in the eighth inning. The score was tied, 2-2. Indians slugger Vic Wertz is said to have "crushed" a pitch that would have been a three-run homer in any other park with any other center fielder. But Mays famously ran it down. On YouTube you can watch that famous catch, and what Mays regards as more difficult and important: his throw back to the infield, preventing Larry Doby from scoring from second base.

Most baseball heroes are linked to numbers – 60 for Babe Ruth, 755 for Hank Aaron, 56 for Joe DiMaggio. But in Willie Mays's case, the timeless image of his catch and throw lifts him to the highest level of sports heroism.

Sherlock Holmes: An Enduring Fictional Hero

Our research on heroism shows that a small but significant portion of the heroes that people claim to have are fictional. Fiction writers can create characters who are unusually clear and prototypical examples of heroes. These characters exemplify the defining traits of morality and competence with no ambiguity and little nuance. They are ideal types, such as Superman or Wonder Woman.

But many fictional heroes are more real and much more interesting on account of their idiosyncrasies, sometimes endearing, sometimes annoying, sometimes both at the same time. Often these heroic figures have sidekicks or partners, who function as straight men by providing a foil for the hero, allowing them to reveal their more human, unique, and engaging characteristics.

One example is the detective Sherlock Holmes. Created by Sir Arthur Conan Doyle in 1887, Holmes is presented through the stories told by his partner, Dr. John Watson. Watson first meets Holmes in Doyle's short novel *A Study in Scarlet*. They are both looking for rooms and decide to move in together at 221B Baker Street. Trying to figure out the kind of work Holmes does, Watson makes a list he labels "Sherlock Holmes – his limits." It starts "Knowledge of Literature – Nil." The same for philosophy and astronomy. His knowledge of politics is feeble, botany variable, chemistry profound, and sensational literature "immense." "He appears to know every detail of every horror perpetrated in the century."

Watson soon learns that Holmes is a consulting detective and quickly becomes an assistant and chronicler of Holmes's adventures. As we learn more about the pair, we come to feel sympathy for Watson having to live with the eccentric Holmes. Holmes rebukes Watson for not using his head – "You see, but you do not observe." He criticizes Watson's stories for being too dramatic and sensational while ignoring their important demonstrations of inference and deduction. Furthermore, Holmes can be quite rude to his housekeeper, Mrs. Hudson, and treats the Scotland Yard police, especially Inspector Lastrade, with disdain.

Still, we find Holmes a convincing hero. His acute mental abilities, his irreverent but dashing style, and his independence in judging the perpetrators of crime make him a compelling figure. He doesn't always follow the letter of the law, but he does act justly and humanely. Although he seems perplexed by women and leaves the "fairer sex" to Watson, we are impressed by his kindness and his admiration for particular women. In fact, the first short story in Doyle's several collections of Holmes mysteries is about the stunning Irene Adler, the character Holmes always referred to as "*the* woman." Holmes admires her character and willingly acknowledges that she outsmarted him.

Several of the Holmes stories – "The Hound of the Baskervilles," "The Speckled Band," and "The Red Headed League" – have kept his legend alive for more than a century after they were written. Some of his verbal jousts, such as the one regarding "the curious incident of the dog in the night-time" ("The dog did nothing in the night-time." "That is the curious incident."), have found their way into everyday conversation. The Holmes character is unique enough yet flexible enough to support stories written by many other authors and portrayals by many different actors, on stage and on screen, the most recent being Benedict Cumberbatch in the 2011 and 2012 Masterpiece Theatre series *Sherlock*. Time will tell whether Holmes will keep providing us a compelling hero template. The signs look good that he will. Both film and television sequels are reportedly taking shape.

Amelia Earhart: Bold Achiever of Mystery

Mystery is an important yet often overlooked aspect of heroism and villainy. Mysterious people and circumstances draw our attention, and the way we resolve those mysteries affects our appraisals of good or evil. Consider the classic movie *Casablanca*, where the audience is drawn to the lead character, Rick, because his past allegiances and present intentions are shrouded in mystery. When Rick makes the right choice in the end, we celebrate his great heroism. Another striking example of a powerful mysterious hero is found in the country & western song "Big Iron." The lyrics describe how the citizens of a town become wary of a mysterious stranger who moves into town and keeps a safe distance from the townspeople. Big Iron eventually defeats the town's villain in a gun battle, eliminating the mystery and catapulting Big Iron to the status of hero.

The details surrounding the deaths of many celebrity heroes, such as Marilyn Monroe, John F. Kennedy, and Elvis Presley, are also replete with mystery, and our efforts to make sense of those details only enhance the heroes' reputations. Such is the case in the remarkable story of the famed aviator Amelia Earhart. Audacious and unconventional, Earhart blazed a trail of achievement and adventure during the 1920s and 1930s that few people, male or female, have since been able to match.

As a young girl in 1907, just a few years after the Wright Brothers' famed first flight, Earhart got her first glimpse of an airplane at a state fair. She was unimpressed. "It was a thing of rusty wire and wood and looked not at all interesting," she said (Butler, 1999, p. 34). During her late teens Earhart attended a stunt-flying exhibition, during which one of the stunt pilots mischievously nose-dived his plane down toward Earhart and her friends. They dove for cover, but Earhart stood her ground. "I did not understand it at the time," she said, "but I believe that little red airplane said something to me as it swished by" (p. 35). At that moment Earhart knew she was born to fly.

Earhart soon became a pioneer in the field of aviation, at first setting records for speed and distance for women, and later breaking flying records independent of gender. Between 1930 and 1935, Earhart set seven women's speed and distance records in a variety of aircraft. On May 20, 1932, five years to the day after Charles Lindbergh's historic flight, she became the first woman to fly from North America to Europe. Earhart felt that her flight proved that men and women were equal in "jobs requiring intelligence, coordination, speed, coolness and will-power" (p. 77). Later, she became the first person, man or woman, to fly from Hawaii to California, from California to Mexico City, and from Mexico City to New York.

In an era when women were encouraged to accept a passive role in society, Earhart shattered convention in both her professional life and her personal life. She married fellow aviator George Putnam but referred to the arrangement as a "partnership" with "dual control." In a letter written to Putnam and hand delivered to him on the day of the wedding, she wrote, "I want you to understand I shall not hold you to any medieval code of faithfulness to me nor shall I consider myself bound to you similarly." Earhart believed in equal responsibilities for both "breadwinners" and retained her own last name rather than becoming "Mrs. Putnam." Aware of his wife's growing fame, George Putnam understood that many people would refer to him as "Mr. Earhart" (p. 133).

In 1937, she made the fateful decision to become the first woman to fly around the world – a total of 29,000 miles. She and her partner, Fred Noonan, departed from Miami on June 1, and by June 29, when they landed in New Guinea, all but 7,000 miles had been completed. Their next stop, Howland Island, covered more than 2,000 miles of open Pacific waters and was by far the most challenging leg of their journey. Shortly after leaving New Guinea, they flew into clouds and rain that made it difficult to use the sun and stars to chart their course. Later, dotted clouds over the ocean may have confused Earhart by casting shadows that resembled the myriad of Pacific islands. No one knows for sure why Earhart never made it to Howland Island. To this day the details of her demise remain a mystery. There has been no shortage of sightings, myths, hoaxes, urban legends, and unsupported claims. The aura of mystery has only heightened the appeal and stature of Amelia Earhart.

Merlin: Supporting Hero of Myth

A good heroic tale can often last for centuries or even millennia – the strength of Hercules, the swashbuckling of Sinbad, or the rise and fall of a king. The Arthurian tales from Britain have persisted for centuries, being retold, modified for changing times, and eventually immortalized in modern literature and film. But behind Arthur's rise to high king, his love for fair Guinevere, and his final death at the hands of his own son, Mordred, there was the wizard Merlin.

While Merlin has often been relegated to myth, the time he lived in was very much real. The withdrawal of the Roman Empire from Britain had left a power vacuum that was soon filled with various strong men and warlords. One of these was Vortigern, who came to power in 426 AD. And this is where history, lore, and myth collide, for it is in the court of Vortigern that a young Welsh boy named Myrddin enters. Vortigern had been told by his court magicians that a mysteriously crumbling tower he sought to build could only be shorn up by a human sacrifice, and that sacrifice had to be a boy with no father. Supposedly being born of a mortal woman and an incubus, Myrddin or Merlin was exactly who Vortigen needed. Merlin somehow convinced the king that it was a pool of water under the tower that was causing the collapse and that if he drained it, he would find two sleeping dragons.

This was where Merlin cast his first prophecy. Once the pool was drained, a red dragon and a white dragon emerged and began to fight. Merlin explained as the red dragon was victorious that this was Vortigern's future. He, as the white dragon, would someday fall to the red dragon. The red dragon represented two brothers, Aurelius Ambrosius and Uther Pendragon. It came to pass as Merlin had described, and he came to serve Aurelius, then Uther, and finally Uther's son, Arthur.

Unlike many other tales of heroism, Merlin's lacks almost any form of personal gain. He doesn't become the ruler of a kingdom for his efforts. Nor does he win the hand of a fair maiden with the possible exception of the fairy Viviane. He nurtured and protected young Arthur, found Excalibur, saw that when Uther fell Arthur was ready to take the throne, and directed the construction of the Round Table. Later tales told of him raising Stonehenge with his magic. In the end he asks nothing for himself, and the legend says that he still lives, awaiting a time when he will be needed again.

In a sense there is truth to the legend, for Merlin still lives on. No story of King Arthur and the Knights of the Round Table would be complete without him. He was cast as a villain in Mark Twain's *A Connecticut Yankee in King Arthur's Court*, a forgotten prince in Mary Stewart's excellent series of novels about him, and the main character in a miniseries and a TV series bearing his name. He even transcended genre and appeared in the science fiction series *Stargate*, where they persistently mispronounced his Welsh name of Myrddin. And certainly he will appear in further novels and movies, no doubt supporting Arthur or some contemporary hero on their quests. He will be there to help.

Like a true hero.

The Chilean Miner Rescue: Protecting a Heroism Narrative

The world always seems hungry for heroes. That appetite was on display in 2010 when 33 Chilean miners were set free after 69 days being trapped under a half mile of rock and rubble. At different times, all 33 miners, or their leader Luis Urzua, or the rescuers, or the Chilean president, or the whole country seemed to be heroes. An undoubtedly great event had taken place, and observers craved to identify the heroes of the historic rescue. The individual who seemed to be the most obvious was Urzua. As the foreman of the crew locked underground, he seemed to have performed magnificently as the group's leader.

Most impressive seemed to be Urzua's ability to get the miners through the first 17 days before a probe finally reached them. During that time the miners had no way of knowing whether they would ever be rescued. Urzua persuaded the men to stringently ration their food and water. They had enough for 48 hours, but Urzua anticipated that the rescue might take much longer than that. At first the men limited themselves to a few bites of tuna fish, some fruit, and a half glass of milk each day. But as the days stretched on, the men were issued rations only every 48 hours. Finally, the outside world made contact with the men, and hopes rose that they might in good time be rescued. Initial estimates were four months. But the efficiency of the rescue operation was truly magnificent. In that context, the behavior of the miners as a whole and of Urzua as leader seemed flawless.

But then other information trickled in that suggested that their story was not so simple or so neat. As the men faced starvation and possible cannibalism, discord and despair descended on the group. While Urzua tried to maintain cohesiveness, subgroups began to form, each with its own agenda. Some planned their own escape. Petty squabbles and even fist fights broke out. Some men refused to get out of bed, seemingly overcome by hopelessness and depression. As food became more limited, and the men had to drink filthy, polluted water, their bodies began to consume themselves. And their minds just waited for death.

Once the miners were contacted and hopes rose for a rescue, a very pretty picture was painted of Urzua's leadership and the miners' response to it. The narrative included the fact that Urzua was the last person to be rescued. It all seemed very tidy. However, while none of the disturbing information given previously was included in most accounts, there were signs that all was not well. For example, only 28 of the 33 miners appeared in early videos sent up to the surface. Where were the others, and why were they not seen?

Once the rescue was achieved, it seemed that what happened below ground would stay there. The men involved had no reason to air their fears, failures, and conflicts in the world spotlight. Even more, perhaps, than the miners, the public had little use for dissonant elements that might diminish the heroic story. Human beings need a steady diet of heroism. The thirst for it seems unquenchable. And few want heroic waters to be polluted by the complexities of human interaction under intense stress.

Constructing Heroic Associations: The Mandela Effect Makes a Good Line Better

There are many iconic quotes or lines from books, movies, and television that crystallize an image of a hero or a heroic moment. In this book we profile traditional hero Nathan Hale and his unforgettable last words, "I only regret that I have but one life to lose for my country." In Clint Eastwood's *Dirty Harry* movies, the image of Clint saying, "Go ahead, make my day," is unforgettable. Such quotes create a clear, sharp, and unforgettable image. But some memorable moments are made more so by readers and audiences making a good phrase even better, thus making the words even more heroic and more memorable.

Several examples are notable. We have written before about the fictional detective Sherlock Holmes and the related importance of sidekicks for many such heroes. For Holmes, that person is his friend and colleague Dr. John Watson. If people know only one specific Holmes quote, it is likely to be this comment to his partner: "Elementary, my dear Watson." That's all well and good, but in the four Conan Doyle novels and his dozens of stories, Holmes never utters that phrase. He says "elementary" often enough, and he frequently says "my dear Watson," but he never links the two. But the two go so naturally together, that they create a better image of Holmes and his relation to Watson than the many phrases that only come close to the memorable combination.

Speaking of Clint Eastwood, people easily recall one of the last scenes in Dirty Harry where the villain is deciding whether to reach for his pistol. He's uncertain whether Harry has any more bullets in his .44 magnum handgun. Harry snarls, "Do you feel lucky?" It's a popular culture phrase. But there's one problem. Eastwood never says it. Rather, he says, "You've got to ask yourself a question: 'Do I feel lucky?'" But the phrase as remembered is more natural and quotable and can be used conversationally more easily. And in fact, Dirty Harry follows up his statement with "Well, do you punk?"

Another example from film: In the well-loved movie *Field of Dreams*, the character played by Kevin Costner hears a voice in his cornfield, "If you build it, they will come." That memorable phrase is often used in conversation. It makes a point about how activity of various kinds can attract others, and it is nicely associated with the characters in the film. Except again, that's not what Costner hears. The voice in the cornfield refers to a single individual, perhaps Shoeless Joe Jackson, or perhaps Costner's father. It says: "If you build it, he will come."

One of television's most iconic series, subsequently made into a number of films and several sequel series, was *Star Trek*. And fans love Captain Kirk's line, "Beam me up, Scotty." This classic phrase underscores the role of one of Kirk's sidekicks, Scotty, who frequently is called upon to transport Kirk safely from danger. But once again, this exact phrase is never uttered.

One final example: Watch the movie *Casablanca* again and listen carefully. Does Ingrid Bergman, playing Ilsa Lund, ever smile at Dooley Wilson, the piano player, and demand, "Play it again, Sam"? The answer is no. She says variations of that line, but never uses those exact words.

Why does this happen? Human beings have a need to organize experience in coherent ways. The tendency to misremember facts about heroes in ways that enhance their heroic image is called the Mandela effect (Goethals, 2023a). We create meaning and construct memories that make the flow of events we encounter even more meaningful. This is especially true as we shape certain individuals into transfigured heroes. Vivid images, such as the Iwo Jima statue in Washington, and pithy quotes, such as "Make my day," stay with us. If we can make them even easier to remember than they are already, our constructive memories will do that for us.

St. Patrick: The Construction of a Legend

It is a well-known psychological fact that people construct a reality for themselves that suits their needs and motives. Often these constructions reflect a blending of fact and fantasy. And so it is with Saint Patrick, the patron saint of Ireland, whose legacy – real and imagined – is celebrated around the world every March 17.

Not much is known about Patrick, and as befits a legend there are some misconceptions. For starters, Patrick was not Irish. He was born in England in the year 420 AD. At about the age of 16, Patrick was captured and taken to Ireland as a slave. During his enslavement, the story goes that Patrick dreamed that God wanted him to escape in a getaway ship. Patrick fled Ireland in exactly this way, returned to Britain, and joined a monastery. After 12 years of training, he became a bishop and, legend tells us, experienced a second revelation – an angel in a dream telling him to return to Ireland as a missionary.

With the Pope's blessing, Patrick returned to Ireland to convert the Gaelic Irish, who were then mostly Pagans, to Christianity. He was quite successful at winning converts, even among the royal families. For 20 years he traveled throughout Ireland, establishing schools, churches, monasteries, and dioceses.

Legend also credits Patrick with teaching the Irish about the concept of the holy trinity by showing people the shamrock, a three-leaf clover. Another tale about Patrick is that he drove the snakes from Ireland. Different versions of the story describe Patrick using a wooden staff to drive the serpents into the sea, banishing them forever from Ireland. The fact that there never have been snakes on Irish soil is immaterial; the truth rarely deters a good legend. Patrick died on March 17, 493 AD, and for centuries the world has celebrated on that day to honor both Patrick and the Irish culture.

In our studies of why people need heroes, we have found that a common reason focuses on a hero's ability to change the world for the better. One respondent to our survey said that heroes "offer hope for good in humanity," and another wrote that heroes "courageously go on journeys that change the world." There is no doubt that Saint Patrick believed he was on a humanitarian mission to spread the word of Christianity to Ireland. The story of his path from slave to saint is inspiring, and there is little doubt that his work forever transformed the Irish people.

We have also found in our studies of heroes that their accomplishments are often exaggerated and, in some cases, fabricated. At the time of Saint Patrick, the Irish culture had a rich tradition of oral legend and myth. Orally transmitted stories are, of course, more prone to distortion over time than are written stories. Today, with regard to Patrick, it simply isn't possible to discern fact from fiction. But then, that isn't the point of any heroic legend, whether the legend is Davy Crockett, Robin Hood, or Saint Patrick. The point of any heroic story is to be entertained, educated, and inspired. On March 17, we'll all drink to that.

Hub Fans Bid Kid Adieu: Ted Williams 70 Years Later

Ted Williams is indisputably one of the sports world's great heroes. He played his last game almost 70 years ago, on September 28, 1960. It's interesting to note that Williams was 42 when he retired that year, deemed too old for his chosen profession, while at the same time, John F. Kennedy, age 43, was deemed too young for his. Furthermore, it's a fitting part of the mythology of baseball that Williams hit a home run in his last at bat. It was a dreary day at Fenway Park, and only about 10,000 fans showed up to watch the sorry Red Sox. The world has changed. It's hard to think that nowadays the last game of a sports icon wouldn't be a huge, overhyped, sold-out event.

But a hero of a different kind was also at that last game for Ted. And he helped define Williams as a hero and helped us understand just what made him a hero. That other hero is the writer John Updyke, then a 28-year-old fan who was in Fenway by accident. Apparently Updyke had "an adulterous assignation that day," but he was stood up (McGrath, 2010). So he decided to go the ballpark. And in a few weeks, he wrote his famous *New Yorker* piece, with the title of this profile, "Hub Fans Bid Kid Adieu" (Updike, 1960).

The article was important in understanding heroism because Updyke focused on some of the crucial things that were heroic about Williams. As McGrath wrote in *The New York Times*, "Updyke identified with the artist in Williams: his focus and perfectionism" and his single-minded dedication to becoming the best in his craft. Williams once said that he wanted people who saw him on the street to say, "There goes the greatest hitter who ever lived." And while many people would argue that Babe Ruth deserves that accolade, Williams holds the all-time record for one of the most important of all baseball statistics. He got on base more frequently than any other player in history, a phenomenal 48.2 percent of the time he went up to bat. (Babe Ruth is second.) While Williams didn't need Updyke to make him a hero, that writer put a human face on Williams's pursuit of excellence. He underscored the importance of dedication and focus for achievement at the highest level.

At the same time, Updyke achieved a kind of heroism on his own, albeit to a much smaller group of admirers. He changed the ways baseball, and to a lesser extent other sports, were written about. For example, he referred to Fenway as a "lyric little bandbox," injecting romanticism and fantasy into accounts of baseball. Red Smith has done that for horse racing. He is often quoted as saying that to get to the Saratoga Race Course from New York City, you "drive about 175 miles north, turn left on Union Avenue and go back 100 years." In 1960, Updyke was one of the first who wrote in that manner for baseball. Of course, Updyke had good material to work with. Williams is a hero based on his exceptional athletic gifts and his dedication to making the very most of them. Was he "the greatest hitter who ever lived"? We wonder what you think. As always, we believe that heroes exist in the eyes of the beholders.

Betsy Ross: The Hero Who (May Have) Sewed the First American Flag

On June 14, 1777, the Second Continental Congress of the United States, meeting in Philadelphia, adopted an American flag. The banner chosen was the now familiar "stars and stripes" that has been saluted and honored ever since. In recognition of Congress's action, June 14 has been observed as Flag Day for nearly a century, since President Woodrow Wilson officially proclaimed the holiday in 1916.

Most Americans know the name Betsy Ross, having been taught that she designed and sewed the first stars and stripes in consultation with none other than George Washington. That account has made her a hero of the American Revolution. But a great deal of uncertainty surrounds the creation of the flag chosen in Philadelphia in 1777.

The idea that Betsy Ross designed that flag took hold in 1870, when Ross's grandson, William Canby, published a paper telling the story of General Washington leading a committee from Congress to Betsy Ross's house to discuss the making of the new country's flag. Some historians note that 1870 was only five years after the end of the Civil War and that the American people were eager for any story that celebrated the nation's founding. They were especially receptive by 1876, the country's centennial year. Thus Canby's account fell on fertile soil. But what do we really know?

Betsy Ross was born Elizabeth Griscom in Philadelphia on New Year's Day, 1752. Her first husband, John Ross, was the nephew of a Pennsylvania delegate to the Continental Congress. Betsy and John ran an upholstery business, but their marriage was short-lived. John, a militia man during the war for independence, was killed in action in 1776. Betsy married twice more but was widowed in both instances. She had two daughters with her second husband, and five with her third. She kept working as an upholsterer until 1827. She died in 1836.

But what role did she have in the creation of the American flag? All that Ross herself ever claimed was that she contributed the five-point star to the flag, replacing the six-point star, because it was easier to make. Ross was one of many women in Philadelphia who sewed flags for the Continental Army, but we really can't know her exact contribution to designing and making the first flag.

Our understanding of heroes emphasizes that heroes and heroism exist in the eye of the beholder. Other writers have offered specific definitions of heroes. In contrast, we have observed who people name as heroes and what traits they say heroes have. We find that almost a third of the people named as heroes are fictional. In that sense it doesn't really matter whether Betsy Ross even existed (she definitely did!) or just what she contributed to the first flag. A narrative has evolved naming her as a hero, identifying her as making an important contribution to the country's founding. That's good enough for us. Her grandson's story, very likely tweaking the truth, makes her a transfigured hero.

Many people call the American flag that has 13 red and white stripes and 13 white stars in a circle on a blue field, the original American flag, the Betsy Ross. We think that's appropriate. Although we don't know all the facts, we do know that Betsy Ross is one of many women who made important contributions to the American founding. In our eyes, they are all heroes.

Pretty Boy Floyd: An Outlaw Hero

Legal briefs often include quotes from song lyrics, including those written by rock, country, and folk artists. Most often quoted is Bob Dylan, followed by the Beatles and Bruce Springsteen. The top three are not very surprising. Number four is more so: Woody Guthrie. On further thought, we know that Guthrie very much influenced Dylan and Springsteen. So his listing makes more sense.

Some of the most quoted Guthrie lines are from his ballad "Pretty Boy Floyd." The song tells of a young man forced by circumstance to become an outlaw, but an outlaw who helps the less fortunate. He is portrayed as a Robin Hood-like character, or one like Jesse James, who robs from the rich and gives to the poor. Guthrie wrote, "But a many a starving farmer, the same old story told, how the outlaw paid their mortgage and saved their little homes." Probably the most memorable pair of lines is the one most often seen in legal briefs, for obvious reasons: "Yes, as through this world I've wandered, I've seen lots of funny men; some will rob you with a six-gun, and some with a fountain pen."

Woody Guthrie's heroic portrayal of Pretty Boy Floyd has had wide influence. A rock band calls itself Pretty Boy Floyd, and Larry McMurtry wrote a quasi-fictional novel portraying him favorably. John Steinbeck contributed to the heroic construction. In his classic novel *The Grapes of Wrath*, published in 1939, the same year as Guthrie's song, the character Ma Joad refers to Floyd as someone driven to crime as a result of hardships of the Great Depression. Floyd is featured in movies and comic books as well, generally as an outlaw with a good heart.

The facts about Charles Arthur "Pretty Boy" Floyd do not tell an obviously heroic tale. He took to robbery as a young man, apparently imitating the exploits of the "Cherokee Badman," a.k.a. Henry Starr, nephew of Belle Starr, the leader of an extended family of outlaws. Newspaper pictures and headlines about Starr were compelling to young boys. After Floyd got his own start on a life of crime, he quickly graduated to many varieties of murder and mayhem. He teamed up with the notorious "Public Enemy Number 1," John Dillinger, and rose to the top of FBI Director J. Edgar Hoover's list of wanted criminals. He and a partner killed the husbands of two women they had become involved with.

But there was another side to the story, the side the song told. Floyd gained the reputation of being kind to people in his adopted state of Oklahoma, and in turn they helped him hide from the law. Most interesting about the legend created by Guthrie, Steinbeck, and others is that so many people seem ready to accept it. Are we predisposed, perhaps through the kinds of archetypes discussed by Carl Jung, to be attracted to strong, active, and perhaps handsome people (note the nickname "Pretty Boy," which Floyd hated) who challenge and defy authority? Is that why we are much moved by Guthrie lyrics such as, "Well, you say that I'm an outlaw, you say that I'm a thief. Here's a Christmas dinner for the families on relief." We need more research on why narratives like this resonate with so many people.

John F. Kennedy's Heroic Mystique

In 2010, prominently displayed in Boston on street lamps and signs was a poster saying "Jack Is Back." It was not clear from a distance what that meant or who Jack was or is. But if you were there and got closer, you would see a picture of John F. Kennedy and read that he was elected president of the United States 50 years ago. Kennedy served as the nation's leader for less than three years but was rated as the 8th greatest president in a 2021 survey of historians, and the Kennedy magic is still strong to many Americans. A half-century after his death, he is still a hero across the country and around the world, especially in Boston. What accounts for Kennedy's status as a hero to so many people after such a long time?

John F. Kennedy was the youngest elected president in US history. He won the election of 1960 at the age of 43, narrowly defeating Richard Nixon. Despite the closeness of the election, his approval rating was over 70 percent when he took office. The public was entranced with his charismatic persona and the sense of action, vigor, and energy that he conveyed. His beautiful wife Jacqueline and young children added a storybook quality to his presidency. Kennedy's popularity continued throughout his term, as he became a champion of public service and emphasized altruism and sacrifice, possibly more than any other president. Very few passages from presidential inaugural addresses are recalled or even recognized. But aside perhaps from FDR's "the only thing we have to fear is fear itself," Kennedy's call to service is the most familiar line from any inaugural address: "Ask not what your country can do for you, ask what you can do for your country." Kennedy is positively associated with the Peace Corps, with the successful resolution of the Cuban Missile Crisis – when the world stood on the brink of nuclear war – and the introduction of what became the 1964 Civil Rights Act.

But part of the Kennedy legacy reflects his tragic death by an assassin's bullet on November 22, 1963, just over 1,000 days into his administration. Research by Dean Keith Simonton (1987) shows that assassinated presidents have higher "greatness ratings" than they might have otherwise. Our own writings discuss the death-positivity effect and how assassinated people are "frozen in time" in a way that keeps their memory fresh and positive (Allison & Goethals, 2008). Also, often metaphors or apt phrases capture an idea or crystallize a feeling about an individual, an event, or even a concept. In Kennedy's case, the play *Camelot* was linked to his administration. For many, the lyrics from the final number of that play captured the sense that many Americans had of JFK's time in office: "Don't let it forgot that once there was a spot, for one brief shining moment, that was known as Camelot."

Kennedy himself would have been unsettled by this sentimental appraisal. At a commencement speech at Yale University in 1962, he asserted that "in our time we must move on from the reassuring repetition of stale phrases to a new, difficult, but essential confrontation with reality. For the great enemy of truth is very often not the lie – deliberate, contrived and dishonest – but the myth – persistent, persuasive and unrealistic." We won't judge how realistic is the heroic image of JFK. As always, that is in the eye of beholder. But we can observe that to many John F. Kennedy is one of America's great heroes of the 20th century.

12 Transforming Heroes

Those Who Forever Changed Our World

One of the last century's most important conceptual advances in the leadership literature was James MacGregor Burns's (1978, 2003) development of the idea of "transforming leadership." The basic notion was described in Burns's 1978 book *Leadership* as the kind of leadership that raises both leaders and followers to higher levels of motivation and morality. Built into this idea was the further notion that leaders can change the motives of followers by helping to satisfy their lower order needs and focusing them on more elevating motives, such as distinguished achievement, moral behavior, or fundamental values. Mohandas Gandhi is an excellent example of a transforming leader who worked tirelessly to focus more cautious Indian leaders on the goal of independence from Great Britain. Central to his success was his unwavering focus on nonviolence and *satyagraha*, or discovery of and adherence to God's truth through universal brotherhood and the force of love. Gandhi wanted people to satisfy but also simplify their basic material needs so that they could focus on higher motives. His complete embodiment of these principles inspired fellow Indians, and other leaders the world over, most importantly perhaps Martin Luther King, Jr. Burns contrasted transforming leadership with *transactional leadership*, in which leaders and followers simply work together for short periods of time to satisfy routine needs.

Bernard Bass (1998) is well-known for empirical studies of what he called *transformational* versus *transactional* leadership, a distinction very similar to Burns's distinction between transforming and transactional leadership. (Although Burns is often credited with the concept of "transformational leadership," he always used the term "transforming leadership" instead [Burns, personal communication, 2012]). For Bass transactional leadership is inspiring and highly motivating leadership that causes people to think carefully and creatively about a group's challenges. Transformational leaders attempt to instill passion and generate commitment rather than merely rewarding followers for effective performance.

DOI: 10.4324/9781003328681-12

The concepts of transformational and particularly transforming leadership apply well to the exceptional individuals whom we here classify as transforming heroes. They are people who are admired for initiating some kind of significant change in the world. They may simply be admired from afar for expressing and embodying important values – perhaps new ones, or perhaps enduring ones that have been overshadowed by other seemingly more urgent priorities – or they may actually engage and inspire people to follow their lead. That is, they may change our values or our behavior, or very often both. Nelson Mandela is an important example of a transforming hero. For some he simply made the values of more peace and reconciliation prominent and powerful. For many others of all colors in South Africa and beyond, he described, modeled, and inspired changes in the ways they thought about and worked with their fellow citizens. He was a transforming leader who became a hero, a transforming one, for the many people who followed his example.

Just as there are many kinds of heroes, within the category of transforming heroes we can distinguish two important subtypes. Some transforming heroes are leaders and heroes in specific domains. For example, the early rock'n'roll star Buddy Holly transformed popular music through his style of writing, singing, and performing iconic songs such as "That'll Be the Day." Other transforming leaders, such as Gandhi and Mandela, transformed the way whole societies were organized. They had a significant impact on people even beyond the borders of their own nations. Some transforming heroes originally have an impact only within a specific domain, but their influence spills over to much broader areas of society. For example, in contrast to Buddy Holly, the so-called King of Rock'n'Roll, Elvis Presley, not only changed popular music but also became a hero to many young men and women by showing that the social order's rules and customs could be altered. People of all ages could be more expressive and enjoy music of many different forms from many different subcultures within American society. It's been said that Elvis reminded young women that they had a body below the waist and that they could move it. If true, that is highly transformational. Similarly, former heavyweight champion Muhammad Ali not only transformed the world of boxing, he embodied a whole new way for African Americans to define themselves and relate to the larger society. In affecting African American identity, he changed the mores of interracial interaction and thus white Americans as well as Black. Along with transforming heroes like Martin Luther King, Jr. and many other ground breakers, Ali nudged the United States of America toward a more equitable society, where phrases such as "liberty and justice for all" really meant something.

Our profiles of transforming heroes include physicist Albert Einstein, whose theories of relativity transformed modern science; Christopher

Columbus, whose trans-Atlantic voyages changed world history; Haitian political activist Miriam Merlet, killed in the 2010 Port-au-Prince earthquake, who fought relentlessly for the rights of women and against the political use of rape; Elvis Presley, who transformed rock'n'roll music; and Princess Diana, whose grace and humanitarian instincts forever changed the world. These and other transforming heroes represent the pinnacle of heroic influence.

Transforming Global Heroes

Muhammad Ali: The Odyssey of a Heroic Champion

Declaring oneself a hero doesn't ordinarily do the trick. But former heavyweight champion Muhammad Ali was an international hero in the eyes of sports fans and ordinary citizens around the world. Ali began calling himself "The Greatest" early in his career and clearly alienated many. People gradually realized that his braggadocio was always part of the act, something that enabled him to perform at his best in the ring and entertain and inspire millions.

Ali's odyssey to heroism was complicated. But by the time of the 1996 Olympics in Atlanta, Georgia, there was no question as to which former American medal winner would light the torch at that year's games. Two

Mohammed Ali

Source: Dutch National Archives, The Hague, Fotocollectie Algemeen Nederlands Persbureau (ANEFO), 1945–1989

years later, it was only a bit of a surprise when corporate America fully endorsed Ali by putting him on a box of Wheaties cereal, "The Breakfast of Champions." The citation on the box credited Ali's impact in sports and beyond: "he was a courageous man who fought for his beliefs" and "became an even larger force outside the ring with his humanitarian efforts."

When Ali, then Cassius Clay, won the heavyweight championship from Sonny Liston in 1964, large portions of white America were uneasy. Although Liston was widely associated with organized crime and seemed like something of a thug, rumors also circulated about Clay being associated with "Black Muslims." Many people found this truly frightening. And although Ali's wit and boxing skills were extremely entertaining, almost as many were turned off by the talking and bragging of "The Louisville Lip" or "Gaseous Cassius." In short order, some of people's worst fears were confirmed. Clay turned to Islam and took the name Muhammad Ali. He became a vocal critic of the Vietnam War and was arrested for refusing to be inducted into the armed services.

Ali's resistance to the draft on the grounds that he was a Muslim minister struck many as ludicrous. But he fought in court for his deferment from the army and eventually won in a unanimous Supreme Court decision. However, his legal struggles kept him from boxing for three and a half years, costing him precious time at the peak of his career. But he had proved the depth and sincerity of his beliefs. At the same time, more and more people believed that he was correct to defend African Americans' rights to their own values and self-respect and in his opposition to the Vietnamese war.

Eventually Ali got the chance to win back the boxing title he had lost while he was banned from fighting, and that he failed to regain when he met Joe Frazier in 1971. The year was 1974, ten years after he first won the title from Sonny Liston. He fought and won a classic battle against George Foreman in the African nation of Zaire, now called Congo. That year he was named "Sportsman of the Year" by *Sports Illustrated*, and it was clear that most Americans had come to embrace a talented and dedicated athlete who had both overcome racial and cultural barriers and had the courage to define himself and to help and encourage other Black Americans to do the same.

After regaining the title from Foreman, Ali fought for several more years. But the numerous punches he had absorbed during his long career made him the victim of Parkinson's syndrome, a neurological disorder which makes motor activity, including walking and talking, extremely difficult. During his entire life, Ali fought outside the ring for those he regarded as his people, and he was, and is, a hero to most of America. His skill, his struggle, his commitment, his charm, and his charisma remain inspirational. He is still one of the most recognized and admired people in the world. Both he and the nation have come a long way since he burst on the scene as a sassy young fighter who perplexed or repelled much of the country. For many, he remains an important hero.

Christopher Columbus: A Globally Transforming Figure

As Columbus Day approaches each October 12, people are drawn to speculation about Christopher Columbus and his unsurpassed impact on the world we live in today. While almost everyone agrees that Columbus was transforming, people debate whether the transformations he triggered were positive or negative. Regardless of where one stands on this issue, there can be no disagreement about the fact that Christopher Columbus and his 1492 voyage to the Americas left an indelible mark on nearly every corner of the globe.

Transforming events do not take place in an historical vacuum. To understand Columbus's motivation to establish a shipping route to Asia, we must look to the city of Constantinople, now Istanbul, Turkey. For centuries, as the capital of the Orthodox Christian Byzantine Empire, Constantinople had been an important center for trade between Europe and Asia. But in 1453, the Muslim Ottoman Empire conquered Constantinople, forcing Europeans to search for a sea route to Asia that would bypass the Muslims.

Interestingly, Columbus may never have attempted his initial voyage had he not held several misconceptions about global geography. He underestimated the circumference of the earth; he overestimated the size of the Asian landmass; and he believed that Japan lay much farther east of China than in reality. He did, however, have an accurate understanding of the prevailing easterly trade winds that would propel his ships from the Canary Islands to lands far to the west. With about 90 men and sailing under the flag of Spain, Columbus's three ships were fortunate to avoid both tropical storms and the "doldrums" – pockets of sea where there is neither current nor wind.

Most of us know the rest of the story. On October 12, 1492, Columbus and his men landed on the island of Guanahani and called it San Salvador. Although he failed to reach Asia, Columbus made the western hemisphere known to Europeans, forever altering human history on a global scale. Until recently, generations of Americans grew up learning that Columbus "discovered" America – a Eurocentric notion that ignored the presence of 50 million Indigenous people inhabiting the Americas in 1492. Moreover, other Europeans, such as the Norse, had ventured to America 500 years earlier. "Columbus's claim to fame isn't that he got there first," explains historian Martin Dugard, "it's that he stayed" (Dugard, 2005).

The heroic interpretation of Columbus is that his daring voyage into unknown waters required courage and conviction. In 1989, US President

George H.W. Bush said that Columbus "set an example for us all by showing what monumental feats can be accomplished through perseverance and faith." Extraordinary changes resulted from Columbus's voyages. The Columbian exchange was established, referring to the two-way transfer of culture, foods, plants, and animals between the continents of Europe and the Americas. The Americas were introduced to crops such as wheat, rice, coffee, bananas, and olives, and animals such as horses, cows, pigs, and chickens. Europeans also received from America many important crops, such as corn, potatoes, tomatoes, lima beans, squash, peanuts, cassava, cacao, and pineapple.

The past few decades have also seen Columbus cast into the role of villain. Deadly European diseases were introduced into the Americas, including diphtheria, measles, smallpox, and malaria. The Americas, in turn, contributed a virulent form of syphilis to Europe. All told, Native American populations suffered to a much greater degree than did Europeans. Epidemics wiped out 80% to 90% of the native populations in Hispaniola, and European settlers enslaved many Native Americans. In fairness to Columbus, the worst of these problems occurred after he died, under the watch of later European governors and colonists.

In preparing this profile, we conducted an online search of "Christopher Columbus: hero or villain" and obtained over 100 online sites debating Columbus's status as hero or villain. It's clearly a muddied picture. All we can say with certainty is that Columbus's voyages had a permanently transforming effect on the world. "Every hero is somebody else's villain," said Felipe Fernandez-Armesto, a scholar and author of several books related to Columbus, including *1492: The Year the World Began*. "Heroism and villainy are just two sides of the same coin" (Fernandez-Armesto, 1991).

Mahatma Gandhi: The Hero of Truth and Peace

In our writings about heroism, we've noted the tendency of the very best among us to be vulnerable to assassination. John F. Kennedy, Anwar Sadat, Harvey Milk, and Martin Luther King, Jr., are prominent examples of heroes who were killed because their vision, courage, and skills threatened the status quo. To this pantheon of fallen heroes we add the name of Mohandas Karamchand Gandhi, commonly known around the world as Mahatma Gandhi.

As with many heroes of social movements, Gandhi's wisdom was acquired through his personal experience with turmoil and pain. While a young man in South Africa in the 1890s, Gandhi was thrown off buses, beaten by stagecoach drivers, and barred from hotels simply because he was Indian. These incidents inspired him to form a philosophy of social justice he called Satyagraha, which encourages the use of nonviolent resistance.

"The Satyagrahi's object is to convert, not to coerce, the wrong-doer," said Gandhi. Satyagraha is a combination of two Sanskrit words, "Satya" meaning *truth* and "Agraha" meaning *pursuit of*. Thus, Satyagraha captures Gandhi's belief that nonviolence is an honest and diligent quest for truth.

After using Satyagraha successfully in South Africa, Gandhi returned to British-controlled India in 1915 and led the greatest anticolonial struggle in world history. He urged Indians to boycott all things British, also using fasting as a method of protest. True to his principles, Gandhi was critical of any violence directed toward the British. "When I despair," he said, "I remember that all through history the way of truth and love has always won. There have been tyrants and murderers and for a time they seem invincible, but in the end, they always fall."

Gandhi also aimed to heal the many ethnic rifts in his country. He opposed any plan to carve up India into smaller nations; doing so contradicted his vision of religious unity. He was saddened by the formation of Pakistan because "Islam stands for unity and the brotherhood of mankind, not for disrupting the oneness of the human family. Those who want to divide India into possibly warring groups are enemies alike of India and Islam." Gandhi urged his fellow Hindus to love and befriend Muslims. He played a central role in bringing about the "miracle of Calcutta" – a miraculous peace between the city's warring Hindus and Muslims.

Throughout his life, Gandhi encouraged respect for all religions, equality of all people, and nonviolence in thought, speech, and action. Indians referred to him as Bapu (Father) and Mahatma (Great Soul). In his famous attire of loincloth and shawl, Gandhi traveled throughout India, usually on foot, inspiring hundreds of millions of people with his message of peace. One of Gandhi's lasting legacies to India is a multiparty democracy that to this day functions peacefully.

Gandhi's assassination in 1948 was followed by an enormous outpouring of grief throughout the world. Most Indians still regard Gandhi, along with Buddha, to be one of the towering figures of Indian history. Martin Luther King, Jr., who later used Satyagraha in his American civil rights movement, said that "Christ gave us the goals and Mahatma Gandhi the tactics." Albert Einstein noted that "generations to come will scarce believe that such one as this ever in flesh and blood walked upon this earth."

Nelson Mandela: The Ultimate Underdog Hero

Our studies of heroism have shown that there is nothing more inspirational to us than an underdog who triumphs over adversity (Kim et al., 2008). When we've asked people to list their most inspirational underdog heroes, the name Nelson Mandela invariably appears more often than any other. No one suffered and sacrificed more for his country than Mandela, who endured 27 years as a political prisoner before assuming his nation's highest office. "In my country," he quipped, "we go to prison first and then become President."

The classic underdog script consists of the following sequence of events: A disadvantaged person, or underdog, is the target of disrespect or oppression by others who hold greater power. The underdog seeks to achieve a noble goal but is repeatedly thwarted by the established power. There is great struggle and pain along the underdog's journey. Courage and persistence are the keys to the underdog's ultimate success. Like "The Little Engine That Could," the underdog eventually prevails and in the process wins over the hearts and minds of nearly all observers.

Mandela's life closely follows this narrative. As a young man, he was a leading member of the African National Congress (ANC), which opposed South Africa's policy of racial separation, known as apartheid. During the 1950s, he was repeatedly banned, arrested, and imprisoned. "When I was first banned," he recalled, "I abided by the rules and regulations of my persecutors. I had now developed contempt for these restrictions. To allow my activities to be circumscribed by my opponent was a form of defeat, and I resolved not to become my own jailer."

After the government outlawed the ANC in 1960, Mandela was captured, convicted of treason, and sentenced to life in prison. His trial attracted worldwide attention and sympathy. At his trial he uttered the famous words, "I have cherished the ideal of a democratic and free society in which all persons live together in harmony and with equal opportunities. It is an ideal which I hope to live for and to achieve. But if need be, it is an ideal for which I am prepared to die."

While imprisoned, he and other inmates performed hard labor in a lime quarry. Prison conditions were harsh; prisoners were segregated by race, with Black prisoners receiving the least rations. Political prisoners such as Mandela were kept separate from ordinary criminals and received even fewer privileges. Mandela described how, as a D-group prisoner (the lowest classification) he was allowed one visitor and one letter every six months. But he did not suffer in vain. His long imprisonment propelled him to international fame and adoration as a worldwide symbol of racial equality.

Released in 1990, Mandela became president of South Africa and took steps to abolish apartheid. He also earned international respect for his efforts to reconcile relations between Black and white South Africans. When his country hosted the 1995 Rugby World Cup, Mandela encouraged citizens of all colors to support the mostly white South African national rugby team, which historically had been loathed by the nation's Black majority. The team was a heavy underdog going into the competition, but miraculously it won the cup. Wearing a team jersey, Mandela presented the trophy to captain Francois Pienaar, who claimed victory for all of South Africa's 45 million citizens. This event was a pivotal moment in healing the rift between white and Black South Africans.

Nelson Mandela's triumph as an underdog certainly makes him a hero in the eyes of millions. He also fits the image of an ideal hero with other qualities such as charisma, intelligence, thoughtfulness, humor, optimism, good height (6' 4"), and good looks. This fact has not escaped the attention of Hollywood movie producers. Mandela has been portrayed by Morgan Freeman (*Invictus*, 2009), Sidney Poitier (*Mandela and de Klerk*, 1997), and Danny Glover (*Mandela*, 1987).

Martin Luther King, Jr.: The Hero of Interracial Peace

Sometimes exactly the right person for the right situation emerges to help resolve a seemingly impossible problem. To succeed, the American civil rights movement of the 1950s and 1960s required a charismatic leader who championed the cause, who commanded respect, who practiced what he preached, and who could stir the hearts of millions of followers. The Reverend Martin Luther King, Jr., was the ideal man for the job.

In our research, we've found that special iconic moments can forever define a hero. Martin Luther King, Jr.'s "I Have a Dream" speech, delivered in 1963 from the steps of the Lincoln Memorial in Washington, is indelibly linked to his passion and eloquence as a transforming hero. Following is a brief excerpt of the speech; note the power of his words:

> *I have a dream that one day on the red hills of Georgia the sons of former slaves and the sons of former slave owners will be able to sit down together at a table of brotherhood.*
>
> *I have a dream that one day even the state of Mississippi, a state sweltering with the heat of injustice, sweltering with the heat of oppression, will be transformed into an oasis of freedom and justice.*
>
> *I have a dream that my four little children will one day live in a nation where they will not be judged by the color of their skin, but by the content of their character.*

Martin Luther King, Jr., is forever associated with the noble goal of achieving a color-blind society. He is a hero to millions of people because he promoted goodwill and freedom for all people of all backgrounds. Much of the sympathy and support he drew to the cause stemmed from his embracing Mahatma Gandhi's principles of nonviolent protest. King also had the unsurpassed gift of establishing an emotional connection to his listeners. His "I Have a Dream" speech is punctuated by a very stirring use of repetition and soaring rhetoric as he inspires the world to share his vision:

Let freedom ring. And when this happens, and when we allow freedom to ring – when we let it ring from every village and every hamlet, from every state and every city, we will be able to speed up that day when all of God's children – black men and white men, Jews and Gentiles, Protestants and Catholics – will be able to join hands and sing in the words of the old Negro spiritual: Free at last! Free at last! Thank God Almighty, we are free at last!"

With this last line, the crowd listening to King erupts in a frenzy of support, love, and hope. The entire speech is a moving, mesmerizing masterpiece. The unsurpassed beauty of its message is combined with a passionate, charismatic delivery. There is no doubt that it is the speech of a legendary, impactful hero.

Our research on heroes reveals that people associate the greatest of heroes with eight specific traits: Intelligence, strength, compassion for others, selflessness, charisma, inspiration, reliability, and resilience. There is no doubt that Martin Luther King, Jr., embodied all of these Great Eight traits. He was exactly the hero that America needed to guide it through painful but necessary social changes. King was indeed a hero who overcame great obstacles to achieve a beautifully noble goal. The only thing he couldn't overcome was the assassin's bullet that killed him in Memphis in April 1968. The world still mourns the loss.

Thomas Jefferson: We Hold These Truths to Be Self-Evident

Most Americans know that the fireworks and hoopla of the Fourth of July are tied to meaningful history. July 4, in the year 1776, was the day that the nation's founding fathers signed the Declaration of Independence in Philadelphia. That date has been celebrated consistently every year thereafter. Many individuals could be considered heroes of American independence, but most people give Thomas Jefferson credit for authoring the Declaration. That document has inspired people all over the world for well over two hundred years. Although Thomas Jefferson was the third president of the United States, he didn't mention that when he dictated the words to appear on his tombstone. He wanted credit for the Declaration, the Statute of Virginia for Religious Freedom, and founding the University of Virginia.

We think Jefferson's words make him one of the most important heroes of America's founding. He persuaded the Continental Congress that "a decent respect to the opinions of mankind" required a statement of reasons for separation from Great Britain. In articulating those reasons, he deftly stated the most fundamental American principles: "We hold these truths to be self-evident, that all men are created equal, that they are endowed by their creator with certain unalienable rights, that among these are life, liberty and the pursuit of happiness." The reach of these ideas can be heard ringing years later in the opening of one of America's most famous speeches, Lincoln's Gettysburg Address: "Four score and seven years ago our fathers brought forth on this continent, a new nation, conceived in liberty, and dedicated to the proposition that all men are created equal."

Although Thomas Jefferson is widely considered a leading hero of American independence, he did not, of course, operate alone. John Adams was the member of the Continental Congress who most consistently pushed and prodded for independence, and he was one of the five men on the committee assigned to draft a declaration. Adams arguably deserves more credit than Jefferson. But heroism and history work in complicated ways, and it is the story of Jefferson's eloquent writing that most powerfully captures the spirit of the founding.

One of the great ironies of US history is that Thomas Jefferson and John Adams both died on the same day. The date was July 4, 1826, the 50th anniversary of the Declaration of Independence. Jefferson died early in the morning. Adams died later in the afternoon, and it is said that his last words were, "Thomas Jefferson still lives." Historian Joseph Ellis argued that Adams was wrong for the moment – Jefferson had already died – but right for the ages – people remember what Jefferson wrote much more than what Adams achieved (Ellis, 2000).

In addition to the Declaration, Thomas Jefferson is known for other acts that served his country well, such as the Louisiana Purchase in 1803, completed during his first term as president. He is also known in less favorable ways, such as for what some scholars consider his hypocrisy regarding slavery. Nevertheless, his ringing articulation of the fundamental values of liberty and equality make him an American transforming hero.

Albert Einstein: The Hero Synonymous with Genius

Heroes change the way we think about the world. They challenge conventional thinking or traditional ways of conceiving everyday phenomena. Perhaps no individual reshaped our thinking about the fundamental laws of nature more than Albert Einstein. So transforming was Einstein's work that *Time* magazine in 1999 named him the "Person of the 20th Century."

In science, the set of assumptions from which scientists work is called a *paradigm*, a term coined by Thomas Kuhn (1962). Any rapid change in assumptions that takes place within the scientific community is called a *paradigm shift*. One example of such a dramatic shift in thinking is Copernicus' proposal in 1543 that the earth rotates around the sun, a view that represented a radical departure from the old notion that the earth was the center of the solar system. Copernicus' new paradigm challenged the established and entrenched way of thinking by completely reframing the way the universe works.

Einstein's paradigm shift was no less groundbreaking. Einstein proposed that space and time are woven into a single fabric, called space-time. He suggested that matter causes space-time to curve and that the motion and properties of matter are, in turn, altered by that curvature. In 1905, at the tender age of 26, Einstein published four seminal research papers on the special theory of relativity, the Brownian motion theory, the photon theory of light, and the equivalence of mass and energy. A decade later in 1915, Einstein published his famous paper on general relativity, unifying Newton's law of gravity and special relativity. The theory spawned some of the greatest and strangest research results in the history of astronomy.

Reinforcing Einstein's status of hero was his unique physical appearance. His image was the perfect embodiment of the quirky mad scientist stereotype. Einstein's hair was long and unkempt, and he sported a walrus mustache. He paid little attention to clothing or fashion. *Time* magazine noted that he was a cartoonist's dream come true. Much to Einstein's dismay, he was instantly recognizable in public. When fans approached him as he took walks near the Princeton campus, Einstein would tell them, "Pardon me, always I am mistaken for Professor Einstein."

In addition to his prodigious scientific achievements, Einstein wrote extensively on topics relating to philosophy (e.g., "The life of the individual has meaning only insofar as it aids in making the life of every living thing nobler and more beautiful"), religion ("Science without religion is lame, religion without science is blind"), war ("Peace cannot be kept by force; it can only be achieved by understanding"), and humor ("Any man who can drive safely while kissing a pretty girl is simply not giving the kiss the attention it deserves").

Einstein's impact on the world was phenomenal, even outside the realm of science. In 1939, he wrote a letter to President Roosevelt, warning him of the possibility of Nazi Germany developing an atomic bomb. This letter is said to have mobilized the United States to create the bomb before Germany did. Einstein was offered the presidency of Israel in 1952 but declined the honor. Also in 1952, a new element named *einsteinium* was discovered and named in his honor.

Einstein also helped transform our perceptions of the role of scientists in society. From his writings it is clear that he believed that scientists have a moral responsibility to improve the human condition. He was an outspoken advocate of pacifism, international cooperation, democracy, and improving the quality of human life. Einstein helped reshape the image of the scientist from a private specialist to a public personality deeply committed to improving the fate of humanity. His heroic leadership was indirect, yet profound.

Princess Diana: The Self-Sacrificing Hero

"Carry out a random act of kindness, with no expectation of reward, safe in the knowledge that one day someone might do the same for you," Princess Diana once said, encapsulating her compassionate approach to life. Princess Diana became a global hero not just for her status as a member of the British royal family but for her extensive charity work and her genuine warmth and empathy toward people from all walks of life. She used her high-profile position to shine a light on various humanitarian issues, including the landmine crisis and the stigma surrounding HIV/AIDS.

Princess Diana's hands-on approach to philanthropy, which often involved directly interacting with those affected by adversity, endeared her to the public and changed the way the world viewed the British monarchy. Her ability to connect with people on a personal level, her tireless advocacy for numerous charitable causes, and her determination to raise her sons with an awareness of and involvement in her humanitarian efforts solidified her legacy as a "people's princess" and a hero to many around the globe.

Heroism has been defined as exceptional behavior directed toward the greater good that involves risk, sacrifice, courage, resilience, and humility (Allison & Goethals, 2011; Franco et al. 2011). Following are illustrations of how Princess Diana checked all the boxes for heroism.

Risk-taking: Diana famously walked through an active landmine field in Angola in 1997 to bring global attention to the plight of those maimed by landmines long after conflicts had ended. This act was not only symbolic but also a very real risk to her own safety.

Self-sacrifice: She often put her personal time and safety aside to comfort those in need. An example of this is her secret nighttime visits to talk to homeless people, which she did on a regular basis, according to her butler Paul Burrell. Her commitment to these causes often came at the cost of her personal time and privacy.

Courage: In the early 1990s, when HIV/AIDS was heavily stigmatized and misconstrued as a disease only affecting certain groups, Diana was photographed holding hands with AIDS patients. This simple act helped break down the immense stigma associated with the disease and changed public perceptions.

Resilience: Diana showed great resilience in her personal life, particularly in dealing with intense media scrutiny and the pressures of royal life.

Despite this, she maintained her focus on her humanitarian work and her role as a devoted mother.

Humility: Despite her royal status, Diana was known for her down-to-earth nature and ability to connect with people from all walks of life. She would sit on hospital beds, listen to people's stories, and show genuine interest and empathy. Her humility was evident in her approach to people suffering from illness or poverty; she treated everyone she met as an equal.

The tragic death of Princess Diana in 1997 can be interpreted as a heroic death through the lens of her relentless pursuit of humanitarian causes and her impact on the world, which did not cease with her passing. In a sense, her premature death cast a spotlight on the very issues she fought so diligently against — the invasiveness of the paparazzi and the media's relentless pursuit of public figures — sparking a global conversation and leading to changes in privacy laws and media practices.

Her death also served to immortalize her legacy and the values she championed. The outpouring of grief and the subsequent reflection on her life's work reinforced the messages she aimed to convey during her life: compassion, empathy, and the importance of human connection. The public mourning and collective tribute that followed emphasized the heroism in her life's actions and the causes she advocated for, from the campaign against landmines to her work with AIDS patients and the destitute.

In the narrative of a hero's journey, the hero often makes the ultimate sacrifice, which can lead to a significant transformation in society. Diana's death, while tragic, prompted a global reckoning with the consequences of a lack of empathy and respect for personal boundaries – principles she herself held dear. Thus, her untimely death can be seen as a heroic sacrifice that catalyzed change and further solidified her role as a humanitarian icon.

Elvis Presley: The Heroic King of Rock'n'Roll

In the first edition of this book, there were a number of nods to Elvis Presley. He was mentioned in the introduction to the section on transforming heroes and also figured in the entry on Buddy Holly, and especially the one about Marion Keisker at Sun Records. But Elvis deserves his own treatment. This is especially true in the wake of Baz Luhrmann's 2022 biopic *Elvis*. Elvis's legacy is further enhanced by the success of his granddaughter actress Riley Keough.

Elvis grew up in Memphis, Tennessee, the only child of working-class parents. Though somewhat introverted and shy, he performed as a singer in high school. He was sometimes bullied both because of his talent and his eccentricity. He absorbed Black music and dressed in ways that were considered too much like the way Black people dressed. After graduating from high school in 1953 he took a job as a truck driver. He then spent hard-earned money at Memphis Recording Studio to make two records. He said that they were for his mother, but it was obvious he wanted to be noticed and perhaps find success as a singer.

Late one day two musicians at the studio were looking for a vocalist. The secretary Marion Keisker, mentioned earlier, asked "What about the kid with sideburns?" In short order Elvis joined guitar player Scotty Moore and bass player Bill Black. They recorded a hit and toured widely in the South. In less than a year Elvis attracted the attention of RCA Records and network television. His first appearance was in January 1956. His style was over-the-top sexy for the day. He became famous, or infamous depending on one's point of view, across the country and around the world with his provocative style. On the 1999 ABC television series *The Century*, narrator Peter Jennings claimed that his presence broke all of the rules. In Howard Gardner's terms, Elvis told a story of self-expression and independence in dress, music, and cultural interests more generally. But there were counter-stories. Elvis was attacked by political, editorial, and clerical leaders for unleashing animal instincts, especially in young women. He plaintively replied, "I don't think I'm doing anything wrong." Millions of young people agreed.

Elvis's commercial success eventually silenced most critics. By the end of 1956 he had top hits with songs "Heartbreak Hotel," "Don't Be Cruel," "Hound Dog," and "Love Me Tender." He had also appeared in his first movie. But the pressures to conform were unrelenting, and soon Elvis toned down his appearance and his performances. He made a number of quite bad movies. Especially after the Beatles and other British bands captivated US audiences, he nearly disappeared from the music scene. He did make a successful "comeback special" for television in 1968. Then he began touring again and made regular appearances in Las Vegas hotels. But under the pressures of performance in his later years he became seriously overweight and addicted to drugs. He died at age 42.

Part of Elvis' lasting legacy is the trail his breakthrough performances blazed for other rock'n'rollers. Thanks to Presley, they could and did perform in a far more expressive and frankly erotic manner than seemed allowable previously. The famous and highly innovative rock star Buddy Holly said that none of this would have been possible without Elvis. Beyond his effect on musicians and performers, he became a model for young people in general to feel comfortable with whomever they were.

Another important aspect of Presley's influence is opening Black music to white audiences. His first hit single, "That's All Right," was written by a Black artist, Arthur "Big Boy" Crudup. Some critics have argued that white singers recording songs written by Black artists constitutes wrongful "cultural appropriation." Others quarrel with the record companies who have short-changed Black artists in their royalty contracts. For Elvis and many others, the music was out there to share and to be enjoyed by all. While the controversy continues, it is clear that Elvis was one of the artists who made Black music more accessible to young white audiences. This has arguably had a significant effect on breaking down racial estrangement and prejudice.

As the so-called King of Rock'n'Roll, Elvis Presley is a widely recognized hero for helping launch a genre of music, and its successors, that has brought artistic pleasure to many people for many years around the world.

Transforming Specific Heroes

Buddy Holly: The Day the Music Died

Generations of rock fans are familiar with the haunting opening lyrics of Don McLean's classic song "American Pie": "February made me shiver, with every paper I'd deliver," and, "I can't remember if I cried, when I read about his widowed bride, but something touched me deep inside, the day the music died." These words refer, of course, to Buddy Holly, one of the icons of 1950s rock'n'roll. Our research shows that the dead are often elevated in our esteem and turned into heroes. Holly illustrates this phenomenon as well as anyone. He, and the men killed with him on February 3, 1959, are frozen in time. The images of those three young rock stars endure in American pop culture history. But Holly is also a hero for what he did in life, not the way he died.

Buddy Holly was an ambitious young musician from Lubbock, Texas. In 1957, at the age of 20, Holly released one of the greatest records in rock'n'roll history, "That'll Be the Day." One of the legends about that song is that a disk jockey in Buffalo locked the studio door and played the song over and over again, for over an hour. True or not, the song was an instant and lasting hit. That tune was followed by many others, most notably perhaps, "Oh Boy," "Peggy Sue," and "Maybe, Baby."

Although Holly's recordings were extremely successful, money problems forced him to join a rock'n'roll tour in the winter of 1959. The tour bus often broke down in freezing weather, and on the night of February 2, the disgusted Holly hired a single-engine airplane to fly him from Clear Lake, Iowa, to Moorhead, Minnesota. With him were rock legends Ritchie Valens ("La Bomba") and J.P. Richardson, "The Big Bopper" ("Chantilly Lace"). The plane crashed shortly after take-off, and the three rockers and the pilot were killed. Other rock stars of the time were fading or retiring, and in some ways the music did die, until the Beatles and others transformed it in the 1960s.

Holly was one of the first rock stars in write, record, and produce his own music. And that music has had enduring influence. The young Bob Dylan saw Holly perform in Duluth, Minnesota, a few days before he was killed and remains indebted to his music to this day. The Beatles chose that name for their band as a nod to Holly's group, the Crickets. The Grateful Dead performed his classic "Not Fade Away" more than any other single tune. Holly's guitar playing, his innovative use of various instrumentations, and his unique blending of a variety of musical traditions were models for other singers, songwriters, musicians, and bands.

Holly himself said that none of what he did would have been possible without the breakthrough performances of Elvis Presley, but Holly's music has had much greater lasting impact. The visual image of Buddy Holly in his thick black-framed glasses, the sound of his guitar, the distinctive hiccup opening the song "Rave On," and his buoyant optimism about making good music will endure. In that respect, the music never died. Rave on.

Sheryl Sandberg: Heroic Leader and Advocate

Sheryl Sandberg has been widely recognized as a hero in both the business world and the realm of women's empowerment. As the COO of Facebook, she has been instrumental in scaling the company into a global tech powerhouse. Beyond her corporate achievements, Sandberg's advocacy for women in the workplace has sparked an international conversation about gender equality. Her book *Lean In* encourages women to pursue their ambitions and has led to the formation of Lean In Circles worldwide, providing a platform for women to support each other in their personal and professional growth. Her personal resilience and commitment to helping others, particularly after the tragic loss of her husband, further cement her status as a hero to many. Sandberg's work continues to inspire, offering a blueprint for overcoming personal adversity while making a profound impact on societal norms and empowering women to strive for leadership roles.

We can think of many specific reasons why Sheryl Sandberg can be considered a hero:

Visionary Leadership

As COO of Facebook, she helped grow the company from a startup to one of the world's most influential technology companies. This demonstrated impressive leadership and business acumen. Joining the company in its early years, Sandberg played a critical role in developing and executing a sustainable business model for the social media giant. Her strategies were instrumental in monetizing Facebook's vast user base, particularly through advertising and data-driven marketing solutions that capitalized on the platform's extensive reach and engagement. Sandberg's leadership was not just about driving revenue; she also focused on scaling the organization's infrastructure, championing a data-informed culture, and nurturing a dynamic and inclusive workplace. Her approach to leadership and growth emphasized long-term vision, adaptability, and the importance of building robust teams, which helped Facebook evolve from a startup into a global entity with substantial impact on digital communication and media. Her influence extended beyond financial success, shaping the company's corporate culture and positioning Facebook as a major player in the tech industry and a fixture in the everyday lives of billions of people.

Advocacy for Women

She advocates for women in leadership roles. Sandberg's book *Lean In* encourages women to pursue their ambitions and supports empowerment in the workplace. She gives women a voice.

Nonprofit Support

She formed the nonprofit organization LeanIn.Org, which offers education and support to women. Her work highlights gender inequality issues and provides solutions.

Resilience

She overcame personal tragedy with the sudden death of her husband and showed resilience in the face of adversity. After the loss, she focused energy on her family and highlighted the difficulties single parents face.

Generosity

She donates large amounts of her wealth to philanthropic causes including social justice, education, and women's empowerment. Her generosity has been heroic.

Way-Paver

As a highly successful technology executive, she broke barriers and served as a role model for women in the tech industry. She paved the way for others.

Courageous Advocate

She speaks openly about issues like sexism, discrimination, workplace policies, and leadership. Her willingness to address tough topics makes her a brave voice.

While Sandberg has her share of critics too, she has made significant contributions as a business leader, feminist icon, and philanthropist that can be considered heroic. She has positively impacted the lives of many women in the modern workforce. In addition, Sandberg has devoted her life to changing the world in big ways and taking huge, heroic risks in doing so. We have argued in our studies of heroism that our most important cultural heroes never shy away from doing whatever it takes to become their best, most heroic selves (Allison et al., 2019). Sandberg is no exception. She once said, "Let me fall if I must fall. The one I become will catch me."

Bill Gates: The Innovative and Philanthropic Hero

In a world increasingly driven by the invisible gears of technology, one man's vision transcended the binary to chart a course toward global philanthropy. Bill Gates, once known as the relentless force behind Microsoft, stood before a packed auditorium not to unveil the latest software but to pledge billions to fight diseases that ravaged the poorest corners of the world. This shift from the digital empire to the front lines of humanitarian crises marked a radical pivot. On that pivotal day, with the announcement of the Bill & Melinda Gates Foundation, Gates committed to giving away a substantial portion of his wealth, an act that redefined modern heroism.

It wasn't just the magnitude of his pledge but the clarity of his mission—to enhance healthcare, reduce extreme poverty, and expand educational opportunities—that underscored his transformation from a titan of industry to a champion of global health and development. Gates's journey into philanthropy reflects the kind of heroism that harnesses power and privilege for the greater good, proving that the most impactful legacy is not about what one builds but what one gives back.

Bill Gates's journey to becoming a tech visionary and philanthropist can be traced back to his childhood and early adulthood, which laid the groundwork for his later innovations. As a precocious child with a keen interest in computer programming, Gates had access to a computer at a young age during a time when they were not widely available. This early exposure to computing at Lakeside School sparked his fascination with software and programming. His supportive family environment encouraged his intellectual pursuits, which was crucial in developing his potential. In his teenage years, Gates demonstrated his entrepreneurial spirit by starting a business with his friend, Paul Allen, showcasing an early ability for recognizing and seizing opportunities.

Gates's enrollment at Harvard University further cultivated his burgeoning talent, although he would later drop out to pursue a vision he passionately believed in – the potential of personal computing. This bold decision to leave Harvard epitomized Gates's willingness to take significant risks to follow his intuition, a trait that would serve him well in the cutthroat business world. His relentless drive and competitive spirit were instrumental in guiding Microsoft through its nascent stages to become a dominant force in the software industry. These formative experiences combined – early access to technology, a supportive family, a natural proclivity for business, and a risk-taking attitude – were the crucible in which the innovator Bill Gates was forged.

Bill Gates's single most important technological innovation is the development of the Microsoft Windows operating system. Launched in 1985, Windows revolutionized the personal computing landscape by providing an accessible graphical user interface that transformed PCs from specialist tools into indispensable machines for the masses. This innovation catalyzed the widespread adoption of personal computers across the globe, fundamentally altering the way people interact with technology in their daily lives and solidifying Microsoft's position as a titan of the tech industry.

During the Covid-19 pandemic, Bill Gates played a pivotal role through his philanthropic organization, the Bill & Melinda Gates Foundation, by mobilizing resources to combat the virus on multiple fronts. The foundation committed substantial financial support to vaccine development, therapeutics, and diagnostic tools, ensuring that advancements in combating the virus could be accessed equitably across the globe. Gates also used his platform to advocate for science-based approaches to pandemic response, including social distancing measures and the importance of widespread testing. His forward thinking had already identified the threat of a global pandemic years before, leading to early investments in pandemic preparedness that became critical when Covid-19 emerged. Through these efforts, Gates not only contributed to the global fight against Covid-19 but also highlighted the importance of collective action and global cooperation in addressing public health crises.

Wayne Gretzky: The Forward-Thinking Hero

Wayne Gretzky is widely regarded as a hero both on and off the ice, known not just for his unprecedented skill and record-breaking achievements in hockey but also for his sportsmanship, leadership, and contribution to the game. Often referred to as "The Great One," Gretzky is celebrated for his humility and grace, as well as his ability to inspire teammates and future generations of players. His dedication to the sport, charitable work, and role in popularizing hockey across North America and beyond have left an indelible mark on the sport and on sports culture. There is no doubt that Gretzky is an enduring icon and a hero to many fans and aspiring athletes.

In our analysis of heroism, we have argued that cultural heroes tend to be ahead of their time (Allison, 2024b; Goethals & Allison, 2019). Gretzky is no exception to this rule. His prolific career offers proof that one of the most important things that a hero can do is to anticipate a positive future and to take steps to make it happen. On the ice, Wayne Gretzky was a maestro of anticipation, as evinced in his iconic quote, "I skate to where the puck is going to be, not where it has been" (Gretzky, 1989). This astute observation has seeped into the popular vernacular, having been repeated in countless self-help programs and executive business meetings.

Heroism scholars have also noted the importance of heroes stepping up to do their heroic work when it is most needed (Kohen et al., 2018). The great Stan Lee once said that "With great power comes great responsibility." The best heroes know they have the power to make the world better and take on the responsibility for acting on their superpower. Again, Gretzky took on this same mantle. He said, "Look at guys like Larry Bird and George Brett and John McEnroe. They all wanted to be the guy under the microscope late in the game or late in the match. So you just take on that know-how that that's part of your responsibility."

Gretzky scored a significant number of game-winning goals during his career. Over the course of his NHL tenure, he tallied 92 such goals. This statistic is a direct indicator of a player's ability to score in crucial moments and directly contribute to his team's victories. Gretzky's performance in the playoffs, when games are generally more critical, was outstanding. He holds the NHL record for the most points in the playoffs with 382 points (122 goals and 260 assists) in 208 games. His ability to elevate his game during the playoffs, when the pressure is highest, is a testament to his clutch abilities.

We have made the argument that celebrities and sports stars can only reach heroic status if they use their physical talents to make the world better for less fortunate people. Wayne Gretzky has been involved in various charitable endeavors throughout his life. His contributions to charity work and community involvement are noteworthy. Gretzky established the Wayne Gretzky Foundation, which is dedicated to providing less fortunate youth with the opportunity to experience hockey. Gretzky has also been involved in supporting health-related causes, particularly those focused on children. He has worked with hospitals and healthcare organizations, participating in fundraising events and campaigns to support medical research and patient care.

Gretzky has also contributed to disaster relief efforts, including donations and support for communities affected by natural disasters. His involvement has helped raise significant funds for recovery and rebuilding efforts. Gretzky has been involved in efforts to support cancer research, including participating in fundraising events and campaigns to aid in the fight against cancer. In transcending the boundaries of hockey to become a symbol of excellence and philanthropy, Wayne Gretzky has redefined what it means to be a hero in the realm of sports and beyond. His legacy, marked not just by unparalleled achievements on the ice but also by his profound impact on communities and lives, continues to inspire a standard of heroism that extends far beyond the rink.

Tom Brady: The Football GOAT Hero

Tom Brady is widely recognized as the GOAT ("Greatest of All Time") in professional football. Others, such as Peyton Manning and Brady's childhood hero Joe Montana, are in the conversation, but Brady's many records, such as ten Super Bowl appearances, seven Super Bowl wins, and five Super Bowl MVPs, pretty much settle the issue. It is ironic that Brady is called the GOAT since for many years the sports world, and sports commentary, distinguished between heroes and their opposite, goats. In baseball for example, Boston Red Sox first baseman Bill Buckner is called a goat for a miscue in a pivotal game World Series game. His overall record is generally set aside in discussions of his career accomplishments. Appropriate or not in evolution of public language, Brady is, for now, the National Football League's GOAT. That is, he is a hero in America's most popular sport.

People are seen as heroes for being highly competent and highly moral. Some heroes are admired mostly for their great skills, in Sherlock Holmes's case for example, keen insight and deductive reasoning. Holmes doesn't register very much on the morality scale, though when he does his actions are portrayed as doing the right thing. In the classic "The Adventure of the Blue Carbuncle," Holmes lets the culprit go rather than turning him over to the inept police, arguing that "I suppose I am commuting a felony, but it is just possible that I am saving a soul" (Conan Doyle, 1892, p. 175). Tom Brady has been involved in a variety of charitable activities, most notably his TB12 Foundation, which works toward "helping athletes maximize their health and potential." He has also been praised for making personal sacrifices for the sake of the team by taking salary cuts so that other players could sign competitive contracts. As a result, for years he was the top quarterback in the league but was paid as if he were in the middle of pack. Still, it is almost exclusively his accomplishments as a player that make him a hero to many. Of course, there are detractors, as is the case with many heroes. Some view him as a villain for so-called Deflategate, by which Brady was temporarily suspended for allegedly causing footballs to be deflated in a playoff game to make them easier to pass. But for most the salient story of one of an underdog rising to the top in his sport.

Brady was a sixth-round afterthought coming out of Michigan in the 2000 NFL draft. He was kept on the team as the fourth quarterback because his coach Bill Belichick thought he had potential. At the start of the next season, Belichick believed that Brady was the best quarterback on the team. However, the starter was the talented and much-admired Drew Bledsoe, who had led the team to the Super Bowl in 1997. But Bledsoe sustained a life-threatening injury in the second game of the 2001 season and Brady took over, and remained the Patriots' starting quarterback for 19 years.

In that first year as quarterback, the Patriots and Brady won their first Super Bowl. When they didn't make the playoffs the next year, both Brady and the 2001 team were viewed by many as a fluke. Then the Patriots won the next two Super Bowls and played deep into the playoffs the next three years, and won all 16 regular season games in 2011, though eventually losing to the New York Giants in that year's Super Bowl. The team experienced unparalleled success for next four seasons but failed to win the league championship again until 2015. That was the team's, and Brady's, fourth Super Bowl victory. They won again in 2017, surging back after falling behind 28-3 the Atlanta Falcons. Brady won a final championship with the Patriots in 2019 but left the team after the next season, only to win a seventh Super Bowl with a new team, the Tampa Bay Buccaneers, in 2021 at the age of 43. His record is unlikely to ever be matched.

Is Tom Brady a hero? For many he is, on the basis of his excellence and accomplishments as a player. His degree of self-sacrifice may also be an element for this who hold him up as a model. People's perceptions differ. As always, heroism is in the eye of the beholder.

Jane Goodall's Enduring Heroic Legacy

Jane Goodall, the famed English primatologist and anthropologist, meets the criteria for heroism through her pioneering work in science, conservation, and humanitarian efforts. Heroism often involves showing remarkable courage, making significant sacrifices for the benefit of others, and having a lasting impact on society. Goodall's contributions can be seen across several dimensions of heroism:

1 **Courage and determination:** Goodall demonstrated remarkable courage and determination by venturing into the Gombe Stream National Park in Tanzania in 1960 at a time when it was uncommon for women to undertake such rigorous scientific endeavors. Her work required physical and emotional resilience, as she navigated the challenges of living in close proximity to wild chimpanzees to observe and record their behavior.

2 **Pioneering research**: She broke new ground in primatology with her discovery that chimpanzees make and use tools, a behavior previously thought to be exclusive to humans. This challenged existing perceptions of the animal–human divide and significantly advanced our understanding of primate behavior, contributing to the field of ethology.

3 **Conservation efforts**: Goodall's work extends beyond research; she is a leading figure in conservation. Understanding the threats faced by chimpanzees and their habitats, she founded the Jane Goodall Institute in 1977, which works toward primate conservation, habitat preservation, and promoting sustainable practices among local communities.

4 **Educational outreach and advocacy**: Her efforts to educate the public about the importance of living sustainably and protecting the environment demonstrate her commitment to advocacy. Through lectures, writings, and media appearances, Goodall has inspired generations to take action for the planet and its inhabitants.

5 **Humanitarian work**: Goodall's ethos includes a strong humanitarian component, emphasizing the interconnectedness of all living beings and the importance of compassion. Her Roots & Shoots program, aimed at empowering young people to initiate environmental, conservation, and humanitarian projects, reflects her belief in the power of youth to drive positive change.

6 **Legacy and influence**: Goodall's legacy is not only in her scientific discoveries but also in her ability to mobilize people toward greater environmental consciousness and kindness toward other living beings. Her life's work exemplifies how one person's dedication can lead to significant societal and environmental benefits.

Jane Goodall's pioneering research on chimpanzee behavior transformed our understanding of what it means to be human and revolutionized the field of primatology. Her work has had a profound impact on conservation efforts, animal welfare, and our understanding of animal intelligence and emotions. Through her books, lectures, and the Jane Goodall Institute, she has inspired millions of people around the world to take action for conservation and animal welfare, and her legacy continues to influence new generations of scientists, conservationists, and activists. Goodall's contributions to science and her advocacy for a more sustainable and compassionate world make her a true icon of conservation and a hero to many. She embodies heroism through her groundbreaking contributions to science, her relentless pursuit of conservation, her efforts to inspire action for a better world, and her unwavering dedication to making a positive impact on society and the environment.

Goodall is known for penning the following memorable quote: "Every individual matters. Every individual has a role to play. Every individual makes a difference," which encapsulates her life's ethos and her heroic contributions to conservation and understanding of primates. This belief in the significance of each action, no matter how small, and the power of individual responsibility has not only driven her groundbreaking research on chimpanzees but also fueled her relentless efforts to inspire others toward environmental stewardship and compassion for all living beings. Goodall's heroism lies in her unwavering commitment to making a difference, one individual at a time.

13 Transcendent Heroes
Influence at Its Deepest Level

In reading about other heroes up to this point, you may have wondered whether we actually placed particular individuals into the right category or type. You may have questioned, for example, whether Gabrielle Giffords is a transitory hero, rather than, perhaps, a traditional hero. Is traditional hero Pat Tillman better regarded as a transitory hero? We have named him a traditional hero because we don't feel that the US military's partial fabrications of his story diminish his genuine heroism. But people can disagree. Indeed, we indicated earlier that the two of us did not see eye to eye on whether Hank Aaron and *Star Trek's* Captain Kirk are transitional or traditional heroes. And as we have written many times, eyes of beholders are where heroes rise, reside, and fall (Allison & Goethals, 2011).

In many cases, placing someone into one category rather than another is difficult, and finally it seems somewhat arbitrary. Furthermore, you may have wondered why certain heroes who would seem to fit a specific category were not found in that chapter. Abraham Lincoln, for example, is on the cover of this book and would certainly seem to be a transforming hero. But he hasn't been profiled thus far. The reason is that we are saving the best for last. Some heroes transcend the categories of our taxonomy. They illustrate more than one kind of hero and more than one kind of heroic influence. For example, we discussed US President Woodrow Wilson as a trending hero. However, he can easily be seen as a traditional hero. We profiled UCLA basketball coach John Wooden when we discussed transparent heroes because many of his efforts to emphasize education and academics as much as athletic achievement were not publicized. But given the way he and his teams changed the way college basketball is played, he could easily be regarded as a transforming hero.

We think it's important to recognize the differing and significant kinds of influence some individuals have had by treating them as transcendent heroes. Abraham Lincoln, as suggested previously, is one of our favorite examples. He seems clearly to fit the transforming hero category. In accomplishing the abolition of slavery and pointing the way toward equal rights

DOI: 10.4324/9781003328681-13

for all Americans, few people have had more impact on US history. Yet Lincoln was also transfigured, during his lifetime and after his assassination. He was, he admitted himself, quite ugly. Yet when a young soldier in the Union army met Lincoln on a visit to a battlefield, he transformed the president's visage so as to perceive heroism in Lincoln's face. He wrote that the president's countenance was "strong yet tender" and that in it "the agony of the life and death struggle of the hour was revealed as we had never seen it before." This transfiguration of Lincoln's face inspired and aroused the motives of this young man. His narrative continued, "With a new understanding, we knew why we were soldiers" (Foote, 1958, p. 803). Thus we see that not only can Lincoln be considered both transfigured and transforming, the psychological process of transfiguring Lincoln had an elevating and transforming effect. One kind of heroic influence led to another. While this transfiguration happened during Lincoln's life, his tragic assassination accelerated the construction of his heroic image. Daniel Chester French's iconic sculpture in the Lincoln Memorial in Washington, DC, creates an unforgettable heroic image of the 16th president. That sculpture along with Lincoln's own words carved into the sides of the memorial complete the heroic transfiguration.

In highlighting Lincoln as a transcendent hero, we want to signal that we have decided to restrict the label "transcendent" to heroes who are clearly transforming as well as having other kinds of influence. The individuals we consider here as transcendent heroes have had an exceptional impact on a significant aspect of world society and warrant being singled out. One clear example is Jesus of Nazareth. Undoubtedly a transforming hero, centuries of iconography have also transfigured him. For some people, Jesus also served as a transitional hero. Former US President George W. Bush completely transformed his life just after his 40th birthday by quitting drinking and becoming an evangelical Christian. For him, Christ was a transforming figure at a transitional point in his life.

Throughout our study of heroism, we have been struck by how many heroes are fictional. Roughly one third of heroes named in our surveys are characters from fiction, whether it be film, literature, or mythology. One such figure who fits the transcendent hero category is Harry Potter. We will see that Potter transformed Hogwarts School and also the realm of witchcraft and wizardry. He is also a transitional hero. He served as an inspiring hero for many young people who have since left him behind as an influential figure. And in fitting the template of the heroic journey discussed so eloquently by Joseph Campbell in *The Hero with a Thousand Faces*, Harry Potter is a traditional hero. His journey included such elements from Campbell as a born calling, help from a wise old man, and struggles with an evil villain.

In sum, we end our study of heroes by profiling those we regard as transcendent. They have had a remarkable influence on our lives and culture.

Harry Potter: The Consummate Archetypal Hero

In the hushed confines of a candle-lit room at Hogwarts, where whispers of past wizarding glories linger like ancient dust, a young boy with a lightning-shaped scar on his forehead grappled with a destiny far greater than his years. Harry Potter, known to the magical world as "The Boy Who Lived,"

Source: Harry Potter and The Philosopher's Stone Original Children's Editions *(Bloomsbury Publishers). Illustrated by Tomas Taylor.*

sat wide-eyed, clutching his wand, not yet fully comprehending the weight of the world that rested on his slender shoulders. It was in his third year, during a treacherous storm that thundered like the battle drums of giants, that Harry confronted the soulless specters known as Dementors.

With a strength that belied his age, he summoned a Patronus, a shining stag of pure light, casting away the darkness. In that moment, with his courage shining as brightly as his spell, Harry Potter transcended the pages of fiction to become a symbol of resilience and heroism for an entire generation. Whether standing defiant against the face of evil or showing compassion to those who had none, Harry's journey was a testament to the power of love and bravery in the darkest of times.

Harry Potter, the protagonist of J.K. Rowling's beloved series, exemplifies the qualities of a hero in multiple ways. Our research on heroism has shown that heroes display the "Great Eight" traits of heroes: Intelligence, strength, charisma, resilience, compassion, reliability, selflessness, and inspiration (Allison & Goethals, 2011). Here's how Harry Potter checks all these boxes:

First, while Harry may not be the top student academically, he shows a quick-witted and resourceful mind during his adventures. He is adept at thinking on his feet and using his knowledge of magic in innovative ways, particularly in duels and when solving mysteries. Second, Harry is strong and courageous. He consistently demonstrates bravery, facing down fearsome enemies like Lord Voldemort, risking his life to save others, and standing up for what is right, even when it means going against authority or his peers.

Third, Harry Potter shows tremendous resilience. Orphaned as an infant, Harry grows up in an abusive household, yet he does not become bitter or vengeful. Instead, he remains kind-hearted and determined, persistently overcoming the trauma of his parents' death and the numerous challenges he encounters in the wizarding world.

Regarding charisma, it can be argued that Harry Potter possesses an important type of charisma, though it may not be the conventional, overtly charming type often seen in traditional leaders. Harry's charisma is more subtle and stems from his authenticity, bravery, and natural ability to connect with others on a genuine level. He inspires loyalty and camaraderie among his friends and even garners respect from those who may not personally like him.

His charisma is also evident in the way he leads by example rather than by command; his actions motivate others to follow him and join his cause willingly. Harry's humility, coupled with his innate sense of justice and his unwillingness to compromise his values, also add to his charismatic appeal. Throughout the series, his presence tends to draw others to him, and he often finds himself at the center of pivotal events not because he seeks out leadership but because others look to him for guidance and motivation.

Related to this are Harry's inspirational qualities. Harry inspires others to fight for good. He is the leader and co-founder of Dumbledore's Army, where he teaches his peers defense against the dark arts. His actions and dedication to combating evil motivate those around him to join the cause and stand up against tyranny.

Finally, Harry Potter's selflessness is woven into the very fabric of his character, evident in his frequent acts of putting others before himself, sometimes at great personal risk. He surrenders his own desires for the greater good, as seen when he willingly faces what he believes to be certain death in the Forbidden Forest to protect his friends and the wizarding world from Voldemort. Throughout the series, Harry consistently risks his safety to save others, such as diving into the icy waters of the Black Lake to rescue his classmates during the Triwizard Tournament or forming Dumbledore's Army to equip his peers with the skills to defend themselves. His readiness to sacrifice his own well-being without hesitation is a defining aspect of his selflessness and heroism.

Through all these qualities, Harry Potter stands as a hero not only in the magical world but also as a symbol of heroism for readers, encouraging them to find the courage and resilience within themselves.

Jesus of Nazareth: The Born Hero

As with leaders, people often ask whether heroes are born or made. In our studies of heroism, we have found that the "born hero" is a rare breed. Extraordinary situations typically bring out the heroes among us. Every Christmas and Easter, much of the world honors the most powerful story of the born hero in the western world. It is, of course, the story of Jesus of Nazareth.

Few people dispute that Jesus was an actual historical figure. He was born about the year 5 BC in what is now Israel. The events of his life have been verified by several Roman historians and other non-Christian figures. Moreover, few people deny that he died by crucifixion around the year 33 AD. His death is described in all four gospels, documented by other contemporary sources, and regarded as a historical event. We also know that during his lifetime Jesus was a transforming leader, inspiring people and elevating them to new levels of morality.

Jesus was, and is, a polarizing figure. During his lifetime, his followers witnessed him perform miracles, and they believed in the new morality that he preached: a message of love, generosity, and forgiveness. But in his day Jesus was also a revolutionary who violated Jewish customs and defied Roman law. Although he did not make the claim explicitly, many Biblical passages imply strongly that Jesus was the son of God. Like Socrates of ancient Greece, Jesus could have spared his own life by offering some defense of the social disruptions he caused. But he did not. His threat to the status quo was deemed too great by Roman authorities, and he was gruesomely executed.

The circumstances surrounding the death of Jesus are largely responsible for the formation of the Christian faith. The gospels tell us that three days after he died, Jesus rose from the dead and was lifted to heaven. The story of the resurrection is a central part of Christianity because it signifies to Christians that God approved Jesus's work on earth and that Jesus lives forever. After Jesus died, many of his followers were burned, stoned, or crucified by Roman authorities. This persecution backfired. As martyrs, these Christians were the source of inspiration for millions of people who began practicing the faith. Today there are roughly two billion Christians worldwide, and Christianity appears to be growing in some parts of the world, such as Asia and Africa. But over the past half-century, Europe has witnessed a significant drop in Christian believers. North America, too, is experiencing a similar albeit slower decline. It is also true that some atheists have become emboldened in their condemnation of religion.

Whether or not you believe that Jesus was the son of God, there is no denying his unparalleled impact on western thought and culture. Historian and author H.G. Wells wrote, "I am an historian, I am not a believer, but I must confess as a historian that this penniless preacher from Nazareth is irrevocably the very center of history. Jesus Christ is easily the most dominant figure in all history." Mahatma Gandhi, a Hindu, had nothing but praise for Jesus, describing him as "a man who was completely innocent, offered himself as a sacrifice for the good of others, including his enemies, and became the ransom of the world." Referring to Jesus's sacrifice at the cross, Gandhi said, "It was a perfect act."

Will Jesus still be worshipped as a hero 2,000 years from now? We cannot even begin to conjecture. As with many transforming heroes, the legend is compelling, the message is powerful, and there are iconic institutions in place to ensure significant staying power.

Abraham Lincoln: A Transcendent Hero

The American Civil War produced many people who are regarded as heroes. In some ways, its losers are regarded as heroes more than the winners. It is hard to find as much adulation in the North for Abraham Lincoln, Ulysses S. Grant or William T. Sherman as there is in the South for Stonewall Jackson and Robert E. Lee.

Still, Lincoln towers above them all in illustrating the different types of heroes that we have identified. We think that Lincoln is certainly a traditional hero. We also hold that he is a transforming hero more than is routinely recognized, and that in interesting ways he helps us understand the concept of transfigured heroes. Since he embodies so many aspects of heroism, he illustrates our overarching type, the transcendent hero, one who combines the features of several different kinds.

First, Lincoln is a traditional hero. He appears on our penny and our five-dollar bill. High school students in many parts of the country still memorize the Gettysburg Address. We are taught that he saved the Union. More important, perhaps, is the way Lincoln was transforming. Prior to the Civil War, slavery was rooted deeply in American society and American politics. Despite the Declaration of Independence's claim that the idea that "all men are created equal" was a "self-evident" truth, slavery was built into and protected by the US Constitution. Although the South seceded because it feared the ways that Lincoln might restrict slavery, he did not enter the presidency to abolish slavery. His goal was to preserve the Union and bring the rebel states back.

But the war had its own dynamic, and by the time of Lincoln's second inauguration, on March 4, 1865, slavery was finished. In his inaugural address that day Lincoln summarized the struggle's evolution perfectly: "Neither party expected for the war, the magnitude, or the duration, which it has already attained." And he went on to underline how transformed the country was: "Each looked for an easier triumph, and a result less fundamental and astounding." Historian Eric Foner has called our attention to that last word, *astounding*. In ending slavery, the war, through its own vicissitudes, changed the country in a way that is, if one thinks about it, simply astounding. Lincoln's central role in that transformation makes him a transforming hero.

Most interesting perhaps, is Lincoln as a transfigured hero. Many Americans have constructed a charismatic, almost god-like image of Lincoln. The irony is that while we are drawn to so many aspects of Lincoln, including his appearance, he was, as he very readily admitted, an unattractive person. When a political adversary accused him of being two-faced, Lincoln asked whether anyone could really believe he would display the face they saw if he had another one.

Yet Civil War historian Shelby Foote, who gained fame during Ken Burns's television miniseries on the war, quotes a soldier who did cognitive work with Lincoln's appearance and saw in it quite heroic qualities. As mentioned earlier, after Lincoln visited the army, the soldier wrote of Lincoln's face: "None of us to our dying day can forget that countenance. Concentrated in that one great, strong yet tender face, the agony of the life and death struggle of the hour was revealed as we had never seen it before. With a new understanding, we knew why we were soldiers." This young man was transformed by the transfiguration he had done himself. Heroism of various kinds is clearly in the eye of the beholder. Of those kinds, transfigured individuals have the most to teach us about how human cognition creates its heroes.

14 Conclusion

Abraham Lincoln, the sixteenth president of the United States

Abraham Lincoln was both a leader and a hero. He led the United States during the Civil War, and in doing so succeeded in both saving the Union and ending American slavery. He is consistently ranked by historians, along with George Washington and Franklin Roosevelt, as one of the greatest of all US presidents. He was also a hero – to many during his presidency, and to many more after his assassination. Among those who revered Lincoln as a hero while he was alive was an African American woman Lincoln encountered when he toured Richmond, Virginia, two days after the Confederate government abandoned its capital. She touched the president's arm as he walked the city's streets and shouted, "I know that I am free, for I have seen Father Abraham and felt him." The moment Lincoln died, his near apotheosis and transformation into a more widely recognized hero began almost instantaneously. Standing at the bedside of the

DOI: 10.4324/9781003328681-14

slain president, Secretary of War Edwin Stanton proclaimed, "Now he belongs to the ages." Millions of people soon saw Lincoln as a martyr (Harris, 2004, p. 205).

There are many other examples of people who have been both leaders and heroes. Alexander the Great was a military leader transformed into a hero. Military historian John Keegan (1987) offers Alexander as an example of "heroic leadership." The name he is known by in itself attests to his status as hero. His heroic transformation, like Lincoln's, was most likely facilitated by his early death. Another example we described earlier is Irena Sendler. A leader of Polish resistance to the Nazis, Sendler became a hero to those she saved and to those who admired her bravery, ingenuity, and sacrifice.

Our purpose in writing this book was to help people develop an understanding of heroic leadership and how it can assume many different forms. Let's briefly reexamine the nature of leadership and how it can manifest as heroic, as villainous, or as something in-between.

What Is Leadership?

Leadership scholars have proposed many different definitions of leadership. Considering a number of scholars' approaches in more detail, we see that there is most agreement regarding the importance of influence, and least consensus on the importance of ethics or morality in understanding leadership. Specifically, scholars differ radically on whether leadership only applies to influence toward moral thought or behavior. Ronald Heifetz (1998) argues that leadership is a term saturated in values, and that when we speak of leadership – for example, saying that the country needs more leadership – we reveal that we understand leadership to be a good thing, something that is moral. On the other hand, Barbara Kellerman (2004b) argues that to call immoral leadership something other than leadership, for example, "power wielding," is to blind ourselves to instances of leadership, such as Hitler's, that we desperately need to understand. She makes the point that writers have not always treated leadership as something moral. Machiavelli, for example, regarded it as far from anything ennobling. Leaving the moral dimension aside, in other respects there is much overlap in the way scholars define leadership.

A good starting point is Hogan, et al. (1994) view that "leadership involves persuading other people to set aside for a period of time their individual concerns and to pursue a common goal that is important for the responsibilities and welfare of a group" (p. 493). They add that their definition is "morally neutral" and that "leadership is persuasion, not domination." It "occurs when others willingly adopt, for a period of time, the goals of a group as their own." The idea that leadership is not domination and that followers willingly go along is consistent with other definitions stating that all leaders have power but that not all power holders are leaders (Burns, 1978; Magee et al., 2005). Some people with power wield it coercively to get people with less power to do their bidding. That, scholars argue, is not leadership.

Heifetz (1998) defines leadership "as an activity . . . mobilizing people to do something" (p. 18). We think this is a useful approach. Heifetz goes on to focus on a "something" he calls "adaptive work," that is, addressing "conflicts in the values people hold" or diminishing "the gap between the values people stand for and the reality they face." Such work typically involves "a change in values, beliefs, or behavior" (p. 22). Leaders must find ways of helping people clarify and perhaps change their values, and think through how they can act to further their values, given reality.

Many scholars choose to offer definitions of leaders as well as or instead of leadership, mostly because defining the latter is a little more complicated. For example, Michael Hogg (2001) defines leaders as "people who have disproportionate influence, through possession of consensual prestige or the exercise of power, or both, over the attitudes, behaviors, and destiny of group members." He adds that leadership is about having "disproportionate power and influence to set agenda, define identity, and mobilize people to achieve collective goals" (p. 188).

Howard Gardner (1995) offers the broadest definition of a leader. He says that leaders are "persons who, by word and/or personal example, markedly influence the behaviors, thoughts, and/or feelings of a significant number of their fellow human beings" (pp. 8–9). Gardner also cites Harry Truman's marvelous quote that "a leader is a man who has the ability to get other people to do what they don't want to do and like it." Most important, as noted previously, Gardner greatly extends our understanding of leadership by contrasting *direct* leadership, as exercised, for example, by Winston Churchill, who spoke to his followers in person or through the radio, and *indirect* leadership, for example, that of Albert Einstein, who generally led through his published work rather than through face-to-face contact. Indirect leadership can be exerted through a range of scholarly or artistic products, such as music, dance, science, political treatises, or literature.

Some leaders lead both directly and indirectly, at different times to different groups of followers or audiences. For example, Martin Luther King, Jr. led directly when he gave his "I Have a Dream" speech in Washington, DC, in 1963. That same year he led indirectly with his "Letter from Birmingham Jail." Both King's ideas and his persona were important elements of his leadership.

The ideas that stories, poems, paintings, performances, and scholarship can influence, and that those who generate these products are leaders, greatly expand our understanding of leadership. It is particularly relevant for linking heroism to leadership. Many heroes influence us through their impersonal works, for example, their words and music, rather than through their personal presence or *persona*. This influence would be defined by Gardner as indirect leadership.

In extending the idea of leadership to examples, products, and accomplishments rather than personally directed influence, the question arises as to whether people who are no longer alive can be considered leaders. When Lincoln gave his Gettysburg address, urging that Americans work to ensure that "government of the people, by the people, for the people shall not perish from the earth," he was clearly exercising leadership at that moment. To the extent that Lincoln's exhortation influences people today, is Lincoln a dead leader? We readily grant heroic status to people who are dead, but calling them leaders may seem to stretch the definition too far. However, in some of our earlier work on people's tendencies to "deify the dead and downtrodden" (Allison & Eylon, 2005; Allison & Goethals, 2008), we argued that leaders are often most inspiring and therefore most influential when they are, in fact, dead. In a number of studies we provide support for the idea that some leaders inspire us the most after they have died. They lead indirectly.

From the authors quoted previously, we can distill a working definition of leadership. It is an activity or product that influences or persuades, but does not coerce, other people to think, feel, or act in particular ways, very often ways that advance the interests or goals of the group to which both the leader and followers belong. Leaders, then, are the individuals who perform the influencing activities or fashion the influencing products. We think that all heroes can be shown to be leaders in accord with this definition. To make this case we need to outline further how we define heroes and heroism.

What Makes Leadership Heroic?

For the past decade, we have argued that heroic leadership is often fashioned by the trials and obstacles that leaders overcame during earlier stages of their life journeys (Allison & Goethals, 2017; Allison et al., 2019). Our basic thesis is that most heroic leaders share a common path of transformative suffering. We see this in real-world leaders such as Nelson Mandela and Malala Yousafzai, as well as in fictional heroes such as Odysseus from *The Odyssey* and Dorothy from *The Wizard of Oz*. While heroic leaders undergo a heroic transformation forged by struggle and suffering, it is important to emphasize that painful experiences by themselves are not enough. Heroic leaders are shaped by a willingness to be humbled, good mentoring, openness to experience, and the leaders' drive to share their enlightened, transformed state with the world (Campbell, 1949; Worthington & Allison, 2018). The heroic end state of this developmental roadmap has been described as *self-actualization* by Abraham Maslow, *bliss* by Joseph Campbell, *integrity* by Erik Erikson, *eudaimonia* by Carol Riff, and *flourishing* by Martin Seligman.

All human beings are capable of undergoing a personal heroic transformation, and thus everyone is capable of becoming a heroic leader. This is the "banality of heroism" principle described by Franco and Zimbardo (2006). Heroic leadership is not reserved for special, iconic individuals but is available to every one of us who is willing and able to become their best selves by traversing the arduous steps of the heroic journey. The journey of heroic metamorphosis culminates with the hero's calling to elevate the morality and motivation of others (Burns, 1978) and promote unity, connectedness, and well-being in followers. Heroically transformed individuals eschew any type of tribal mentality and help disparate groups unify in becoming part of something greater than themselves.

A quick glance at political leadership around the world makes it very apparent that not all leaders are heroically transformed. We must all choose whether to heed the call to undertake the transformative journey or to remain stuck in lower stages of development. Unfortunately, untransformed leaders can rise to the top of the political ladder. These leaders do not appeal to "the better angels of our nature," as Lincoln once did, but rather to the darker impulses of our nature. These darker impulses represent qualities such as hatred, division, and selfishness.

A question of vital importance to the world is this: How do we distinguish the good leaders from the bad ones? What sets apart the heroic leaders in our world from the villainous leaders? Answering this question is not as easy as it seems, for while we prefer to see heroes and villains as polar opposites, the reality is that only a fine line separates heroes from villains (Allison & Goethals, 2011). This fine line explains why people may agree on the definition of heroic leadership yet disagree who specifically meets the criteria for heroic leadership. In the US during the 2010s and 2020s, people who agreed that *courage* and *wisdom* are required for heroic leadership often vehemently disagreed whether Donald Trump checks these two boxes. What litmus test can we, as responsible citizens, use to distinguish the true heroic leader from the false one?

The Container versus the Content of Leadership

We have come up with a framework for discerning heroic leadership based on the idea that it important to differentiate between the *container* for leadership and the *contents* of leadership (Goethals & Allison, 2019). The container for leadership is the vessel that houses the expression of leadership.

For example, the container can be flashy in color (charisma) and made of strong materials (resilience). Although one cannot tell from the leadership container whether the leader is a hero or a villain, people tend to assume that flashiness and strength are indicative of great leadership. This was Nazi Germany's mistake in the 1930s. Adolf Hitler was a strong, confident, compelling figure who exploited people's tendency to over-value the container of leadership and overlook the contents of leadership.

Consider the Great Eight traits of heroes (Allison & Goethals, 2011). It can be argued that five of these heroic traits also describe villains: *smart, strong, resilient, charismatic,* and *inspiring*. When we examine Kinsella et al.'s (2015) 12 central traits of heroism, seven of these qualities can also arguably be considered traits of villains: *brave, conviction, courageous, self-sacrifice, protecting, determined,* and *inspiring*. These are all features of the leadership container, not the contents. We are left with the unsettling conclusion that it is easy for human beings to leap to the conclusion that *container greatness* equals *content greatness*. We've called this mistake the *heroism attribution error* (Allison, 2023; Beggan et al., 2023). It almost goes without saying that our human tendency to focus on style over substance can lead to disastrous choices of leaders.

What are the contents of heroic leadership? The traits unique to heroism appear to fall on the moral dimension of heroism more so than on the competence dimension. The Great Eight traits unique to heroism are *selfless, reliable,* and *caring*, and the Kinsella et al. (2015) traits unique to heroism are *moral integrity, selfless, saves others,* and *helpful*. It would seem that the morality of heroism focuses on concern for others, on a "self-less-ness" that underscores a heroic transcendence of boundaries between the self and others.

This selflessness dimension of heroism was emphasized by Joseph Campbell (1949) in his description of the hero monomyth. Describing the hero's journey, Campbell (1949) wrote, "where we had thought to be alone, we shall be with all the world" (p. 25). Heroes want to unify the world. Villains want to divide us. Almost without exception, this sentiment of unification is expressed by every cultural hero, including Martin Luther King, Jr., who said: "Whatever affects one directly, affects all indirectly. I can never be what I ought to be until you are what you ought to be. This is the interrelated structure of reality." Albert Einstein (1950, 47), moreover, wrote: "A human being is a part of the whole, called by us 'Universe,' a part limited in time and space. He experiences himself, his thoughts and feelings as something separated from the rest – *a kind of optical delusion of his consciousness. This delusion is a kind of prison for us*, restricting us to our personal desires and to affection for a few persons nearest to us. Our task must be to free ourselves from this prison by widening our circle of compassion to embrace all living creatures and the whole of nature in its beauty" (italics added).

Heroic Leadership Is Service to Others and Love in Action

We acknowledge the obvious truth that heroism and heroic leadership are slippery concepts, difficult to pin down, easily misunderstood, and open to interpretation. Still, we argue that despite the elusive nature of heroism, it always consists of service to others. Heroism, in short, is love in action (Allison, 2023; Goethals & Allison, 2019). By extension, heroic leadership is leadership aimed at promoting a state of unified loving kindness for all human beings.

Defining heroism and heroic leadership as "love in action" emphasizes the essential mission of both heroism and leadership. All heroic leadership deeds, whether direct or indirect, are motivated by love and compassion. This concept is supported in various ways. First, many heroic acts arise from altruistic motives – risking oneself to help others, safeguarding innocent lives, or upholding shared values. Such selflessness demonstrates love not only for humanity at large but also for specific individuals facing challenges. By taking action to assist when needed, heroes show love through deeds rather than just words or emotions. Heroic acts often stem from empathetic connections to those in distress, indicating that love significantly influences our reactions to crises. When we observe someone else suffering or being treated unfairly, our instinct to intervene stems from our concern for them and a desire to ease their pain. This compassionate drive illustrates love manifesting in tangible actions that promote fairness, justice, and well-being.

Again, we note that this message of love is often lost among people focused on the container of heroism in lieu of the contents. A strong and flashy leader has a property that psychologists call *salience*, meaning that the leader stands out and captures our attention. A salient leader is attention-getting for all the wrong reasons. We can become so enamored with the salient leader's container that we overlook the leader's flawed contents. Doing so leads us to commit the Warren Harding error, or the heroism attribution error. Salient leaders are dangerous leaders because they can appear larger than life. They may satisfy our thirst for heroes but at great cost to us individually and collectively. We hope that this book helps you, the reader, develop a more critical eye in discerning true heroic leadership.

References

Adler, J. (2006). *Freud in our midst*. http://www.myspace.com/32661578/blog/101412768

Allison, S.T. (2023). Constructions of heroism. In S.T. Allison, J.K. Beggan, & G.R. Goethals (Eds.), *Encyclopedia of heroism studies*. Springer.

Allison, S.T. (2024a). Heroic lag. In S.T. Allison, J.K. Beggan, & G.R. Goethals (Eds.), *Encyclopedia of heroism studies*. Springer.

Allison, S.T. (2024b). Heroism attribution error. In S.T. Allison, J.K. Beggan, & G.R. Goethals (Eds.), *Encyclopedia of heroism studies*. Springer.

Allison, S.T. (2024c). Definitions and descriptions of heroism. In S.T. Allison, J.K. Beggan, & G.R. Goethals (Eds.), *Encyclopedia of heroism studies*. Springer.

Allison, S. T., & Beggan, J. K. (2023). Hero illiteracy. In S. T. Allison, J. K. Beggan, and G. R. Goethals (Eds.), *Encyclopedia of Heroism Studies*. Springer.

Allison, S.T., Beggan, J.K., & Goethals, G.R. (Eds.). (2024). *The encyclopedia of heroism studies*. Springer Publishing.

Allison, S.T., & Eylon, D. (2005). The demise of leadership: Death positivity biases in posthumous impressions of leaders. In D. Messick & R. Kramer (Eds.), *The psychology of leadership: Some new approaches* (p. 295–317). Erlbaum.

Allison, S.T., Eylon, D., Beggan, J.K., & Bachelder, J. (2009). The demise of leadership: Positivity and negativity in evaluations of dead leaders. *The Leadership Quarterly, 20,* 115–129.

Allison, S.T., & Goethals, G. R. (2008). Deifying the dead and downtrodden: Sympathetic figures as exceptional leaders. In C.L. Hoyt, G.R. Goethals, & D.R. Forsyth (Eds.), *Leadership at the crossroads: Psychology and leadership*. Springer.

Allison, S.T., & Goethals, G.R. (2011). *Heroes: What they do and why we need them*. Oxford University Press.

Allison, S.T., & Goethals, G.R. (2014). "Now he belongs to the ages": The heroic leadership dynamic and deep narratives of greatness. In G.R. Goethals et al. (Eds.), *Conceptions of leadership: Enduring ideas and emerging insights*. Palgrave Macmillan.

Allison, S.T., & Goethals, G.R. (2017). The hero's transformation. In S.T. Allison, G.R. Goethals, & R.M. Kramer (Eds.), *Handbook of heroism and heroic leadership*. Routledge.

Allison, S. T., Goethals, G. R., & Kramer, R. M. (2017). Setting the scene: The rise and coalescence of heroism science. In S. T. Allison, G. R. Goethals, & R. M. Kramer (Eds.), *Handbook of heroism and heroic leadership*. Routledge.

Allison, S.T., Goethals, G.R., Marrinan, A.R., Parker, O.M., Spyrou, S.P., & Stein, M. (2019). The metamorphosis of the hero: Principles, processes, and purpose. *Frontiers in Psychology, 10,* 606.

Allison, S.T., & Green, J.D. (2020). Nostalgia and heroism: Theoretical convergence of memory, motivation, and function. *Frontiers in Psychology, 11,* 3682.

Allison, S.T., & Hensel, A. (2012). Sensitivity to the changing fortunes of others. *Personality and Social Psychology Connections.* https://spsptalks.wordpress.com/

Allison, S.T., & Hutchins, R. (2024). Amalgamated heroes. In S.T. Allison, J.K. Beggan, & G.R. Goethals (Eds.), *Encyclopedia of heroism studies.* Springer.

Allison, S.T., Messick, D.M., & Goethals, G.R. (1989). On being better but not smarter than others: The Muhammad Ali effect. *Social Cognition, 7,* 275–296.

Allport, G.W. (1985). The historical background of social psychology. In G. Lindzey & E. Aronson (Eds.), *The handbook of social psychology.* McGraw Hill.

Aronson, E., & Linder, D. (1965). Gain and loss of esteem as determinants of interpersonal attractiveness. *Journal of Experimental Social Psychology, 1,* 156–171.

Auden, W.H. (1973). *Selected poems.* Faber.

Augustine of Hippo. (1998). *Original written in 398 AD, confessions.* Oxford University Press.

Bales, R.F. (1958) Task roles and social roles in problem-solving groups. In E.E. Maccoby, T.M. Newcomb, & E.L. Hartley (Eds.). *Readings in social psychology* (pp. 437–447). Holt, Rinehart, & Winston.

Bass, B.M. (1998). *Transformational leadership: Individual, military, and educational impact.* Lawrence Erlbaum.

Baumeister, R.F., Bratslavsky, E., Finkenauer, C., & Vohs, K. (2001). Bad is stronger than good. *Review of General Psychology, 5,* 323–370.

Baumeister, R.F., & Tierney, J. (2011). *Willpower.* Penguin Books.

Beggan, J.K., Allison, S.T., & Goethals, G.R. (2023). *The hazard of great leadership.* Cambridge University Press.

Bocchiaro, P., Zimbardo, P., & Van Lange, P.A.M. (2012). To defy or not to defy: An experimental study of the dynamics of disobedience and whistle-blowing. *Social Influence, 1,* 1–16.

Bradley, M. (2010, July 8). LeBron goes from Cleveland to Miami, from hero to villain. http://blogs.ajc.com/mark-bradley-blog

British Psychological Society. (n.d.). British Psychological Society Annual Conference, Enniskillen, Co. Fermanagh, UK.

Burgess, C. (2000). *Teacher in space: Christa McAuliffe and the Challenger legacy.* University of Nebraska Press.

Burns, J.M. (1978). *Leadership.* Harper & Row.

Burns, J.M. (2003). *Transforming leadership: A new pursuit of happiness.* Atlantic Monthly Press.

Butler, S. (1999). East to the Dawn: The life of Amelia Earhart. Da Capo Press.

Campbell, J. (1949). *The hero with a thousand faces.* Bollingen Series 17. Princeton University Press.

Campbell, J. (1988). *The power of myth.* Anchor Books.

Campbell, W.J. (2012). *The military's 'fabrication'? No, Jessica Lynch was WaPo's story.* http://mediamythalert.wordpress.com/2012

Canellos, P.S. (2010) *Last lion: The fall and rise of Ted Kennedy.* Simon and Schuster.

Carruthers, P., Laurence, S., & Stich, S. (2005). *The innate mind: Structure and contents.* Oxford University Press.

Cialdini, R.B., Borden, R.J., Thorne, A., Walker, M.R., Freeman, S., & Sloan, L.R. (1976). Basking in reflected glory: Three (football) field studies. *Journal of Personality and Social Psychology, 34,* 366–375.

Cohen, W. A. (2010). *Heroic leadership: Leading with integrity and honor.* Jossey-Bass.

Conan Doyle, A. (1892). *The adventure of the blue carbuncle.* George Newnes Ltd.

Cook, E.T. (2012). *The life of Florence Nightingale.* University of California Libraries.

Crysel, L.C., Cook, C.L., Schember, T.O., & Webster, G.D. (2015). Harry Potter and the measures of personality: Extraverted Gryffindors, agreeable Hufflepuffs, clever Ravenclaws, and manipulative Slytherins. *Personality and Individual Differences, 83,* 174–179.

Darion, J., & Leigh, M. (1965). The impossible dream (The Quest). In D. Wasserman, J. Darion, & M. Leigh, (Eds.), *Man of La Mancha.* Broadway musical.

Davies, H. (2004). *The Beatles.* W. W. Norton Publishers.

Dehaene, S. (1997, October 27). What are numbers, really? A cerebral basis for number sense. http://www.edge.org/3rd_culture/dehaene/dehaene_p2.html

Dugard, M. (2005). *The last voyage of Columbus.* Little Brown & Company.

Einstein, A. (1950). Letter. *New York Times,* falseMarch 29, 1972.

Ellis, J.J. (2000). *Founding brothers: The revolutionary generation.* Knopf.

Erikson, E.H. (1959). *Identity and the life cycle.* International Universities Press.

Eylon, D., & Allison, S.T. (2005). The frozen in time effect in evaluations of the dead. *Personality and Social Psychology Bulletin, 31,* 1708–1717.

Fernandez-Armesto, F. (1991). *Columbus.* Oxford University Press.

Festinger, L. (1954). A theory of social comparison processes. *Human Relations, 7,* 117–140.

Fiske, S. T., & Taylor, S. E. (2017). *Social cognition: From brains to culture.* Sage.

Foote, S. (1958). *The Civil War: A narrative, Fort Sumter to Perryville.* Random House.

Franco, Z., & Zimbardo, P.G. (2006). The banality of heroism. *Greater Good, 3,* 30–35.

Franco, Z. E. (2017). Heroism in times of crisis: Understanding leadership during extreme events. In S. T. Allison, G. R. Goethals, & R. M. Kramer (Eds.), *Handbook of heroism and heroic leadership.* Routledge.

Franco, Z.E., Blau, K., & Zimbardo, P.G. (2011). Heroism: A conceptual analysis and differentiation between heroic action and altruism. *Review of General Psychology, 15,* 99–113.

Gabriel, S., & Young, A.F. (2011). Becoming a vampire without being bitten: The narrative collective-assimilation hypothesis. *Psychological Science, 22*(8), 990–994.

Gardner, H. (1995). *Leading minds: An anatomy of leadership.* Basic Books.

Gladwell, M. (2005). *Blink.* Little, Brown, and Company.

Goethals, G.R. (2023a). Cognitive construction of heroism. In S.T. Allison, J.K. Beggan, & G.R. Goethals (Eds.), *Encyclopedia of heroism studies.* Springer.

Goethals, G.R. (2023b). Mandela effect and heroic perceptions. In S. T. Allison, J. K. Beggan, & G. R. Goethals (Eds.), *Encyclopedia of heroism studies.* Springer.

Goethals, G.R., & Allison, S.T. (2012). Making heroes: The construction of courage, competence and virtue. *Advances in Experimental Social Psychology. 46,* 183–235.

Goethals, G.R., & Allison, S.T. (2019). *The romance of heroism and heroic leadership: Ambiguity, attribution, and apotheosis.* Emerald.

Goethals, G.R., & Allison, S.T. (2025). The construction and presentation of heroes and heroines. In K. Lee (Ed.), *A cultural history of fame in the modern age*. Bloomsbury Press.

Goldschmied, N., & Vandello, J. A. (2009). The advantage of disadvantage: Underdogs in politics. *Basic and Applied Social Psychology, 31*, 24–31.

Goldschmied, N., & Vandello, J. A. (in press). The future is bright: The underdog label, availability, and optimism. *Basic and Applied Social Psychology. 34*(1), 34–43.

Gretzky, W. (1989, January). Wayne Gretzky: I skate to where the puck is going to be, not where it has been. *Sport, 23*(1), 16.

Harris, W.C. (2004). *Lincoln's last months*. Harvard University Press.

Harvey & Riggio, R.E. (2011). *Leadership studies: The dialogue of disciplines*. Edward Elgar.

Heifetz, R.A. (1998). *Leadership without easy answers*. Harvard University Press.

Hogan, R., Curphy, G., & Hogan, J. (1994). What we know about leadership: Effectiveness and personality. *American Psychologist, 49*, 493–504.

Hogg, M.A. (2001). A social identity theory of leadership. *Personality and Social Psychology Review, 5*, 184–200.

Invictus. (2009). Eastwood, C. (Director). Warner Bros. Pictures.

Johnson, H.H., & Morton, J. (1991). *Biology and cognitive development: The case of face recognition*. Blackwell.

Jung, C.G. (1969). *Collected Works of C.G. Jung, Volume 9 (Part 1): Archetypes and The Collective Unconscious*. Princeton University Press.

Jung, C.G., & von Franz, M.L. (1964). *Man and his symbols*. Doubleday & Co., Inc.

Kahneman, D., & Tversky, A. (1979). Prospect theory: An analysis of decision under risk. *Econometrica, 12*, 263–291.

Kassin, S.M., Fein, S., & Markus, H.R. (2010). *Social psychology* (8th ed.). Houghton Mifflin.

Keegan, J. (1987). *The mask of command*. Viking.

Kellerman, B. (2004a) *Bad leadership: What it is, how it happens, why it matters*. Harvard Business School Press.

Kellerman, B. (2004b). Review of Bad leadership: What it is, how it happens, why it matters. *Harvard Business Review*.

Kidd, D.C., & Castano, E. (2013). Reading literary fiction improves theory of mind. *Science, 342*(6156), 377–380.

Kim, J., Allison, S.T., Eylon, D., Goethals, G., Markus, M., McGuire, H., & Hindle, S. (2008). Rooting for (and then abandoning) the underdog. *Journal of Applied Social Psychology, 38*, 2550–2573.

Kinsella, E.L., Igou, E.R., & Ritchie, T.D. (2019). Heroism and the pursuit of a meaningful life. *Journal of Humanistic Psychology, 59*, 474–498.

Kinsella, E.L., Ritchie, T.D., & Igou, E.R. (2015). Zeroing in on heroes: A prototype analysis of hero features. *Journal of Personality and Social Psychology, 108*, 114–127.

Klinnert, M., Campos, J.J., Sorce, J., Emde, R.N., & Svedja, M. (1983). Emotions as behavior regulators: Social referencing in infancy. In R. Plutchik & H. Kellerman (eds.), *Emotions in early development, Vol. 2, The emotions*. Academic Press.

Kohen, A., Langdon, M., & Riches, B.R. (2018). The making of a hero: Cultivating empathy, altruism, and heroic imagination. *Journal of Humanistic Psychology, 59*, 617–633.

Kuhn, T. (1962). *The structure of scientific revolutions*. The University of Chicago Press.

Lee, J., & Hancocks, P. (2011). Workers endure astere conditions in averting nuclear disaster. articles.cnn.com/2011-03-29/world

Lightfoot, G. (1972) *Don Quixote*. Warner Brothers Records.

Loeb, V. (2003, April 3). She was fighting to the death. *The Washington Post*.

Lumet, S. (1957). *Twelve angry men*. Sidney Lumet, director. MGM.

Magee, J.C., Gruenfeld, D.H., Keltner, D.J., & Galinsky, A.D. (2005). Leadership and the psychology of power. In D. Messick & R. Kramer (Eds.), *The psychology of leadership: Some new approaches* (pp. 287–306). Erlbaum.

Mandela. (1987). Singh, P. (Director). Polymuse Entertainment.

Mandela and de Klerk. (1997). Chadwick, J. (Director). Showtime Networks.

Mar, R.A., Oatley, K., Hirsh, J., Dela Paz, J., & Peterson, J.B. (2005). Bookworms versus nerds: Exposure to fiction versus non-fiction, divergent associations with social ability, and the simulation of fictional social worlds. *Journal of Research in Personality, 40*, 694–712.

Marcus, G.F. (2005). What developmental biology can tell us about innateness. In P. Carruthers, S. Laurence, & S. Stich (Eds.) *The innate mind: Structure and contents*. Oxford University Press.

McGrath, C. (2010, September 28). *The 50th anniversary of Ted Williams' last game—and Hub Fans Bid Kid Adieu*. The New York Times.

McPherson, J.M. (1988). *Battle cry of freedom*. Oxford University Press.

Meltzoff, A.N., & Moore, M.K. (1995). Infants' understanding of people and things: From body imitation to folk psychology. In J.L. Bermudez, A. Marcel, & N. Eilan (Eds.), *The body and the self* (pp. 43–69). MIT Press.

Monin, B., Sawyer, P.J., & Marquez, M.J. (2008). The rejection of moral rebels: Resenting those who do the right thing. *Journal of Personality and Social Psychology, 95*, 76–93.

Monroe, I. (2012). Bayard Rustin: One of the tallest trees in our forest. http://www.huffingtonpost.com/irene-monroe/bayard-rustin_b_1371165.html

Murphy, C. (2006, August 25). *Looking for fame in all the wrong places*, 34. Chicago Tribune.

Myers, D.G. (2010). *Social psychology* (10th ed.). McGraw-Hill.

Piaget, J. (1952). Autobiography. In E. Boring (Ed.), *History of psychology in autobiography*. Clark University Press.

Pinker, S. (1991). Rules of language. *Science, 253*, 530–535.

Schein, E.H. (1992). *Organizational culture and leadership*. Jossey-Bass.

Schultz, C. (1956). This is a 'security and happiness' blanket...All little kids carry them. In *Good grief, more Peanuts*, 25. Penguin Press.

Simonton, D.K. (1987). *Why presidents succeed: A political psychology of leadership*. Yale University Press.

Sophocles. (2001; 429 BCE). *Oedipus The King*. Simon & Schuster. (B. Knox, trans.).

Sorenson, G., & Hickman, G.R. (2002). Invisible leadership: Acting on behalf of a common purpose. In C. Cherry & L.R. Matusak (Eds.), *Building leadership bridges* (pp. 7–24). James MacGregor Burns Academy of Leadership.

Sternberg, R. (2011). Leadership and education: Leadership stories. In R. Riggio & M. Harvey (Eds.), *Leadership studies: The dialogue of disciplines* (pp. 161–170). Edward Elgar.

Stogdill, R.M. (1974). *Handbook of leadership: A survey of theory and research*. Free Press.

Sturdivant, R.T. (2021, January 11). A lone Black officer faced down violent US Capitol mob, fooled them to save lives I Reese's Final Thought. WUSA9. https://www.youtube.com/watch?v=lVYD6YkKfpY

Taylor, S.E., Peplau, A.L., & Sears, D.O. (2006). *Social psychology* (12th ed.). Prentice Hall

Updike, J. (1960, October 22). Hub fans bid kid adieu. New Yorker.

Vandello, J.A., Goldschmied, N.P., & Richards, D.A.R. (2007). The appeal of the underdog. *Personality and Social Psychology Bulletin, 33,* 1603–1616.

Vezzali, L., Stathi, S., Giovannini, D., Capozza, D., & Trifiletti, E. (2014). The greatest magic of Harry Potter: Reducing prejudice. *Journal of Applied Social Psychology, 45*(7), 105–121.

Weir, T. (2012). LeBron James expresses regret about "The Decision." content. usatoday.com/communities/gameon/post/2011/12

White, T.H. (1978). *In search of history: A personal adventure.* Harper & Row.

Winnicott, D. (1953). Transitional objects and transitional phenomena. *International Journal of Psycho-Analysis, 34,* 89–97.

Worthington, E.L., & Allison, S.T. (2018). *Heroic humility: What the science of humility can say to people raised on self-focus.* American Psychological Association.

Yukl, G. (2013). *Leadership in organizations.* Pearson.

Zimbardo, P. (2008). *The Lucifer effect: Understanding how good people turn evil.* Random House.

Zimbardo, P. (2012). Heroic imagination project. http://heroicimagination.org

Index

Pages in *italics* refer to figures and pages in **bold** refer to tables.

Printed in the United States
by Baker & Taylor Publisher Services.

Printed in the United States
by Baker & Taylor Publisher Services